Understanding DeFi

The Roles, Tools, Risks, and Rewards of
Decentralized Finance

Alexandra Damsker

Beijing · Boston · Farnham · Sebastopol · Tokyo

Understanding DeFi

by Alexandra Damsker

Published by O'Reilly Media, Inc., 1005 Gravenstein Highway North, Sebastopol, CA 95472.

O'Reilly books may be purchased for educational, business, or sales promotional use. Online editions are also available for most titles (*http://oreilly.com*). For more information, contact our corporate/institutional sales department: 800-998-9938 or *corporate@oreilly.com*.

Acquisitions Editor: Michelle Smith	**Indexer:** BIM Creatives, LLC
Development Editor: Shira Evans	**Interior Designer:** David Futato
Production Editor: Aleeya Rahman	**Cover Designer:** Karen Montgomery
Copyeditor: nSight, Inc.	**Illustrator:** Kate Dullea
Proofreader: Sharon Wilkey	

March 2024:   First Edition

Revision History for the First Edition

2024-02-23:   First Release

See *http://oreilly.com/catalog/errata.csp?isbn=9781098120764* for release details.

978-1-098-12076-4

[LSI]

Table of Contents

Preface

Decentralized finance, or DeFi, is just about finance without banks. It's one of the core use cases for blockchain, which is really an innovation in accounting. DeFi will eventually be a key part of finance for people, and one of the primary ways people earn returns on their assets, whether fiat or cryptocurrency. Banks need competitors, and so do DeFi protocols. Together, they will allow people to get the highest and best returns on their assets for the lowest cost and risk.

This book is not about promoting specific DeFi protocols, or even about promoting the current state of DeFi. It is about understanding the entirety of the space—where it fits into blockchain, its core elements, how to operate in the space, and the future of DeFi.

People who enter blockchain—and even those who have been in it for years—tend to have a sort of "Swiss cheese" knowledge: very deep and detailed in some areas but almost nonexistent in others. Accordingly, this book has significant background information, explaining the history and technology of blockchain and the key concepts of finance. This is to ensure that readers have a more complete understanding of how these fields merge in the DeFi industry, and what the potential and limitations truly are.

How Is This Book Organized?

This book starts by laying down the foundation for the reader to understand the basic principles and history of both blockchain and DeFi. It moves from there to the tools of DeFi and how to build in DeFi. It then covers the current state of DeFi, and how protocol users make money on various types of protocols. Finally, it concludes with a look at the future of DeFi, and potential areas of growth and benefit.

Who Is This Book for, and What Will You Learn?

This book is for anyone, whether from a business or technical background, who needs a grounding in the blockchain and DeFi space and wants to build compliantly and productively. It is also for anyone who wants to learn how to operate protocols or invest money in the DeFi space. Finally, it is for anyone who wants a great explanation of how things work in blockchain and/or finance, without getting bogged down in acronyms and jargon. You don't need to have any prior knowledge to use this book.

The book is not intended to be a detailed, language-specific, step-by-step analysis and implementation guide for building DeFi protocols for a specific set of requirements. After reading this book, you should have the understanding and knowledge to help design, build, and operate successfully within the DeFi arena, however it progresses.

After reading this book, you should also have ideas of what works in DeFi and what doesn't, where risks lie, and where you are comfortable operating and even innovating. Users need to know what questions to ask developers when considering new protocols, and many need the knowledge contained in this book to understand what to ask—or if the protocols even make sense or are just failures that haven't operated long enough to fail.

Tutorials are great for working through specific needs, but a fundamental understanding of these core concepts is needed to allow teams to build correctly and compliantly—two things sorely missing in the current and already failed protocols in DeFi.

Conventions Used in This Book

The following typographical conventions are used in this book:

Italic
> Indicates new terms, URLs, email addresses, filenames, and file extensions.

 This element signifies a tip or suggestion.

 This element signifies a general note.

This element indicates a warning or caution.

O'Reilly Online Learning

 For more than 40 years, *O'Reilly Media* has provided technology and business training, knowledge, and insight to help companies succeed.

Our unique network of experts and innovators share their knowledge and expertise through books, articles, and our online learning platform. O'Reilly's online learning platform gives you on-demand access to live training courses, in-depth learning paths, interactive coding environments, and a vast collection of text and video from O'Reilly and 200+ other publishers. For more information, visit *https://oreilly.com*.

How to Contact Us

Please address comments and questions concerning this book to the publisher:

O'Reilly Media, Inc.
1005 Gravenstein Highway North
Sebastopol, CA 95472
800-889-8969 (in the United States or Canada)
707-827-7019 (international or local)
707-829-0104 (fax)
support@oreilly.com
https://www.oreilly.com/about/contact.html

We have a web page for this book, where we list errata, examples, and any additional information. You can access this page at *https://oreil.ly/understanding_defi*.

For news and information about our books and courses, visit *https://oreilly.com*.

Find us on LinkedIn: *https://linkedin.com/company/oreilly-media*

Follow us on Twitter: *https://twitter.com/oreillymedia*

Watch us on YouTube: *https://youtube.com/oreillymedia*

Acknowledgments

I'd like to thank everyone who provided support, understanding, and kindness to me in the process of writing this book. I'd particularly like to thank the following people:

Thanks to Shira Evans, my development editor, and Michelle Smith, senior acquisitions editor, for being so incredibly helpful, patient, supportive, and wise during this entire process. Thanks to the many editors at O'Reilly for their help and assistance in making this book a reality.

Thank you to Patrick O'Connor-Read for his valuable and insightful review and suggestions to improve the quality of the book.

Special thanks to my husband, Keith, and daughters, Kira and Juliet, and puppy, Scooby. They have been exceptionally patient in letting me write; (mostly) tolerated my frustration at the industry, the process, and other things over which I had no power to change; and only occasionally resorted to pelting me with chocolate to make me stop complaining.

(To be fair, Scooby didn't really do anything during this process but demand tummy scratches, which, it turns out, is significantly less productive than it sounds. Still, he's an exceptional puppy, so I am officially acknowledging he is a Very Good Boy.)

They're an excellent family.

CHAPTER 1

Introduction to DeFi

DeFi is shorthand for *decentralized finance*. That's generally what you hear when you ask about DeFi, as if that clears up all the confusion. But for most people, that definition doesn't do a thing to clarify what DeFi is, what it does, and why anyone would want to use or build a DeFi application. So let's fix that. After all, the most important characteristic about any decision is that it's an informed one. And you can't make an informed decision in DeFi unless you know what you're working with.

DeFi runs on blockchain platforms or decentralized applications (called *DApps*). Understanding the basics of blockchain is the core of understanding how DeFi works and why, so we're going to cover that first, so you can follow along with the specifics of DeFi. After all, it would be pretty hard to explain the benefits of a Bryant pivot versus an Iverson step back if you have no working knowledge of the rules of basketball. You need to understand the boundaries of the game before you take on the advanced plays, so we have to help you understand what blockchain is and how it works before we get into one type of blockchain application. In this chapter, you'll learn what blockchain is and how it evolved, what decentralization is, what traditional finance and decentralized finance are, and the differences between them.

General Warning to Readers

For those reading this and thinking they don't need a lawyer, or a CPA, or any other paid advisors:

1. This book is to give you a strong *general* grounding in DeFi and the issues surrounding the field.

2. This book isn't your lawyer. Your lawyer is your lawyer.

3. This isn't a book designed to detail these regulations for specific situations, so your particular issue is likely not covered in depth.

4. I *strongly* encourage everyone developing, investing in, contributing to, or using applications in DeFi to find an attorney who specializes in this area to determine whether they are subject to Know Your Customer (KYC)/anti–money laundering (AML) or other regulations.

5. Read 1–4 again.

What Is Blockchain, Anyway?

Has anyone ever lied to you before? Has someone ever promised you they would do something and then not done it? Most of us have had some experience being on the receiving end of a lie, from the Tooth Fairy to a ghosted Tinder date. People promise to pay for drinks "as soon as I get my check" and then disappear off the face of the earth—or pretend there was no obligation to pay, or they didn't even get the drinks in the first place. Checks get bounced, accounts get overdrawn, families invest in companies and stop speaking when they fail. People lie. But, unfortunately, they aren't kind enough to tell you when they're lying. Decisions stall in various efforts to check facts and complete due diligence, and people get screwed.

But people still need to work together. We need to buy and sell stuff. We need to collaborate and join resources to innovate. So what do you do when you need to work with people but can't trust them? You need a trustless system. You need something that doesn't require trust—something that assumes that people are lying—and still operates effectively, transferring rights without conflict. You need blockchain.

Blockchain can be an intimidating topic. It's a field full of people throwing around obscure words and technical theories, designed more to keep earlier adopters feeling like members of a special club than educating people on the technology.

But even with the best of intentions, it's a pretty complex topic. It combines philosophy, theories of economic and monetary policy, microeconomic modeling, and a sizable chunk of behavioral psychology. With the "crypto bro" culture and meme-heavy jargon, it's hard to find a solid foothold to build your knowledge on. Discussions of blockchain and DeFi can make anyone feel like they're back in middle school, afraid to ask questions or even comment.

But it's important to remember that blockchain is just a technology. When we think about technology, what is the first thing we think about? Usually some form of hardware (computers, smartphones, weird old switchboards with dozens of wires and women bound to relentless patriarchy). But what is technology really? The best definition is probably one like this: it solves problems people have, using scientific knowledge. That's it. It has no real ulterior motive. When you pair a scientific understanding of the world (how things work by principle, not observation) with a specific context (calculate this faster, use fewer people, do work humans can't, extend the ability of humans, etc.), you get technology. Cars, sneakers, airplanes, hair dryers, toothbrushes—all types of technology. It feels threatening only when you are in the generation above the generation of mass adoption.

At its heart, blockchain is a technological implementation of Yuri Ijiri's seminal accounting innovation, momentum accounting (also known as triple-entry bookkeeping).[1]

A Brief History of Accounting

I hear you thinking: "Wait, what? I thought we were talking about blockchain. I would never buy a book on accounting. Ever." Before you start hunting for the receipt (and stop doing that!), I know. I agree. Accounting can be incredibly boring—except that it inspired the greatest of all innovations: writing.

Ancient Sumerian tablets, containing some of the oldest writing, are actually simple receipts: "I gave you this for that." Merchants tallied their accounts at the end of the day, to derive a view of cash flow. And when you think about it, it makes sense. I mean, what's the thing you want to keep track of the most (aside from any kids or pets)? Your money.

Turns out we've been trying to track value—money we have, debts we're owed, debts we owe—since humans started to understand what "my stuff" meant. Let's look at what we've come up with over the millennia, starting with single-entry bookkeeping.

---

1 Yuji Ijiri, "Momentum Accounting and Managerial Goals on Impulses," *Management Science* 34, no. 2 (February 1988): 160–66.

Single-Entry Bookkeeping

IOUs are the oldest form of accounting, known as *single-entry bookkeeping*. This allowed people to begin to trade without having to carry items with them. An IOU in some form is an incredible innovation. Farmers, for example, had few options before this: either wait at the farm and hope buyers stop by (limited market opportunity) or cart around giant bales of harvested grain to a marketplace to access more and higher-volume buyers (high cost of opportunity). Being able to access marketplaces without dragging around bales of grain provided much greater opportunity for sale. In addition, marketplaces could be attended off-season, so farmers could buy things all year, not just for the short period in the fall when grain was harvested and ready for sale. This opened up the world of off-season purchasing with an early form of credit.

All this resulted in extra income, which could be used to improve farm efficiency, hire more labor, and improve the ability to support more children. More children meant more money, either by providing free labor to the farm or becoming employees to outside entities, bringing in salaries. In addition, the more frequent market exposure allowed more opportunity for culture and knowledge exchange, which is the basis for human innovation.

Payment in advance, whether by seasons or days, allowed people to buy things before they actually had the money. In effect, the IOUs were the first credit cards—physical proof that the debt existed and could be collected. This is the core of provable transfer of resources, and how humans were able to expand to nearly every inch of habitable land on Earth. The ability to keep records and learn vicariously is the foundation for all technology—and all human knowledge.

However, as transactions spread beyond the people in one's town or village, the limitations of single-entry bookkeeping began to reveal themselves. A simple receipt didn't show that anything was received in exchange, nor did it protect against fraud or theft.

In addition, businesses had become large ventures. People started to realize that when expenses are investments, they should look different from expenses that are simply repeat spends of consumable goods. (For example, $10,000 spent on pencils should look different to a company's financial picture than $10,000 spent on equipment to manufacture the product sold, and both are different from $10,000 as a one-time payment to set up an overseas subsidiary.) We needed a better system to keep up. Enter double-entry bookkeeping.

Double-Entry Bookkeeping

In the 11th century, bankers of the medieval Middle East created *double-entry book-keeping*, likely culled from a version of the Indian Jama-Nama system. This was revolutionary because it required both parties to enter both sides of a transaction, assuring greater accuracy and reliability, as well as account for expenses and revenue as they actually impacted the total company, rather than simple cash flow. This is the move from recording "I owe you one bale of grain" to "You gave me three goats, so I owe you one bale of grain."

Now parties could trade not just existing goods, but future goods, with a way to account for goods and services owed and paid. Transactions could be carried forward and still remain in each day's records, so that revenue and debt accrued but not paid could still be kept current. This took off in the 1300s with the Genoese empire, and by the 1600s it had become the common method of recordkeeping among the major trading empires. Massive movements of goods, services, and capital across borders resulted, in large part because the method of accounting for these flows between strangers did not require trust—only proper records and proper receipt. This was the true beginning of globalization.

Then...we kind of got stuck. Remember, there were tens of thousands of years between the first humans hanging out by the magic fire and the creation of single-entry bookkeeping, and a few more millennia to the leap to double-entry bookkeeping. Accounting isn't exactly a field that drives innovation. When something works, we tend to keep to the status quo until that status quo simply doesn't work any longer.

Massive Fraud, or the Status Quo Officially Doesn't Work Any Longer

But then, in 1997, the Asian banking crisis happened. What were previously considered stalwart banks making conservative investment and capital management decisions turned out to be an intertwined mess of favoritism and personal enrichment at the expense of shareholders and deposit holders. This was later termed "crony capitalism": expensive short-term capital and development funds went to inside parties and/or inefficient, poorly managed companies, rather than to those offering the best or most profitable business propositions.

Quickly on its heels came the accounting scandals of the 2000s. Enron, WorldCom, HealthSouth, Tyco, AIG—the early 2000s are a ghostly graveyard of blue-chip companies that were cheating shareholders with "creative" accounting techniques, often backed by the most widely respected independent accounting companies in the world. Respected "Big 6" accounting firms like Arthur Andersen and KPMG were suddenly connected to shady inside business practices.

As the world stared into a gaping hole where millions in revenue should have been, a flaw of the double-entry system was brutally exposed. With the double-entry system, everything is accounted for in arrear, and anything can change or be changed from the moment of entry up until the accounts are audited by an impartial third party. Unaudited accounts were subject to any sort of editing with any sort of rationale, by accident or intention, which did nothing to help people making current and future decisions based on those entries. People started to realize that the mere act of keeping books wasn't sufficient. Third-party auditing was mandatory to maintain any sense of reliability or trust.

How Accounting Can Be Like Building an Ikea Table—in a Bad Way

Accounting *in arrear* means that your records reflect events that happened in the past, not current or future events. For example, say you're a landlord. You get paid on the first of every month, but you do your books on the last day of each month. At the end of the month, you sort through the cash you've received and the expenses you've paid, and you try to match them up.

Sometimes (if sometimes means a *lot*), you don't have an exact match. You end up with something I think of as the bookkeeping version of "extra parts" when you get something from Ikea. You think you're done building, but then you see these handful of screws and bolts and think, "Crap. Did I need those?" You can keep them or toss them, but when those leftover screws and bolts represent actual cash, you don't usually feel like just tossing that in the trash (and doing so might be illegal).

You have to figure out where to put these bits of extra revenue or expense, calling it something like "extra rent" or "fixture purchase" to account for it. It might not seem like a big deal, but these bits add up quickly and can result in major crimes like tax fraud or debt default. You see how the opportunity (and temptation) for accidental or intentional fraud is both very high and very easy. A number of companies figured this out, too. It did not end well. (Thanks, Enron.)

Triple-Entry Bookkeeping

In 1988, Dr. Yuji Ijiri, professor at Carnegie Mellon University and president of the American Accounting Association, wrote a monograph discussing a new accounting revolution: *momentum accounting*, or *triple-entry bookkeeping*.[2] This was less of a sea change in the accounting and business communities than you might expect. More like a puddle change. This was likely because almost no one read it.

---

2 Ibid.

Momentum accounting is a method of accounting that helps forecasting; it tells you how fast or slow a company is growing. But it required something double-entry bookkeeping doesn't have: facts. As you saw earlier, double-entry bookkeeping provides a reason for a debit (money you owe) or credit (money someone else owes you).

As Dr. Ijiri describes:

> [Accounting moved from] single entry [bookkeeping], which just records what happened, to double entry, where what happened has to be explained by reasoning by another account—if you don't have [an] explanation, you can't have an entry.

But it still leaves open the risk of mistake or fraud. If you want to be able to use bookkeeping for prediction, you need something solid to base your prediction on, not guesses or something that may be misremembered or, worse, something both parties colluded on. Something that can't be altered or edited or "revised creatively." And from this, we get the idea of a permanent ledger that records in real time—a system in which both parties keep a record of the transaction, *but so does the system itself.*

Do you see the sea change here? Triple-entry bookkeeping moves to the logical third dimension of accounting, which is not just a record and a reason, but also an auditable trail. Many have discounted the impact of this methodology, or the relationship of triple-entry bookkeeping to blockchain. However, this revolution is the heart of the functionality of blockchain.

But one person did read the monograph, eventually. And it turns out that one person recognized the genius of this innovation. On June 26, 2005, Ian Grigg, a financial cryptographer and later member of the Satoshi Nakamoto Institute, posted this:

> It was widely recognised since David Chaum's designs first appeared that the new "digital certificate" model of money was not aligned or symmetrical with accounting techniques such as double entry bookkeeping. Many people expected the two to compete, and indeed many money systems avoided combining them; this is I believe one of the few efforts to integrate the two and show them as better in combination than apart.

Arrear Versus Arrears

In arrear means *after the fact*—e.g., payment after the service has been rendered. This is like hiring a cleaning service to clean for the month of August, and the company bills you on August 31. You are paying in arrear.

In arrears means *behind*—e.g., payment that is late. If you hired that cleaning service for August, and payment is due August 31, but you don't pay until October 1, your payment was made in arrears.

Triple-Entry Accounting

The digitally signed receipt, an innovation from financial cryptography, presents a challenge to classical double-entry bookkeeping. Rather than compete, the two melded together form a stronger system. Expanding the usage of accounting into the wider domain of digital cash gives three local entries for each of three roles, the result of which we call *triple-entry accounting* (*https://oreil.ly/kw7dk*):

> This system creates bulletproof accounting systems for aggressive uses and users. It not only lowers costs by delivering reliable and supported accounting; it makes much stronger governance possible in a way that positively impacts on the future needs of corporate and public accounting.[3]

This is the core thesis of what later became blockchain technology. As digital cash was maturing (through online banking, ATM machines, etc.), Grigg noticed the failure of double-entry bookkeeping to account for potential fraud and mistakes in the system. More importantly, however, he created a solution. By pairing the digital certificate of digital cash with a triple accounting system, capital movement could be more reliable and secure, and less subject to fraud. Eventually, this method of recordkeeping wasn't just about recording financial transactions. The recordkeeping *became* the financial transactions.

Confused? Let's clarify by seeing it in action. Welcome to the emergence of Bitcoin.

The Bitcoin Revolution: The First Blockchain Use Case

In October 2008, an unknown individual or entity going by the name of Satoshi Nakamoto published a paper titled ""Bitcoin: A Peer-to-Peer Electronic Cash System" to the Cryptography and Cryptography Policy mailing list (*https://oreil.ly/5-5fY*).[4] Nakamoto described creating tokens, called *bitcoin*, which represented individual digital certificates moving through a chain of transactions. Nakamoto advocated creation of encrypted blocks to track these transactions through time, as they were happening.

While many count this as the genesis of blockchain, it is really the origin of a single practical application method of an auditable trail transfer system. This application is what we generally term *blockchain* (named for the chain of encrypted block transactions). It is this application, the *Bitcoin blockchain*, that is the model for all currently developed blockchain technology, but it is important to remember that this is just one part of the true innovation—an auditable trail transfer system.

---

3 See Ian Grigg's June 26, 2005, post and correlating paper, posted to FinancialCryptography.com.

4 Ian Grigg is widely considered to be either the identity behind the mysterious Satoshi Nakamoto persona, or one of a small group who collectively named themselves or were affiliated with Nakamoto.

The Bitcoin blockchain was based on a compilation of the token-based interbank transfer accounting system of the 1960s and 1970s (still in use), a digital cash innovation from the 1980s known as Hashcash (the encryption method is actually called *hashing*), and this basic concept of using tokens as the substitute digital certificate.

Does Blockchain *Have* to Look Like the Bitcoin Blockchain?

Remember that the current structure of blockchain, including the Bitcoin blockchain and all the other tokenized blockchain, isn't the only way to create this system of verified, immutable, auditable trail accounting. Nakamoto was offering only an example, not a definitive methodology, of auditable trail transfer technology.

It's probably not even the best way to do this—more efficient methods of immutable digital signature recordkeeping are out there and will likely emerge in the next two to three years. Blockchain platforms could also be done without being peer to peer, or listing all transactions since genesis, or without using tokens, or many other ways. The token-based system of the Bitcoin blockchain is just the one we came up with first, and now it's our default method for the moment.

We have a bit of time to see alternatives and determine if we like them better or if they have major advantages over the token structure we have now. Not much time, though— we're at the point in technology development that looks like a race between innovation and standardization.

When the internet had enough users that people started thinking about commercializing and generating revenue, the focus moved from creating new types of networks and protocols to standardizing the ones that existed (the Transmission Control Protocol/Internet Protocol, or TCP/IP, eventually in combination with the Hypertext Transfer Protocol, also known as HTTP—that thing you don't even notice anymore at the start of your web address: *http://*), and requiring all new additions to conform to these standards. It became more important for all the networks to communicate with one another than find newer, better protocols. The same occurred with VHS, CD formats, etc. A certain standard format or rule structure has to win so developers can focus more on things to do with the technology instead of how to create the technology. Users then move from early adopters, who are willing to learn new ways to access and use every type of technology and play around to figure out hidden potential, to the mass group of users who are willing to learn only one type of access and are generally less focused on exploring the technology's potential (what it could do with more help) and more focused on gaining value from the technology (applications that do stuff for users). This point is called *mass adoption*, and we're reaching it now in blockchain.

To summarize, blockchain technology is an application pairing triple-entry book-keeping with digital certificates. Its primary use case is to prevent fraud or mistakes in double-spending digital money or assets. It isn't the so-called peer-to-peer transfer (without a bank) that is revolutionary, though excluding banks from transactions is always a positive development, according to me. It's the new instant auditability that is revolutionary. The ability to have real-time transfers of value between parties that is based on verifiable facts that we can audit, or track, at any given time is incredible. We aren't relying on someone's word or opinion that a transaction happened between parties and someone was or wasn't paid. We aren't hoping someone didn't end up with bookkeeping "extra parts" they're trying to shove somewhere illegally.

With blockchain, we know that each party (1) agreed to enter into a transaction with the other (both used private keys or passwords to sign off on the transaction), (2) agreed to exchange a specific amount of value with each other (an amount of the underlying token, coin, or asset represented by a token), and then (3) actually exchanged that value. How do we know this? Because the *transaction closed*. It is listed as a transaction between the parties on the blockchain. If those three conditions didn't exist, the transaction wouldn't exist on the blockchain. So no more guessing, missing numbers, or extra parts.

This is particularly important because, in United States law, legal contracts require meeting of the minds (agreement to enter into a transaction that is mutually understood by both parties) and consideration (an exchange of value) reflecting both quantity and price. As you can see, all these elements may be met by having a closed blockchain transaction between parties.

People call blockchain a "trustless system." It is an entirely trustworthy system.

Ethereum and the Smart Contract Revelation

The Bitcoin blockchain is the primary use case and application of auditable trail accounting for digital cash or currency. Bitcoin is nothing more than a coin representing a value, and each bitcoin can be broken into 100 million subcoins called *satoshis*, or *sats*.[5] Bitcoin (or sats) is the coin that gets transferred from wallet to wallet, and it represents a cash value. You can see what the value of bitcoin is on any of the marketplaces on which it trades, converted into various fiat currencies or other cryptocurrencies. People buy it from other people or from crypto exchanges (trading for fiat currency) or in exchange for goods or services.

---

5 A satoshi is one 100-millionth of a bitcoin, just as a penny is one 100th of a US dollar.

Is Bitcoin a Currency?

Many people believe bitcoin could be a substitute for fiat (government-issued currency, such as the US dollar). But it is fundamentally impossible for bitcoin to be a currency.

First, bitcoin is deflationary, meaning it is in limited supply, with the intention that the limitation will drive up the value of each individual bitcoin. There will be only 21 million bitcoin minted—*ever*. Regardless of need or demand, if some are accidentally lost or burned, that's it. No more. And that's as much a problem as something that's inflationary, or in limitless supply. Currencies need to have a supply that can expand and contract as needed, so supply and demand meet as perfectly as possible. Why? Because the purpose is to keep a currency as stable in value as possible, not have it rise or drop. Currencies have to be stable and predictable, which means they need to be adjustable and nonvolatile. Having 21 million, no more, no less, means it is not adjustable.

Which leads us to the next problem: volatility, or wild fluctuations in value. Price volatility is a hallmark of assets, and it can be great—it's what makes your tiny investment in a stock shoot up in value...or plummet, and you lose everything. Price fluctuations are not great for currency. You don't want to have to add a level of guesswork onto every transaction regarding something called asset risk.

For example, let's say you pay for a new iMac with cash. You are worried about whether you need that computer, if it works well for your needs, if you are paying too much for it. The store is worried only that you might run off without paying. All the concerns are *transactional risk*—related to the exchange that is the reason for the transaction.

But what if you decide to pay for that iMac with Apple stock instead? Now you're still worried about whether the computer is what you need, you're not being overcharged, etc. But you also have a new level of concerns—what if that Apple stock goes way up tomorrow? Then you lost out on all that upside and paid way too much for that computer. The store is worried that Apple goes way down tomorrow, and it will lose money on the sale. Those issues with the Apple stock are *asset risk*. You have a second set of issues when you use assets to conduct transactions that you don't have when you conduct transactions with currency.

People hoard bitcoin for just this reason, and are concerned about facing loss or losing potential upside when exchanging bitcoin for goods or services. Why? Because it has potential upside and loss—it's volatile, and you can't fix that volatility without supply adjustability.

So—it's an asset.

But then people started stretching this concept of auditability of transactions. What else could you transfer between wallets? Does it have to be bitcoin? Could it be something else or represent something else? Absolutely. Here are some things you could transfer:

- Coins representing value on other chains
- Tokens representing a promise, ownership, or interest in something digital or physical
- Tokens representing a patent or other intellectual property
- Tokens representing digital or physical art
- Tokens representing anything digital, such as music, AI code, or a novel
- Tokens representing a "skin" for your avatar in a game
- Tokens representing an equity interest in a project or company
- Tokens representing the right to sublet your apartment or house

But could you do it on the Bitcoin blockchain? The first step was to figure out if the Bitcoin blockchain could handle smart contracts.

Smart Contracts

Smart contracts were originally created by Nick Szabo, an American cryptographer and computer scientist, in 1994. These didn't start off as what we currently think of as *smart contracts*: self-executing programmable logic that initiates whenever an agreed state exists, can stop on set conditions, and can automatically start over countless times.

Szabo was initially focused on the idea of a transaction protocol that automatically executes or documents a set of actions based on the terms of a previously agreed set of terms. Several attempts to create functional smart contracts and a smart contract platform on the Bitcoin blockchain failed. An early NFT (nonfungible token, see "Nonfungible tokens" on page 136) platform was even created, called Counterparty. However, none of these made any inroads in adoption or gained significant traction.

How Does a Smart Contract Work?

A smart contract works like a vending machine. Modern vending machines date back to the 1880s and are basically a simple smart contract. Prices are associated with particular snacks, for example, which are all identified with a basic letter and/or number code. When a person puts in money and enters their selection, they are agreeing to the terms of the machine (if you want item E5, you must pay $1.00) and simultaneously triggering a set of mechanized actions, currently aided with software. This triggered execution checks the value of the money deposited and then releases one of the

---

requested items. After releasing it, the machine stops automatically, and resets to wait for another event.

This ability to start automatically on being triggered, execute according to agreed terms, and then stop automatically requires a Turing complete device or language. *Turing complete systems* are able to solve any problem, given enough time, processing power, and proper instructions. They can also communicate with any other Turing complete system.

So, why would you ever want to make a Turing incomplete system? Because Turing complete systems are hard to create, are far more complicated, and, like all complex things, a lot can go wrong. So it's understandable that when the original developers were building the complicated blockchain, they wanted to keep the already new and complicated blockchain process as simple and predictable as possible. They left the Bitcoin blockchain Turing incomplete, and they made sure it did the one task it was assigned constantly and consistently. And it does. It mines bitcoin, processes transactions, and transfers one asset (bitcoin) from wallet to wallet quite well. But that is all it does. And to add in more possibilities, they needed a new blockchain—one that was designed for more complex actions. A Turing complete system. And that's how we got Ethereum.

Ethereum's Innovation: Self-Executing Programming →
Smart Contracts

Finally, in December 2013, a 21-year-old developer named Vitalik Buterin released a whitepaper on his blog proposing a new vision of audited trail technology, moving beyond the financial use case evinced by Bitcoin and the Bitcoin blockchain.[6] He considered the Bitcoin blockchain to be a weakly executed form of smart contract, and it was not able to support Turing complete applications. He proposed an alternative platform, named *Ethereum*, that would be a stronger and more malleable, Turing complete system, using a token-based approach to execute transactions involving *any* digital asset.

These self-executing transactions are based on starting principles agreed to by the parties, then recorded by digital certificate tokens known as Ether that function on the Ethereum platform. He made these self-executing, or smart, contracts initiated and halted by use of *Ether* tokens and clear logic systems. This was an incredible step forward—no more waiting for payments or approvals.

---

6 Vitalik Buterin, "Ethereum White Paper: A Next-Generation Smart Contract and Decentralized Application Platform," *Ethereum*, 2014, *https://ethereum.org/whitepaper*. Updated and revised by the Ethereum Foundation.

For example, say a company makes instrument sensors to ensure that highly sensitive instrumentation is being maintained within a small, specific range. This company wants to sell access to its instrument sensors to large clients, and it has a business model requiring monthly installment payments of $750. This could present a problem for the company—it no longer has physical possession of the sensor, so it either requires constant oversight of the payment schedules of every individual client, or it runs the risk of the sensors being used without payment. It also presents a risk to the customer: if the amount is paid but an error occurs in recording payment, payment is not recorded, or the instrument company fails, then the sensors will not operate, and the sensitive instrumentation and equipment could be severely damaged. Now the sensor company can protect both itself and the client by attaching the sensing trigger application to Ethereum's blockchain.

Since this is an auditing network, first and foremost, everything is initiated when the contract terms are placed on the system. Here, those terms would be something like (in very simplified form) "if $750 is deposited into the company account on the first of each month, turn the instrumentation sensor on, and leave it on until the last day of the month," and set as a loop until the termination day or event of contract. On the first day of each month, the smart contract triggers an oracle to check the company's account.[7] Provided that the conditions are met ("$750 was deposited today into the company account by the client"), the instrumentation sensor will start or continue running until triggered to stop. No human intervention is required, nor permitted. To confirm that the terms of the contract are met, the contract and each execution is clearly tracked and traceable on the platform.

Think about that. It's pretty incredible. You don't need a department of people to confirm payment, verify transactions, chase down clients for collection. You also don't need to be a huge company that can afford that much overhead and cost. If the sensor (or whatever you make) is working, you were paid. If you don't get paid, it doesn't work. This is how we start making the transition from the records tracking the transaction to becoming the transaction itself. So the tokens that reflect the transactions now start having independent, not assigned, value. They represent the value of real transactions. And you don't need to be the size of IBM to afford using this system; anyone can do it.

So now we have the ability to transfer assets anonymously (Bitcoin blockchain), and the ability to do more complex actions like programming asset transfers and automating transfers based on prior programmed conditions (Ethereum). Blockchain is officially a Thing now, so we need to discuss the basic tenets of blockchain that define the ethos most projects require. This is an extrapolated list made by empirical

---

7 An *oracle* is a piece of data-sensing software that leaves the blockchain platform to retrieve external data.

observation (i.e., I created the list after talking to a lot of people and looking at more projects than any human should).

Tenets of Blockchain (According to Me)

Here's the list of what I believe to be the basic tenets of blockchain:

- Open
- Shared
- Distributed
- Consensus
- Permanence
- Anonymity
- Trustless

Open

Open here refers to two different concepts: open ledger and open source.

Open ledger refers to the type of transparency that exists in most of blockchain. Go to any industry event, and you'll hear about 70%–75% of the speakers mention "transparency" as a core value of blockchain. But that isn't really what exists—or what people want. Blockchain has an odd sort of half-transparency that we'll call public-private. The transactions are all public, which means you can literally track an asset as it passes from one person to another, and you can see that someone paid x amount for y. But the identities of the parties are all private. We transact through *wallets* (discussed more in the section "A Word on Wallets" on page 41), which are our means of accessing the blockchain—just as your ATM card lets you access your bank account. Your bank account exists and chugs along without requiring your interaction or attention, but when you want to see what it's doing or withdraw or deposit assets or funds, you need that ATM.

That wallet is a mix of letters and numbers, and although your wallet is your unique set of letters and numbers, it's very hard to tell who specifically owns any particular wallet, unless you own a unique item. (Your wallet can be identified as yours in a number of ways. For example, by seeing some of the assets held in it, like a one-of-one NFT or token someone knows you've bought, NFT you bought, or, if you are the biggest holder of a particular token, locating the wallet that holds the biggest chunk of that particular token. Note that there are ways to fix these issues quite easily.) Otherwise, anyone could be the owner of any wallet. This open ledger really means public transactions with private parties.

Open source code is very different from traditional web or app development. Most traditional development uses a closed source code, which is more or less proprietary to the founding team and company and is kept confidential, as intellectual property is considered a valuable asset.

Blockchain is often (though not always) driven by community first, and that leads to viewing development as a communal project, which means using base code that is free and available to anyone who wants to use it. It is usually hosted on GitHub or another decentralized site, and anyone can view the code and borrow it. Many open source projects also allow open commenting and even editing—anyone can develop on these projects, and they become very community-focused. While a few projects are based on closed source code (particularly if a private chain or an identity-based application), this is generally not considered "acceptable" within this space.

Shared

Shared here refers to a shared ledger. Every computer that operates a particular blockchain platform is called a *node*, and each one shares the exact same record of transactions (the blockchain ledger). This is not one communal list of transactions; it is a full ledger that is replicated on every node. This way, no one can edit the ledger independently and create false transactions. That would be rejected by everyone else's version of the ledger, and the false transaction, and who inserted it would be obvious. This keeps the list of transactions legitimate and prevents fraud. We like that—especially when we're talking about money.

Distributed

Being concept of *distributed* isn't well understood in this context. We're talking about the fact that no one controls the ledger. It's related to the preceding shared concept: the ledger is the same across all the nodes. But distributed goes a bit further. This means that everyone has the same copy—but also that no one controls it.

There's a lot of confusion between the terms "distributed" and "decentralized," and people learning about DeFi aren't sure which one applies to blockchain. (People who have been in DeFi for years aren't always sure, either.) So let's talk about the difference, and the problems with saying that anything in blockchain is fully decentralized.

Distribution versus decentralization

Blockchain technology is, in its ideal state, both distributed and decentralized. Let's clarify what this terminology really means, starting with Figure 1-1.

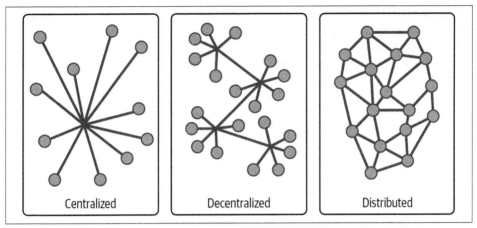

Figure 1-1. Different ways to build networks: centralized, decentralized and distributed (Image credit: nakamo.to)

Decentralized in this context is talking specifically about control. Decentralized systems have control shared among a certain number of independent parties—the more independent people, the more decentralized. For example, open source software, like Linux, is decentralized—the code is created and modified by independent developers who jointly develop the base software and any derived applications. There is no overarching master parent entity controlling all. Everything is entirely independently created and deployed.

The internet as it currently stands is (sort of) decentralized. No one entity controls the internet. However, a few key players, like internet service providers ("portals" to the internet, like Facebook/Meta and Google), telecom companies (like Spectrum and Verizon), some governments, and even internal employer home pages, serve as bottlenecks that either redistribute users to the various sites or stop them from being able to move freely around the internet. We call this "federated," because the parties are all independent—but there aren't many of them and they can (and often do) collude.

"Distributed" and "co-located" describe where the parts of the system are physically located. In a *distributed system*, all parts of the system are located in different places, like on the different nodes of the platform. For example, people-distributed companies have executives and staff who do not share a main office. Personnel may not even share the same city or country. They rely on technology to convey information such that all parties remain current on the goings-on of the business.

Co-located systems, on the other hand, have all parts of the system in one place. Companies with all primary personnel coming to the same office are co-located, as is a software company with all servers and personnel located in one place. Everyone is nearly instantaneously aware of whatever they need to know, because it happens on-site.

Distributed, Co-located, and Decentralized...?

Note that you can be distributed and centralized, or co-located and decentralized—decentralization is about control, not location. But we'd be lying if we said being co-located didn't make it a *lot* more likely that the system is also centralized. It's just much easier to control something when you're all together in one place.

Blockchain systems are certainly distributed, in that all parts are not just located in different locations, but every access point, or node, running that blockchain has access to all the information on the system. So, in essence, all system information is located on every system access point. Each node has all the information you would expect to find on a central database; no central headquarters or tacky badges on lanyards required.

Decentralization of blockchain, however, is a bit trickier. Most of the current systems are controlled at some point (or many points) by a relatively small group of people. These could be miners (if tokens are mined), governance token holders (the people who get to vote on stuff the platform or application does or doesn't do), or both. So, one of the biggest problems of blockchain is that it can be manipulated by just a few people agreeing and forming a choke point. Most of the time, it isn't intentional. It just takes time for a small founding team to build something that's distributed broadly enough at all points to be called fully decentralized. It's not really a coincidence that one of oldest platforms, Bitcoin, is our most decentralized. But even Bitcoin still has bottlenecks of control. To really understand decentralization issues in blockchain, we have to explore it a bit deeper.

Three types of decentralization

The problem of decentralization is really that it's difficult not only to express in various situations, but also to understand. Fortunately, Vitalik Buterin, one of the key founders of both Bitcoin and Ethereum, already thought through a bunch of this for us and conveniently wrote it down.[8] He's brilliant, and great at explanations, so I encourage everyone to read his Ethereum whitepaper (you should also read his blog

---

8 Derived in part from Vitalik Buterin, "The Meaning of Decentralization," *Medium*, February 6, 2017, *https://oreil.ly/sjTEN*.

and other papers—and if he gets into graphic novels or screenplays, we should all probably start reading those, too). But we're going to distill a bunch of that down here so we can apply it toward blockchain and DeFi specifically. I'm kind of extrapolating at will here, so apologies in advance to any purists who look at it as dogma.[9]

Also, that's weird, because none of this is dogma. Stop doing that.

So, as we mentioned before, when we talk about "centralized" and "decentralized" here, we are talking about states of control, or governance. A centralized system has one individual or group of individuals controlling the entire system, while a decentralized system has its governance spread out among all the members.

An example of a centralized system would be the Chinese yuan exchange rate with other currencies. (I'm simplifying a lot here, so bear with me.) Until 2015, China's yuan exchange rate remained fixed relative to a basket of currencies. China kept the yuan's value pegged to within 2% of that basket's value. It wasn't based on the market rate for the yuan. It wasn't based on any opinion of the yuan. It was based on a rate that was fixed by the Chinese government and, possibly, an underground coven in the mountains of Tibet. I'm speculating on that last one, but really, it's as likely as any other valuation method, because we just have no idea how this thing was set. The yuan was entirely centralized, with all control resting with the Chinese government.

What's in That Chinese Basket, Anyway?

If you try to find out what the basket of currencies are, you will come up with a version of this conversation:

"What's in the basket?"

"Currencies of China's main trading partners."

"Oh, great—which ones are those?"

Decentralization can happen in many ways, or all these ways together (italicized text taken directly from Vitalik's post). These are as follows:

Architectural
> *How many physical computers is a system made up of? How many of those computers can it tolerate breaking down at any single time?*

---

9 Hopefully, my good intentions will stave off hate.

Political

> How many individuals or organizations ultimately control the computers that the system is made up of?

Logical

> [Do] the interface and data structures that the system presents and maintains look more like a single monolithic object or an amorphous swarm? One simple heuristic is: if you cut the system in half, including both providers and users, will both halves continue to fully operate as independent units?

Vitalik lists a bunch of examples of variations in political, architectural, and logical centralization or decentralization, but the point is that you can have one or more levels of decentralization. You can adjust your level of decentralization. With this in mind, asking, "Is it decentralized?" isn't going to give you the information you want. You have to ask, "How decentralized is it?" In blockchain, you probably want to focus mostly on architectural and political decentralization—which are, unfortunately, the most likely to be centralized in some manner.

Architectural decentralization

Architectural decentralization is important because this reduces the likelihood of the system crashing because of a node computer breakdown, system hack or other attack, or forced shutdown due to political pressure. (Each of these has happened to the Bitcoin blockchain.) Distributing the system among a wide number of nodes has two benefits: it reduces the likelihood of crashing, and as a bonus it also reduces the ability of private or government actors to control or shut down a particular blockchain.

Political decentralization

Political decentralization is what most people are referring to when they talk about the need for "decentralization in blockchain." It's really about two types of political control: governance and consensus.

Governance is the process that figures out which rules control a system, how to execute those rules, and what the system (or members of the system) do to enforce the rules and deter rule-breakers. For example, holders of the Rally (RLY) governance coin are able to do things like these:

- Approve proposed updates to the application
- Define rights for internal pre-minted "creator" coins
- Determine the rate of return for a staked correctly validated vote
- Determine whether a staked coin should be confiscated because of a falsely validated or fraudulent vote

Consensus, on the other hand, is the voting method that determines whether a measure passes or a block of transactions should be closed and the next block opened. This happens via an agreed-on method of voting that includes the percentage of vote required to pass various actions. "Reaching consensus" means using the existing governance methods to find a common agreement that a particular block of transactions or proposal should be added to the chain (transactions) or adopted (proposal).

Tolerance and decentralization

Why does decentralization even matter? The theory is that systems that are decentralized are less likely to fail because they have three types of resistance to failure, or tolerance:

Fault tolerance
> The decreased likelihood that a complex system with lots of parts and redundancy will fail accidentally because too many parts would be required to fail simultaneously.[10]

Attack tolerance
> The decreased likelihood that a complex system will fail intentionally because it's too expensive to attack and destroy it because there aren't central access points; you have to attack the entire system at once.

Collusion tolerance
> The decreased likelihood of multiple parties acting maliciously in tandem.

These reasons have flaws, unfortunately.

Fault tolerance is drastically lowered when, for example, all the parts are manufactured in the same location. For example, most mining equipment required to process proof-of-work transactions come from four major manufacturers, two of which dominate market share.[11] Similarly, most blockchains have nodes that run identical software. A bug or virus that affects one node would impact all of them.

Attack tolerance is generally lowered as efficiency improves. This is a natural condition of the current iterations of blockchain: typically, scalability is attained by reducing pathways to processing, which reduces the cost of attacking the remaining nodes. Systems like delegated proof of stake or large mining pods reduce the attack cost as well by making it more likely for attackers to attack the nodes actually processing.

---

10 Simple systems may be more secure, technically, because they have fewer overall points of access or potential breach, but the statistical likelihood of failure is higher because fewer things are required to fail to have the simple system not work. Each component of a simple system is simply more important. (Ha.)

11 Jamie Redman, "Bitcoin ASIC Miner Manufacturing Domination: Bitmain and Microbt Battle for Top Positions," Bitcoin.com, June 22, 2020, *https://oreil.ly/EuNe7*.

Hardware is much easier to spot than tokens, so proof-of-work nodes present much greater risk of attack than any other kind of consensus/processing method.

Collusion tolerance is generally lowered the more concentrated blockchain control is, either by mining power or token holding. Having large mines or nodes all co-located, especially in a country that promotes restrictions on blockchain, encourages collusion, even if only to evade local prosecution or expulsion. If your large token holders or miners all know each other and can get together for tea to discuss what's happening on-chain, or they all show up at the same conference and wave hello to one another, you may have a significant collusion problem.

Fortunately, there are ways to address this in platforms and DApps. The following options will add a degree of security in your chain or DApp:

- Add in true randomization (such as quantum randomization), or at least some form of pure proof of stake, which allows any token holder to be a voting node and reduce predictability.
- Distribute nodes geographically.
- Use varied and competitive software and hardware developers.
- Identify core developers or nodes publicly (this one is less popular, as "doxxing" removes anonymity and is often avoided by those interested in working in blockchain).
- Use a complex consensus method like proof of work combined with proof of stake, or other combination system.
- Keep software and protocol developers separate and unknown to one another to the greatest extent possible to avoid commonality and easy collusion.
- Limit concentrations of mining power and/or token holding, and establish severe penalties for surpassing limits.

Consensus

We've covered a bit of consensus already, but a consensus method is a validation method for all nodes.[12] There are around 14 consensus methods as of the time of this writing, the earliest of which is the proof-of-work method described in the Nakamoto Bitcoin whitepaper.[13]

---

12 *Nodes* are computers supporting a blockchain platform or application by lending theirs processing power or voting validation to the platform or DApp for stability and governance.

13 See "The Bitcoin Revolution: The First Blockchain Use Case" on page 8 for a description of the paper. This paper is referred to as the "Nakamoto whitepaper."

This really just means you need a method that determines how you will process transactions (hashing or encrypting them in the process), who gets to be part of the voting or closing process (mining, staking, etc.), what percentage of votes constitutes agreement, the actual voting method, and how the votes are counted. Most chains want this as automated as possible, and they use a combination of algorithms and smart contracts to make this easy to execute but difficult to fake for an outside attack.

Permanence (or Immutability)

Immutability is the inability to erase, undo, or insert transactions after a block is closed. is a This is a really important part of the technology. Erasing and undoing transactions in financial recordkeeping is the heart of most fraud. These are transactions that are kept "off book," ignored, deleted, isolated, and otherwise separated from the bulk of the financial transactions, giving an often drastically different financial picture.

Remember, at its heart, blockchain is an accounting ledger. The ability to avoid manipulating past entries or creating false ones is at the core of blockchain. We'll look at the example of Enron shortly.

However, like all features, the inability to undo transactions can have bug-like problems. This is why, when assets are stolen—e.g., someone steals bitcoin from an exchange or wallet, other assets are illegally obtained by con (a "rug pull" or "honeypot") or straight hack—it is impossible to stop or undo the transaction. The transaction must be voluntarily reversed by the thief initiating a transaction back to the person robbed. As you can imagine, this doesn't happen often. There are some "white hat" hackers who do this to test for security holes, then return assets after they report the breach, and collect a bounty. Unfortunately, you're more likely to find your assets on a black market site than back in your account with a note saying, "Ha ha. Just kidding."

The inability to insert transactions is another major feature of blockchain. Blocking and hashing, a process that is described in the Nakamoto Bitcoin paper, links every transaction in the past to all future transactions. Early blockchains, including the Bitcoin blockchain and Ethereum, used a consensus method called *proof of work*, in which a block of transactions are hashed, or encrypted with a randomized code, then combined with all other concurrent and past transactions, and reencrypted. This makes it nearly impossible to extract a single transaction from the past and alter or add in a transaction that doesn't have the proper links to all past transactions, including the randomized encryption codes. Because current transactions are inextricably linked to past transactions, it is nearly impossible to insert or alter a transaction outside the chain of all previous transactions accidentally. Fraud is immediately noticeable, because it cannot have all prior transactions, correctly hashed, with the correct tagging (the header) to insert with new transactions. This means that you can't alter past transactions or insert new ones to justify past decisions, and no delete button or discussion with accounting will allow past transactions to be viewed in a different light or amended so they look better to shareholders. Any attempt to fraudulently insert a transaction is blatantly obvious.

How Fraudulent Transactions Are Obvious: A Proof-of-Work Example

Imagine you are at a train station platform, waiting for a 20-car freight train to pull up and load your valuable product so it can be delivered to its buyer.

While you're waiting, an engine (we'll call this Train 1) drives up and says, "Hey! I'm that 20-car freight train you were looking for! Go ahead and get that product onboard." At the same time, another train (Train 2) pulls in, and says, "No, stop! *I'm* the 20-car train, and that engine is just trying to rob you!" You see that both Train 1 and Train 2 look identical from the front—but one of them will take your goods to the buyer, and the other is clearly fake. What to do?

You lean forward and see Train 2 has a bunch of rail cars pulled behind it. Train 1 isn't even an engine—it's a stumpy car painted to look like an engine with nothing behind it, and a driver yelling "choo choo!"

Using all your powers of logic and reason, you quickly realize that Train 1 is lying about being a 20-car freight train. You load your product on Train 2 and call the police on the idiot trying to steal goods with a stumpy fake engine and pretending it's a train.

Similarly, a fraudulent transaction or set of transactions will show up as a cropped chain, not the full hashed chain. This stumpy set clearly doesn't belong, and any miner agreeing that the fake transaction is real is just like anyone agreeing the fake Train 1 is actually the real Train 2: a bad actor conspiring to make the bad transaction seem legitimate.

This is what immutability really means—you can't hide things that are fake.

Of course, as with all things, this has a "bug" side as well. Processing the entire chain whenever a block of transactions closes requires more and more energy as the blockchain grows. This is the cause of the environmental risk often discussed, and one of the primary reasons most of blockchain technology has moved beyond the original proof-of-work consensus method to other, far more energy conservative approaches, like proof of stake.

We should also note that the permanence that prevents fraud also prevents easy pivots when building. It's taken over five years for Ethereum to move from proof of work to Ethereum 2.0's proof-of-stake system. It is that hard to pivot. You have to plan very far ahead to deal well with roadblocks and potential barriers and failures. This is the opposite of the common traditional web and application approach of building a minimum viable product, testing it out continuously, and altering as the market deter-mines. None of that is possible, and certainly not in a beta version. In blockchain, you build and succeed or fail in public. These prior offerings have great lessons for us in understanding how other people have approached problems and how their decisions turned out. Since we can't pivot, we have to study these past offerings in detail, and work in as much flexibility as possible, to allow for the ability to recover and add a bit of agility to a very structured system.

How Would Blockchain Have Prevented a Case of Real-Life Fraud?

Let's look at what this means in a practical example. In 1999, Enron attempted to merge with a German utility company called Veba, in what would have been a merger of equals. During due diligence, Veba discovered something that caused them to call off the merger. It has long been speculated that the cause of the failed merger was Veba's discovery of Enron's off-book accounting,[14] which removed millions of dollars of debt off its books by hiding the money in limited purpose vehicles (LPVs) owned by Enron.

Had Enron's transactions been conducted using blockchain technology, hiding this debt would have been impossible. All the transactions would have involved two par-ties, with the blockchain itself tracking every transaction. Using LPVs that were inter-nally owned and controlled would have been readily discoverable to anyone with access to the blockchain, as it would have been clear that Enron was simply conduct-ing transactions with itself, not an independent third party. Putting transactions on the blockchain makes this kind of accounting fraud nearly impossible.

Now, that is not to say tampering with a blockchain is impossible. Any system has multiple weak points, and blockchain is no different. Other weak points follow and will be discussed in much more detail later in this book:

Wallets
> Wallets are accounts that stay electronically linked to the internet, either because they are controlled by another site or exchange (*hot wallets*) or simply remain on the internet (*warm wallets*). Each of these can be attacked by viruses or theft, including theft from the platform itself if it's a hot wallet.

---

14 This is an "open secret" in the securities community. Though no official statements have been made regarding the failed Veba merger, numerous investigative reports indicate the link between Enron's books and the failure of the merger. The most cited appears to be "Enron's Many Strands: Early Warning: '99 Deal Failed After Scru-tiny of Enron Books" by Edmund L. Andrews et al. in the *New York Times*, Jan. 27, 2002.

False consensus

False consensus, or virtual control, of the blockchain is really a risk of too few holders of tokens or too few nodes—it recentralizes control. False consensus occurs when the tokens or nodes are held by one or a few entities that own or control over 50% of the blockchain's tokens (the *51% attack*). As blockchains progress, more nodes are added, distributing control to more people and reducing this risk. Bitcoin, unfortunately, is particularly subject to this risk, as the *HODL* (buy and hold) philosophy has resulted in mining and hoarding, rather than distribution of assets.

As a result, 10% of miners control 90% of mining capacity, and only 50 miners (0.1%) control close to 50% mining capacity.[15] While balances by intermediaries have been increasing since 2014, the top 1,000 investors control around 3 million BTC (approximately 20% of the bitcoin in circulation), while the top 10,000 investors control approximately 5 million BTC (approximately 33% of the bitcoin in circulation).[16] All that means lots of bitcoin in few hands, which is a point of centralization. The more these holders act together, the more we can see that this small group can exercise an enormous amount of power over the chain when acting together.

Phishing and bad invitations

This remains one of the biggest reasons fraud persists, especially among wallets. People click links they shouldn't, give away seed phrases (which you should *never* do), and/or invest in projects based on false premises or fraud. This is still a huge problem in the industry.

Failed security protocols

Attacks also attacks result from failed security protocols or protocols that have a deliberate "back door" left in the code to allow later attack when more assets are on the chain. An example is one entity holding two of the three authentication keys required for a multisignature (multisig) wallet, allowing internal theft and fraud (see, e.g., the $66 million theft from Bitfinex).

Currently, these are being addressed by new voting protocols and adjusting loss across users. These are temporary resolutions, at best, and are addressed in a later section of this text. I'll discuss details on how these smart contracts are actually triggered in "A Word on Wallets" on page 41.

---

15 Study done by National Bureau of Economic Research, released October 2021.

16 Ibid.

Anonymity

Anonymity here refers to that concept I mentioned earlier: public transactions, private parties. The platform or application has to protect the identity of the parties, and it does this by providing randomized wallet identifiers (letters and numbers) and using protocols that do not directly identify parties whenever possible.

Legal requirements regarding money laundering and securities issues, among other things, prevent this from being as anonymous as most in the system would like. Most try to keep these identity requirements to a minimum, and stress the importance of keeping identifiers to as small an amount as possible.

Trustless

As noted previously, one unique aspect of blockchain is that it *expects* bad actors. It expects a certain amount of fraud to be part of the system and deals quite well with it. If you want anonymous parties and public transactions, you need to be able to have agreements and actions execute by themselves, or the delay in getting every party to agree to a contract or offer will be so long and work intensive that the blockchain would be unusable.

What Does Any of This Have to Do with Finance?

That's a great question. We have a bunch of information on blockchain, but what does this have to do with finance—and what is finance, anyway?

I already went through accounting; I'm not going to make it worse and start adding in a bunch of math and statistics to discuss finance and financial tools. Let's talk about what traditional finance (or TradFi) is and how money flows in economies—and why this sucks for most people, leading to the rise of DeFi. It's exciting stuff that leads to you making more money with the money you have, so let's get started!

What Is Finance?

Finance, in general, can best be described as money making money. When you hear people say you need to "put your money to work," they are often speaking of putting your money into some sort of financial tool so you can generate more money with it. How does that work? Through the magic of interest and time—especially compound interest, which we'll discuss in this section.

When you put your money into a standard bank account, you get access to three powerful tools: the ability to store your funds in a safe location, the ability to convert someone's debt to you into cash that is available for use, and the ability to convert your money in whatever form it exists to digital cash, which is now the primary form of payment. It's difficult to buy most goods and services in the US without some form of digital payment—either a credit or debit card. This is the fundamental problem of the unbanked: it's not that they have zero access to funds; it's that they have no cheap or convenient way to store it, which is why predatory lenders like check-cashing companies and pawnshops are able to prey on them so easily. This was one of the first problems blockchain intended to solve—the ability of banks to preclude people from accessing their basic services, forcing them to use services with extremely high interest payments that create debt that is functionally impossible to pay off.

If you are lucky enough to have a bank account and access to those tools mentioned, you also get the ability to earn interest on the money you deposit. This is like earning rent from the bank because it gets to use your deposited money, and the bank earns interest on the investments it makes—with your money. But interest rates have not been particularly high since the 1990s, and most people earn little to no interest on their deposits—even though the bank is still using their money, and making a lot of money on it. We're going to discuss how that happens next.

How Money Flows in Banks and Economies

Now, let's talk about how money flows between retail customers (people like us, not institutions or funds). When you deposit money in your account, you might think this cash sits in a vault, ready for people to take it out. It does not.

Most economies flourish only with economic activity—that is, when money changes hands. This is what happens when you buy or sell goods or services. Economies like lots of activity; it makes people who make goods or offer services richer, which, in theory, makes them hire more people, who earn money that they can, in turn, spend on more goods and services. All this spending and making and hiring means the government doesn't have to support people through entitlements like welfare.

Entitlement programs cost money, which has to be generated through taxes. Raising taxes does not endear any elected official to their constituency (especially in the US), so most view entitlements, and the increases in taxes they require, as a last resort only. Everyone spending money means the money is getting redistributed without the need for increased taxes—which, of course, makes lawmakers extremely happy. The fact that redistribution always seems to go from the same people and to the same people is not something they like to focus on.

Most governments view the role of government as primarily to monitor redistribution, not to enforce a more equal flow of money to and from parties. As a result of this redistribution and money flow goal, they do not particularly want money to sit idle in vaults or under beds. When money sits, it doesn't get redistributed, and that leads quickly to requirements for broad government support—and tax increases. Even China, with its economy that is actively managed by the government, as opposed to the US system of economic management through free markets, experienced trouble with the tendency of many Chinese families to save up to 30% of their income. They had to encourage spending to release those funds, which was a big trigger for the growth of the middle and upper classes we've seen in the past few decades.

So, we imagine banks full of stacks and stacks of cash—but now we know that it is against government interest to have it just sitting there. So what did they do? They required banks to hold only a small amount of cash, which is called the reserve ratio. This reserve ratio varies depending on the total amount of eligible deposits each day, but ranges from 0% to 10%. That's it. Ten percent of deposits are kept on hand. Some banks choose to keep more on hand to make sure they can pay out more depositors on demand, which is called *excess reserves* and is another range that banks set themselves according to their perceived needs (the *liquidity ratio*). Note that the liquidity ratio can be reduced or removed whenever the bank wants.

Also, banks can borrow money from the central bank (the Federal Reserve in the US, or Fed) simply by asking—and are not turned down. This overnight loan to cover the reserve ratio means that all banks can effectively leave *nothing* in their vaults and assume the Fed will help them if they need to pay out depositors because they want to take money out of their accounts.

Banks Are Using *Your* Cash—and Not Paying for It

So, what do they do with the millions of dollars we depositors so generously leave with them? Banks put this money to work. They enter into a variety of financial instruments, lending out your money in mortgages, small business loans, personal loans, and many other types of interest-bearing offerings. And there's that word again, interest. Let's take a little detour to understand what interest really is.

When you loan out money, think of it like renting out a truck. The person you loan it to either takes the keys and goes (if you know them), or leaves maybe a copy of their license and a credit card authorization (if you don't know them—to make you feel comfortable loaning out your truck to a stranger). When the truck is due to be returned, they return the truck. The truck has to be in the condition you loaned it—no extra scratches, dents, or missing parts. You get everything back exactly as you loaned it out. But what else do you get? You get a rental payment—the amount you charge for loaning out your truck. That is your incentive to loan out your truck. You are getting paid for it, which is the cost of rental, and the price of you being without your truck because someone else is using it.

Now, instead of a truck, imagine you are loaning out money. You loan it out, with collateral if you don't know or trust the person, or without if you feel certain they will repay the money. You get your money back in full; they don't get to keep part of it. But on top of that, you get a payment for renting out your money. That's interest.

Interest is the rental fee for loaning out your money. The rate is high if you think the person you are loaning the money out to will probably pay but aren't sure they will pay back everything or pay on time. You want to get more money because there is more of a chance you could lose it, and you might have to borrow money to cover your own expenses. If you can borrow it at a certain rate, like 3%, you want to make sure that you loan it out at a higher rate, something like 5% or 6%, so that even if you have to borrow money to cover your own mortgage payments and bills, or even go to court to collect the money you are owed, you still charged enough to make a profit. That's why the rate you can borrow money at is so important to know. If you thought you could borrow at 3%, but it turns out that when you need money you can get it only at 7%, loaning your money out at 6% would make you lose money if anything goes wrong. Remember, you can't use your money while you are loaning it out. If it isn't repaid, you have to find money somewhere. You have your own lenders to worry about. Many people don't bother to understand this basic concept, which is why they end up losing money in financial instruments.

So, now we know that the government doesn't want big chunks of money sitting and doing nothing, and banks have to leave only a small amount (if anything) in their vault for depositors. What are they doing with all those deposits? They are lending them out—and earning interest! They have millions of dollars of your money (and mine, and everyone else who has an account there), and they turn that money around and loan it out, charging a range of interest rates for it. It would be nice if they guaranteed that the money would be available as loans for the same community that deposited money in accounts with that bank. That would be circulating money from the community to the community, in larger amounts than any individual could do on their own.

But, unfortunately, they do not do that. They loan to the people who can pay them the most money, who they believe will repay their funds with certainty. And generally, that is not the small businesses of the local community or individuals. It's the large companies and high-net-worth individuals.

So, you aren't getting that money loaned back out to you. But, at least you get a piece of that interest your money is generating, right? No. The bank keeps all of it. That is what is forming the base amount of its revenue—all those dollars it earns. The bank does that by loaning out your money and then putting it back in the bank only long enough to give people their money when they request it (this is just your typical bank withdrawal from your account). But all those interest payment profits the bank made on the money you generously, if unknowingly, let it borrow free of charge? The bank keeps that. And if you've ever paid a bank fee, or an ATM fee, or a low balance fee, or a wire fee, then you just paid them to use your money.

On top of that, let's talk about access. You see the banks making all this delicious cash for far less risk than investing in a stock or coin, or starting a company. So you decide you'd like in on this great deal. So you ask the bank if you can put some cash in those investment tools also. Just a little bit to add to its pool and give you a nice return in a few months. Easy peasy, right? Nope.

Your bank offers you crappy option one: an interest-bearing account. This account has a minimum balance and often a limit on transactions per month, along with a fee for many services. And for all this, you get an interest rate of 1%. If you're lucky.

No? Welcome to crappy option two: a certificate of deposit (or CD), generally requiring you to lock up your minimum investment for a period of six months. The minimum amount is, on average, $5,000—meaning you need $5,000 *extra* dollars you can't touch during the lockup period (six months!), for the incredible interest rate of... 1.36%.[17]

My goodness, these are both shockingly crappy options with a huge amount of expense and very little upside, you say? You're correct. Banks do not care about providing access to investment tools to anyone who does not have $5,000 as spare cash. But between zero investable cash and $5,000 in investable cash lives around 95% of the population. That banks don't care about. At all.

And that's the problem with traditional finance: most people don't want you to be able to do it. Especially banks.

What Is Decentralized Finance, and Why Is It Important?

Decentralized finance (*DeFi*) is money making money, like centralized finance, but without using banks. Does it sound more interesting already? I think so too.

Instead of banks controlling access to financial tools, anyone can get access to the magical tools of interest and time to generate and maintain generational wealth. No one will limit your access based on your income, your last name, your ethnicity, your address, your education, your alma mater, your parentage, or even your legal status within a country. If you want access, you get it.

That, of course, presents its own problems. With no financial educational requirements in most school systems around the world, those with knowledgeable people in their house or immediate environment have a clear advantage over those who do not. And the people with that kind of knowledge floating in their environment more often than not are already wealthy. Those who are not wealthy don't have Uncle Joe, who runs the Derivatives desk at Citi, pop on over to run through cash flow, risk management, and the time value of money. The rest of us are more likely to get a list of people (relatives and predatory lenders) and food banks to turn to when the money runs out before the end of the month. It's hard to worry about investment strategy and

---

17 National average interest rate as of October 2023. Note that minimum amounts and yields vary tremendously by bank and personal credit and banking history of applicants.

cost-benefit analysis when you are trying to make sure your kids are fed every day, especially when you aren't.

So the openness of DeFi is a bit illusory. Anyone can participate, but the advantage clearly lies with those who have the background to understand what is happening in real time. And those people are the already wealthy investors, who have access to both traditional finance (TradFi) via banks, and nontraditional finance, through DeFi.

Access and risk comprehension aside, DeFi applications work similarly to TradFi in principle. You loan someone money for a set interest rate, and you get back your money plus interest rate returns. That's pretty much where the resemblance ends.

Although the terms used will be described in much greater detail as we move into the mechanisms of DeFi, some of the key differences between DeFi and TradFi are summarized in Table 1-1.

Table 1-1. TradFi versus DeFi

	TradFi	DeFi
Length of investment	One month to five years for most interest-bearing offerings, and indefinite for interest-bearing savings accounts.	Some loans (flash loans) are the length of the transactions, others for minutes or hours. Some are for days or even a month.
Investment currency	Fiat	Stablecoins and/or asset-backed tokens, primarily incentivized governance tokens
Interest rates, on average	Banks are giving, on average, 0.06% for interest-bearing savings accounts, 0.07% for money market accounts, 0.14%–0.27% for certificate of deposit accounts (longer term = higher interest). Compare that with the average rates banks are getting, which range from 3% to 36% (longer term = *lower* rate). This difference between rates banks give and rates banks get is the net interest margin, which is the biggest source of profit for banks.	1%–5% for simple staking on a chain, 1%–6% for liquidity providers, 2%–10% for lending platforms, 60%–80% or more for yield farming and aggregators.
Compounded/ simple	Annual percentage rate, which does not factor in compounded interest	Annual percentage yield, which does factor in timing and amount of compounded interest
Custodial	Yes—your investment is locked up for a predetermined period.	Rarely. Most are noncustodial, and you can exit the transaction once concluded (flash loan) or at will (staking, liquidity provider, etc.).
Identities	Parties are aware of one another, including detailed identifying information such as Social Security number.	Parties identified by wallets; not otherwise known to each other.
Qualifying	Minimum amounts and credit score may apply	No qualifications other than sufficient collateral
Collateral	Collateral is required for loans as borrower, and minimum balances function as collateral base.	Collateral determines amount of loan.

Conclusion

In this chapter, we've learned about the basic structure of blockchain, the key aspects of blockchain, characteristics that describe blockchain, and its applications, some of which also cause difficulty in blockchain use or development.

We also discussed the key principles of both traditional and decentralized finance, and the reasons that decentralized finance, or DeFi, is so incredibly important. Next we're going to talk about current development in DeFi applications and platforms, and understanding the main tools of the DeFi system.

CHAPTER 2

The Building Blocks of DeFi

We've talked about blockchain as a whole; now let's talk about the individual terms describing the building blocks of DeFi and how they fit together. These building blocks are protocols, platforms, decentralized applications (DApps), wallets, stablecoins, and governance tokens. Remember that Bitcoin and ETH (the base token of Ethereum) are permitted on nearly all DeFi chains because they are well established and the most liquid of the assets available. I am not explaining them further in this chapter, but they are also building blocks of DeFi.

After that, we will discuss some of the use cases of DeFi.

Protocols

Protocols are just a set of rules and procedures. DeFi protocols are the rules and procedures for lending and borrowing without using banks. These protocols are used in one of two things: a platform or a DApp. Let's discuss the difference between the two.

Platforms

A *blockchain platform* is just like any technology platform. It establishes the environment, or basic rule system, that will allow applications to run. Blockchain platforms, as they currently stand, have a few basic requirements and one main issue to resolve. As you'll see in Figure 2-1, platforms deal with these requirements and issues differently, and that's what makes the key distinctions between various platforms.

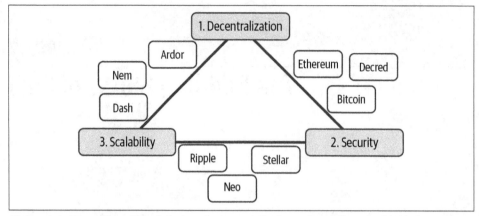

Figure 2-1. Examples of blockchain solutions and where they fall in the blockchain tri-lemma (adapted from an image by Toshitimes)

This section details what you need to consider in building a blockchain platform. It's not a complete or exhaustive list, but it will get you building properly.

A Trilemma Solution

First, you need a *trilemma solution*. The blockchain trilemma is based on a classic issue in international finance regarding the three competing requirements of national monetary policy, only two of which can be achieved at any given time.

Initially defined in the blockchain field by Vitalik Buterin,[1] the premise is that, because all nodes process all transactions (all blockchains are held in their entirety on each node), all blockchain protocols are limited by the abilities of its slowest, least secure node. Accordingly, anyone trying to innovate in blockchain will have to address three competing interests, only two of which can be met by a blockchain solution. The interests are decentralization, scalability, and security.

Decentralization

The blockchain is distributed across nodes and not controlled by any single node or subgroup of nodes. The removal of any node or subgroup of nodes will not break the blockchain. And no single node or subgroup of nodes is able to solely dictate which transactions, proposals, code, policies, or adaptations will pass or fail. Most chains aspire to this, but the Bitcoin blockchain is the most decentralized.

---

1 The trilemma solution was defined by Vitalik Buterin in the Ethereum Wiki at *https://eth.wiki/sharding/Sharding-FAQs*. Note that this description is quite useful to blockchain developers but not as useful to users.

Scalability

The blockchain should have the ability to bring on nearly unlimited users without requiring a similar rate of nodes onboarding, with no decrease in transaction processing speed, and the transaction processing speed should approach or exceed the speed of centralized database transactions. This is the most difficult issue to solve, and the one most are trying to include as part of their solution. The benchmark on this is 64,000 transactions per second (tps), a near-mythical barrier that is Visa's maximum transaction speed. At the time of this writing, the platform closest to achieving this is Solana at 50,000 tps. However, as explained later, this number will be a low-end barrier with the advent of new technologies, including nonsharded directed acyclic graphs (DAGs) like Hedera or the new object-oriented programming models from Aptos and Sui, and the future incorporation of quantum computing into blockchain.

Security

The blockchain should be able to maintain its integrity against hacks and malicious attacks. This is actually one of the most interesting aspects of blockchain: because blockchain developers don't assume hackers are strictly outside bad actors, but could also be some of the nodes and/or users, the developers develop the system to withstand both internal and external malicious action.

Personally, I find this fascinating, because it acknowledges a simple truth about human nature: bad actors are everywhere, and they don't always conveniently announce themselves as masked robbers with guns blazing, shooting their way into secured areas. They are quite often internal actors, or ones who exploit weaknesses that aren't known or addressed. This is one of the first problems addressed, in fact, with a principle called *Byzantine fault tolerance*. The problem really lies in the fact that security and scalability are inversely related. The more secure something is, the harder it is to move things quickly or add a bunch of new users. The faster a system moves, the harder it is to make sure nothing gets broken. (Hence the constant demand in Silicon Valley to "move fast and break things." Because that's what happens when you move fast.)

The most secure chains operate on a proof-of-work consensus method, such as Bitcoin blockchain and Ethereum 1.0. These are blockchain's earliest technology and its most secure, but also the most expensive, most work intensive, slowest, and most environmentally damaging.

While some projects have claimed to have solved for all three interests, none have, in fact, resolved this trilemma. So, when selecting the type of blockchain you want to build, or the platform your DApp should sit on, think of the nature of the problem, and which two of the three issues take priority over the third. For example, financial transactions, including DeFi, tend to favor scalable, secure platforms. The priority in money transactions is making sure the transfer is fast and secure, at the expense of a certain amount of decentralization. And this is what you see, in fact. Some chains, such as Cardano, focus on the scalability and security, while preserving as much decentralization as possible—but not at the expense of scalability and security. DeFi is an excellent fit for this type of chain.

Identity protocols tend to favor decentralized and secure transactions, at the expense of speed (scalability). Gaming DApps, on the other hand, favor scalability and decentralization, at the expense of security.

Remember that blockchain projects, including DeFi projects, are still fundamentally startups. The order of operations must *always* be (1) find a problem many people have that they will pay to solve, (2) figure out a solution to the problem that is at least 10 times better than the current best option(s), and then (3) choose the technology that best serves your solution. Many people discover a new technology and skip right to step 3, without understanding the nature of the problem or the ideal solution. *Always* make sure your platform selection is grounded in the nature of the problem you are addressing, not the solution you have in mind.

Deployment Network

A platform requires a system to store, process, and maintain data. Instead of a centralized database maintained on either servers or cloud space, blockchain platforms are deployed via individual or grouped computers running the architectural base and related client software (both discussed next). These computers are called *nodes*.

An architectural base

The architectural base is the structural base of the platform. In blockchain, this is fundamentally the block-based recordkeeping system. Beyond that, enormous variation exists. A few of these variations can include languages, smart contracts, and/or software libraries.

You can use any language that works—and people do. These include C++ (Bitcoin), Python (Hyperledger), Solidity (Ethereum), Rust (Solana), and Substrate (Polkadot).

Smart contracts are the programs that drive the whole system. To execute a smart contract, the language must be Turing complete, or able to execute on a trigger and then stop automatically. Some chains, like the Bitcoin blockchain, are not Turing complete, while others, like Ethereum, are Turing complete. Most chains are Turing complete at this point in time.

Libraries are generally as flexible as languages. Most platforms have an existing library and software development kit (SDK) to ensure easy and interoperable application development.

A common token

Blockchain currently runs on smart contracts that are triggered by tokens specific to that platform (which may also permit other tokens that are wrapped to fit the platform's token, which is discussed in more detail in Chapter 4).

A common client software

The platform will need some sort of operational software to allow nodes to run the platform. This software must be easy to download with an SDK or something similar to make it easy to adopt. The system must have a firewall to protect any other data that may be on the node, and function as an independent sandbox with limited, if any, offline interruption.

Application access (automated or bespoke)

Currently, in our token-based system, platforms must have a way to easily allow applications to interact with the platform. Applications may use the platform's native token, or they may develop their own native token suitable only for use on that specific application. In the event the application uses its own native token, the native token of the platform must also be accepted.

Ethereum revolutionized a method to automate token development for applications by creating pre-minted tokens (the ERC-20, ERC-1155, ERC-721, etc.). This massively reduced the cost of creating a compliant, compatible token by offering preformatted tokens that were designed to work on the Ethereum system, but can be tailored to individual applications within a particular category, such as fungible (representing an interchangeable item), nonfungible (representing a unique, noninterchangeable item), or other category of use.

Most platforms now offer a standardized token to assist with and encourage application development. Not requiring a team of developers to create each smart contract is a major cost and time benefit. Bitcoin blockchain is the most conspicuous of those that do not offer standardized tokens.

Virtual machine

A *virtual machine* allows a platform (or application) to operate on a standard computer without the cost of required hardware and closes off the new (or "guest") operating system in a secure environment that has no access to the computer's main operating system or data. It allows a safe "sandbox" to run a separate operating system to see how it works or, in the case of nodes, run the platform (or application) without having to invest in a separate computer with necessary hardware. It also compresses data so that it can travel across systems (including across platforms) without crashing a system or being susceptible to either corruption or hacking.

Not all platforms use virtual machines. Ethereum's virtual machine is probably the best known. They have benefits and detriments that are beyond the scope of this book but well worth exploring if you are building a platform.

Decentralized Applications

An *application* is a software system created to perform a particular task, or to enable a user to perform a specific function. It runs on a particular type of platform, and it is the main point of interaction for users.

DApps are similar to traditional applications. They run on a platform operating system. However, instead of being run on a centralized server, they run on a blockchain platform. As discussed in Chapter 1, these distributed, decentralized platforms are a direct, peer-to-peer network that conducts direct transfer of assets between wallets instead of running through a controlled intermediary like a server.

The following are the four main elements of a true DApp.

Incentivized

Those who run nodes and provide stability and security to the node must be incentivized to contribute to the security and functioning of the chain. Most often this is in the payment of the platform token, the DApp token, or another incentivized governance token.

Decentralized

All the records of a public blockchain must be stored or accessible by each node, so none have an advantage in understanding process or building reputation.

Blockchain-Based Protocol

The founding team of the application, or the community if it exists prior to the application being developed (rare, but possible), need to select a blockchain platform and a protocol. There are many ways to select a platform, but primarily the platform is selected because it has a community of people interested in using and supporting the application, or it has a base protocol that is advantageous for the application. Ideally, the platform has both. The base protocol is generally a representation of the type of problem the platform is looking to solve and the choice the founding team of that chain made with respect to the trilemma (discussed in "Platforms" on page 35).

Open Source (Maybe)

This means the chain should be governed autonomously by the nodes, with changes all conducted by consensus of its users and/or nodes (depending on the type of change). Open source requires the base code of the chain to be available for adoption by third parties and able to be audited by anyone willing to review the code. Most platforms currently run as open source in name only.

A Word on Wallets

Wallets are yet another misnomer in the blockchain space (along with cryptocurrency, smart contract, and many others). Many people think wallets hold digital currency, NFTs, and other assets. They don't—they just hold the access to a list of transaction "receipts" that live permanently on various blockchains. Think of it more like a private portal, and the portal reads all the connected blockchain platforms and DApps, and it compiles a list of your assets based on transactions that are connected to that wallet's address.

Assets and coins don't actually move into or out of wallets. *Ownership* moves, and is permanently recorded on the blockchain as a series of transactions. So, while you see a balance of coins and images of art or other assets you hold in your "account," what you are really seeing is a representation of the receipts of your wallet's transactions.

Your wallet has two keys, a public key and a private key. Your *public key* is what people use when they want to send you something. It's money *into* your account. You also have a *private key*, which is the authorization to send assets *out of* your account. So, public key is assets in, private key is assets out. If you want to buy something or gain access to anything, you need your private key, which is basically a confidential password, to tell your wallet to send an appropriate token to trigger the platform or DApp smart contract. If someone else gains access to your private key, they immediately have the ability to send or spend anything in your wallet. It effectively becomes their wallet.

You may have heard about the importance of seed phrases. A *seed phrase* is a list of 8–12 words randomly generated by your wallet. Most wallets have only one seed phrase, and no other can or will be generated. If you have your seed phrase, you can avoid being shut out of your wallet. If you forget your private-key password, or your password is somehow compromised, entering your seed phrase will force the wallet to generate a new private-key password. If someone gets hold of your seed phrase, they can effectively change your password and lock you out of your wallet for good.

Custodial Versus Noncustodial

With a *custodial wallet*, some other party, not you, maintains ownership. *Noncustodial wallets* give you all the access but also the risk of not remembering or losing your private-key password and/or seed phrase; there is no recourse if this happens.

In a custodial wallet, someone else holds the keys to your wallet "portal," like Coinbase wallet or most wallets attached to DApps or exchanges. If you lose your private-key password, they can generate a new one, because they hold the seed phrases (and thus hold ultimate possession over your wallet assets). However, in the far more secure noncustodial warm and cold wallets, you are the only person who holds your unique seed phrase. If you lose it or it is stolen, there is literally nothing you can do to recover your assets other than file an action against the offender (if you know who it is).

Wallets come in many varieties, but we generally categorize them as hot, warm, or cold.

Hot wallets

Hot wallets are attached to something like an exchange or other application. They tend to be run through a cloud or other database operator and can be accessed from any device. They are controlled by the exchange or application, which lets you have access to the wallet for the purpose of conducting transactions on that exchange (or what have you). You do not own the private or public keys to this wallet.

Benefits include the fact that transacting on that exchange is simple and efficient and you can ask for recovery or a new private key if you forget yours. Detriments include the fact that the attached exchange owns the public and private keys, not you. You also do not have any access to the seed phrase. This means the exchange can lock you out and seize all or a portion of your assets if they choose. This has occurred more than once, and redress is very difficult.

This is considered the least secure wallet class.

Warm wallets

Warm wallets live on single desktops or mobile applications (not the cloud). They are constructed by software that must be downloaded onto whatever access point you choose. These wallets, such as Trust Wallet and Brave Wallet, are noncustodial, so you, not the application, own your keys. These are more secure, provided a bug or virus isn't introduced, and can be taken offline if you wish to do so. If you lose your keys and/or seed phrase, there is no recourse, and you cannot access the assets in your wallet.

Cold wallets

Cold wallets store your private keys in a separate device, which looks like an elongated thumb drive. The current market leaders are Ledger and Trezor, though there are others. As with warm wallets, these are noncustodial, and you retain the rights and responsibility of your public and private keys and seed phrase. You can take these completely offline and allow no access until connected to the internet and a chain. These are the most secure of the wallets.

How do wallets work?

Two things trigger smart contracts, generally speaking: a token released from a wallet, or an oracle.[2] This is why wallets are so important—they function as the intermediary that tells the blockchain what you want to do on a particular DApp or platform. When you click a particular button, like Buy or Sell or Trade or Play or Enter, you are really using your private key to authorize your wallet to transfer a token from your account to the account of someone else (the DApp, another party, an exchange, etc.). The wallet checks to see whether your public and private keys match and, if so, initiates a smart contract on the blockchain platform or DApp. The receipt of the transaction, "asset A was removed from wallet A's account" and the matching "asset A was added to wallet B's account," is now listed as a transaction on that blockchain.

So, really, your wallet is your personal record of asset ownership. You and your counterparty are using double-entry bookkeeping to record your transaction in your respective wallets, then confirming that transaction with the third party: the blockchain. Voilà! Triple-entry accounting, via your wallets.

Your wallet must recognize the token or asset being transferred to or from your account, so make sure your wallet accepts as many of the tokens or assets you are

---

2 *Oracles* are, broadly speaking, bits of data from the outside world. They are sent from the blockchain (by another triggered smart contract) or by a centralized database that reports the results to a particular blockchain. This data can be any piece of information, from the balance in a traditional bank account to the weather on a particular day to the functionality of a particular sensor. The data either triggers a smart contract (for example, "move asset A to wallet B if the results are X or greater") or refrains from triggering a smart contract ("do nothing with asset A if results are less than X"). The *oracle problem* in blockchain refers to blockchains being independent, secure, and isolated platforms. They run on a secured system driven by consensus. They have no innate ability to get information from outside the blockchain, or any innate way of tracking and confirming the quality of the data the oracle brings back. Asking about the weather in a particular city, for example, may result in different answers by different web sources or sensors. To validate the authority and quality of any data ("this information is from the National Weather Service—safe data, use acceptable" or "this information is from Aunt Jo's lawn thermometer with IoT access, and is located outside the city required—unsafe data, use unacceptable") would require a huge upgrade in power and complexity for any node, and because all nodes share an identical ledger, it would require the upgrade in all nodes or lack consensus. This is extremely expensive and not viable in any system designed to have rapid transactions and/or scale, or exponentially grow, quickly. Oracles have other issues, but this is the primary one, and a concern the community is still working to resolve in a scalable manner.

interested in, regardless of platform, as possible. If you attempt to transfer a token or asset to a wallet that does not accept it or does not have an account for that type of token or asset, that unrecognized token or asset will fall into a digital void, *and it is impossible to recover.*

Are There Any Problems?

Anyone can send something to your wallet if they have the public key, and, for the most part, anyone can look into any wallet and see what is being held. "But remember," you are thinking, "these are anonymous transactions. How can anyone see into my wallet?" Good question. Anyone can see any transaction on a public, or permissionless, blockchain.[3] These are public transactions, but private parties. So, currently, anyone can look into a wallet, but no one knows a particular wallet belongs to you, specifically, unless you self-identify.[4]

Some wallets are identified because of the assets in there, or the volume of a particular asset held. If you know a particular person bought a particular NFT, for example, and you find that particular NFT in an account, you can be reasonably certain you know whose wallet you have found. For this reason, you can't really trust anyone who says buy X currency/asset/NFT because Y (famous person) did. You have no idea if that item was purchased by Y, or if someone just sent it to Y's address, unsolicited.

Similarly, you have to be careful in accepting free items into any wallet, because it may contain a tracker that allows someone to connect your wallet to you and/or hack the wallet to gain access to your keys. Strategies such as using many wallets, or using only new or empty wallets for drops or connections to the blockchain, have become useful.quite

---

3 Blockchains have two main types: permissioned and permissionless. *Permissionless* systems are most of the blockchains you've heard of. They are open to the public, and you don't have to request access to conduct a transaction on one. You just hook up your wallet to Ethereum, or Tezos, or Cardano, or whatever, and off you go. *Permissioned* blockchains are private chains, usually used internally by a particular company or shared among a few private parties. Examples include the internal Walmart chain, used for supply chain management, or private chains used on the Hyperledger system. You need to ask permission to access them, and generally all wallets are hosted, internal wallets. They are not used to transact financial business as much as track, verify, and/or pull data from internal networks.

4 A massive push is being made internationally, including but not limited to the US, to introduce identity procedures for all wallets and exchanges pursuant to the FATF Travel Rule changes, detailed in Chapter 3. Some form of identity is likely for the majority of wallets and exchanges that connect in any way with fiat. In addition, "crypto-sleuths," like ZachXBT, and tracking firms, such as Chainalysis and CipherTrace, specifically focus on identifying wallets and/or tracking transactions to the original parties. Other "whale tracking" sources will find and track wallets belonging to whales, or large token holders, of various chains to anticipate market movements. These actions are rarely done for people who are not wealthy and/or operating in questionable assets or circumstances.

Stablecoins

Stablecoins—a hot but are very misunderstood topic—are one of the earliest and most popular applications in DeFi. At their heart, they are intended to have the core functionality of currency, without the centralized control of fiat. Understanding the difference between an asset and a currency is extremely important in understanding how coins differ in both value and use. To do this, we need a better understanding of how money flows in an economy, the purpose and distribution of fiat currency, why a decentralized currency is necessary, and flaws with the current crop of stablecoins. (If you were inclined to highlight and star any section, it would probably be this one.) Let's get started!

Asset Versus Currency

Understanding the differences between assets and currency isa key issue that's commonly misunderstood. Generally speaking, volatility is a great quality for an asset but a terrible quality for a currency. In this context, *volatility* is the tendency for a price or market value to fluctuate. You want volatility in your assets—you want that price to move, because that's how your $100 investment in a coin or stock in 2015 can grow to $1,000 in 2019 (a 10× return, which is what angel investors typically call a win). Of course, it's also what can make your $100 investment worth $5 in 2019. Volatility can work for you or against you, which is what makes investing a risk. You mitigate this risk carefully by researching the assets you invest in, understanding the risk involved in the investment, and making an informed decision based on your own risk profile.

Currency, on the other hand, is most useful as a medium of exchange. It has a predictable value that fluctuates within a very narrow band of values. Say you and I decide to enter into an agreement: you will deliver wheat for my farm for the year, and I will pay you $10,000 at the end of the year. We both know what we're signing up for, and the risk is limited to standard contractual risk: you fail to deliver wheat, the wheat is spoiled or otherwise unusable for the purpose intended, I fail to pay, I refuse delivery for unpermitted reasons, etc. We have only *transactional risk*.[5]

---

5 Transactional risk is defined in Chapter 1.

Now, if we use a medium that fluctuates wildly, we add the risk of conversion to all that other transactional risk. For example, if we contract for 10,000 bitcoin, at the end of the year that could be worth $500,000—in which case I lose based on conversion value, because I've overpaid you, possibly so much that I declare bankruptcy. Or, it could be worth $500, in which case I've underpaid you, possibly more than you can recover from. Now we face *asset risk*,[6] on top of transactional risk.

And it doesn't apply only to contracts. Say I decide to pay for a coffee at my local café, Barbux, in bitcoin. We close the transaction, and I take my coffee. The next day, I check the price of bitcoin, and it has risen 20% in value. I realize I have missed out on that gain and paid too much for my already overpriced Barbux half-caff triple shot froofaccino. On the other hand, if I pay in bitcoin and it drops 20% in value, I've underpaid Barbux.

And this problem perpetuates up the supply chain. Every vendor in the chain would have to weigh the risks of accepting versus not accepting bitcoin as payment. So instead of just completing transactions, there is an extra decision with additional risk that has to be calculated at every decision. This delays transactions, as various issues like market timing, delayed closing, conversion and exchange costs, and more have to be weighted. Consider it like an example from Chapter 1, paying for products at the Apple store with Apple stock (also an asset). You would have to weigh the volatility and potential future value of the stock every time you make a purchase, especially if the purchase is for a depreciating asset like electronics or a disposable consumer product like coffee. With the already complex decision process involved in spending resources, the pace of commerce would slow to a crawl.

Enter Stablecoins

To deal with this issue of volatility, a new class of cryptocurrency was developed. Stablecoins are, as their name implies,[7] a category of cryptocurrency designed specifically to avoid the volatility issue. The entire purpose of a stablecoin is to maintain a set value within a narrow range.

---

6 Asset risk is defined in Chapter 1.

7 One theory indicates that stablecoins derive their name from pegging to a stable fiat currency, but the point of creating a financial alternative to fiat is the underlying belief that fiat and the system underpinning it is unstable and untrustworthy.

That sounds familiar, doesn't it? Because it is designed to act like a simple medium of exchange—these are a type of currency. They remove the issue of volatility so people can use them for payment without worrying that they are going to suffer conversion risk. Uses include basically anything you would use fiat for (real costs, like rent, goods and service, and debt repayment), as well as a way to store value for people with hyperinflationary fiat (discussed in more detail later in this chapter) or to store value on-chain.[8]

The other primary use for stablecoins is DeFi, and we will discuss this in detail later in this chapter, as well as in Chapters 4 and 5. Stablecoins are a major part of DeFi, so understanding what these are and how they work is key to understanding DeFi.

Stablecoins work similarly to fiat currencies that are hyperinflationary or volatile. They want to inspire trust in their utility as a medium of exchange and retained value, so they start by declaring a fixed ("stable") target value. This value is their *pegged* value, or the value for which each stablecoin is redeemable. Most stablecoins (and volatile fiats) are pegged to the US dollar, which means they have a declared value of $1. But they could be pegged to anything—1 euro, 20 yen, the average value of a mix of cryptocurrencies, 1 troy ounce of gold, the cost of premium dog food to feed five full-grown huskies for one day, the shipping cost of one pint of Ben & Jerry's ice cream from Vermont to California, or whatever you want. It must be a fixed, known range or value that can be externally verified. The more likely it is to stay fixed, the better. This is why hyperinflationary or volatile assets or currencies are not good pegs, and why a stablecoin pegged to Bitcoin or other volatile cryptocurrency isn't likely to happen in the near future.

After picking their peg, stablecoins then have to figure out a stabling mechanism. This is how they are going to maintain that peg. Unfortunately, simply declaring something to have a specific value doesn't work to establish that value. There are a number of methods that have evolved to do this. However, most stabling mechanisms are effective only in the short term, which means they may work over a period of

---

8 This was a popular method of storing value after exiting an investment, but without the heavy transaction costs and time lag of converting to fiat and back to crypto. The idea is that, once you cash out of a position, it is better to leave it on-chain in a stablecoin, so it is easier to transfer back to a cryptocurrency when a position opens. This theory was largely based on a period where it was difficult to get into "secondary currencies" (now called "alt-coins"). Before the burst of current access that began in 2019, many people did not have fiat on-ramps to crypto exchanges, and/or were not able to purchase bitcoin legally. So people bought a stablecoin, such as Tether, to hold assets on-chain until they could be converted to bitcoin or other assets. During that same period, you were required to hold Bitcoin or Ether to purchase any alt-coin—direct access was not possible. In fact, many early holders of Bitcoin were just stocking up on Bitcoin to have it ready to transfer into another coin when an offering was available. Both of these problems caused Tether and Bitcoin to gain much larger usage out of necessity, but most coins can be purchased directly on an exchange, and an on-ramp is available for most fiats at this point. The current theory of keeping assets on-chain may also be from a mistaken belief that crypto has no tax implication until it's converted back to fiat, but this is untrue in the US.

months or even years but are 100% likely to fail over the long term. Here, failure means the value of the stablecoin "breaks," or is worth less than the declared target value. This could mean a market price a few pennies under the target value, or a market price of zero. Anything other than the target price means it has broken and is now unstable. Let's take a look at current options for stabling mechanisms.[9]

Types of Stablecoins

In this section, I'll tell you about types of stablecoins.

Backed by fiat

A stablecoin that is backed by fiat is by far the most popular. Its declared target value is maintained by holding a reserve of a fiat currency, like US dollars or euros or Swedish krona.[10]

"Backed by fiat" means that for every stablecoin issued, one unit of fiat is purchased by the stablecoin team and held in reserve, which generally means physical units of fiat in a physical vault. When the holder of the stablecoin decides to "cash in" the stablecoin, or convert it back to fiat, the fiat from the reserve is used to buy back the stablecoin, which is then burned or destroyed to maintain the exact ratio of 1 stablecoin to 1 unit of fiat reserve. Many examples exist, but one of the best known is Tether, and its collateralization is expressed as "one Tether equals one US dollar (1 USDT/$1)," and is accomplished by purchasing one unit of fiat (e.g., one dollar) for each stablecoin sold (e.g., one Tether).

Of course, if it were that easy, everyone would use this method. Unfortunately, as those who experienced the crashes of the Argentine peso, the Thai baht, the Nigerian naira, and the Mexican peso know, this method has many problems. Essentially, one country is controlled by the fiscal and monetary policy of another country's central bank (or central banking ministry). The controlling country (which we'll call the "parent country," or "parent fiat"), however, isn't considering the controlled country's (which we'll call the "subcountry" or "subfiat") economy when making decisions. Eventually, the economies diverge—the policies followed by the parent country are

---

9 Central bank digital currencies (CBDCs) are *not* cryptocurrency, much less stablecoins, so not included in this section. A detailed discussion is included in Chapter 3.

10 The fiat held in reserve is not required to be the same fiat as the target value. So, you could have a stablecoin with a target value of $1, and hold euros or yen as the reserve. Stablecoins have historically held only the same currency as the target value.

not the same as those preferred by the subcountry, because they have different base economies, resources, and priorities.[11]

Along with this economic divergence, we have the real issues of what happens to countries with pegged fiats. First, it is very expensive to maintain a peg to another economy. The subcountry needs to have huge reserves of capital to manage the supply of currency to maintain the peg. They have to constantly adjust the currency supply to maintain the peg, which is extremely complicated, because many forces are acting on the parent fiat, including foreign countries conducting their own manipulation on the parent fiat to benefit their own countries' economies. It is difficult under the best of circumstances, and requires capital controls the subcountry may not have or wish to institute, as well as a level of financial discipline many countries find cumbersome under the best of circumstances. Most populations find this tough, if not impossible, to live with—especially considering the next two problems we're about to discuss: no growth and inflation.

Second, the growth rate of the subcountry slows. Without the ability to move the value of the subfiat relative to other currencies, both imports and exports can be disadvantageous to the subcountry, and the cost of real wages is likely to rise because of the peg. There is also a tendency toward protectionist policies (e.g., "buy local!"), which further slows growth. Now, if the country is a wealthy or even middle-income country, this is often offset in large part with an increase in foreign direct investment. However, wealthy and middle-income countries rarely find themselves in need of a parent peg. Lower-income countries have almost no offsetting investment, which brings growth to a standstill.

As a result, we have the third problem: inflation. At the outset of the pegging system, inflation is generally stemmed to very low levels. Accordingly, the newly trustworthy subfiat now becomes desirable as a mode of preserving value. This means people start saving the subfiat, which removes it from circulation. More subfiat has to be issued to maintain the peg, which results in inflationary pressure—often without any counteracting deflationary pressure.

---

11 This is an a priori argument—if the two countries had similar size economies with similar resources, and made similar decisions based on similar priorities, they would de facto have similar outcomes and both be making similarly healthy (or unhealthy) financial decisions. However, the subcountry's economy has such significant risk that it requires the parent economy's fiat as collateral to secure its own. The parent country clearly does not—it is significantly healthier and more trustworthy than the subcountry, and the parent fiat is significantly safer, hence it is the target currency value.

Eventually, the pressure to maintain the peg becomes unsustainable for the subcountry, and the peg breaks.[12] This is often referred to as "the worst week of our lives," and life savings are wiped out in a day. Inflation then balloons enormously, and it takes years to recover, if recovery is possible.

Now, imagine all of the above, but without any capital controls to constantly adjust supply—only purchased reserves of parent fiat that floats on the market. The demand created by the stablecoin's purchase of the parent fiat every time it issues a stablecoin makes that parent fiat incrementally more and more expensive with every coin issuance. At some point, the purchase of one more unit of fiat (e.g., one more dollar) is more expensive than the coin issued, and cash reserves cannot be purchased without forcing the stablecoin into a loss position, a position that only increases with every stablecoin issued and fiat unit purchased.

Let's look at the biggest stablecoin in the world both by trading volume and market capitalization, Tether (USDT). Tether's claimed stabilization method is pegged 1:1 with the US dollar. However, the sheer volume of dollars it would need to hold to meet that claim would alter global economies, so doubt on its claim has been pervasive. As Tether recently revealed, it could not support more than 3% of Tether's current circulating supply in liquid US dollars.[13] Not 100%—only 3%. As a result, it has been buying assets other than the parent fiat, including Treasury notes and other assets that weren't nearly as liquid as the parent fiat they insisted backed every Tether stablecoin. As we later found out, approximately 60% of the backing assets included unnamed commercial loans with a variety of risk, and other negotiable paper instruments that were redeemable within 90 days.[14] Fully 24% of Tether is unbacked.

Lest you think only Tether has this problem, the next largest currency, the Circle dollar (USDC), which also claims to maintain a 1:1 peg with US dollars, has been issued subpoenas questioning its ability to have 100% liquid backing. Circle released an attestation that it is only 61% backed with "cash and cash equivalents," including

---

12 Many cite Hong Kong's long-standing peg (a limited range of permitted exchange rate relative to the US dollar) as a contradictory example, but there is significant evidence that this peg is not genuinely maintained and has broken in whole or in part. That is a discussion for a much longer book than this, but well worth researching and considering, and determining whether this particular use case supports or contradicts this mandatory breakage thesis.

13 The notorious "Tether pie charts" revealed how little cash Tether actually held, even though it had always been touted as a 1:1 (one Tether to one dollar) coin. It has since deleted these charts, but fortunately they've been preserved at: https://oreil.ly/EIzX0.

14 This includes a $1 billion loan to Celsius, a blockchain DeFi platform, which is against Tether's own terms of service at the time of the loan issuance, which states, in part: "Tether will not issue Tether Tokens for consideration consisting of the Digital Tokens (for example, bitcoin); only money will be accepted upon issuance," as stated in https://oreil.ly/sjgcD.

overseas certificates of deposits, the remainder being clearly less liquid municipal and corporate bonds.[15]

Pegged currencies that are 100% collateralized by the parent fiat are either a strictly temporary undertaking or a manipulated undertaking.

Backed by commodities

Coins that are backed by commodities such as gold or silver are very similar to those collateralized by fiat. The underlying commodity is held in reserve in an amount equal to the total circulating value of the stablecoin. The reserve amount is bought or sold to account for the supply of stablecoins.

While any commodity can be used as the underlying reserve, gold and silver have been the historical choices because of their ease of identification, divisibility, fungibility, relative rarity, ease of mining, and general nonreactivity (it doesn't rust or degrade much relative to other commodities). Examples of this in cryptocurrency are Digix Gold (DGX), Paxos Gold (PAXG), and Diamond Standard (DIAM—backed by diamonds).

However, being backed by commodities has the same problems as collateralization by fiat. At some point, the demand created by the reserve has too much impact on the price of the underlying commodity, and the cost of maintaining the reserve is very high. In addition, it has the following disadvantages.

Downward economic pressure. The pressure on maintaining an economy of any size on available reserves raises the price of each following ounce, which makes the entire market difficult for companies with industrial use of the underlying commodity and competing economies with commodity backing. Commodity-backed currencies tend to be very volatile, particularly in the short term.[16] This usually passes in the long run, unless the underlying commodity is prone to discovery of new deposits or is near depletion of current deposits.

There is strong deflationary pressure on gold- or silver-backed currencies, particularly. This may sound like a good thing (and is the raison d'etre for those who support

---

15 There is no detailed breakdown of what percentage of the 61% "cash and cash equivalents" actually consists of US dollars in Circle's report. See Nikhilesh De, "Circle Reveals Assets Backing USDC Stablecoin," *Coindesk*, July 20, 2021, *https://oreil.ly/SSUev*.

16 Barry Eichengreen, *Globalizing Capital: A History of the International Monetary System*, 3rd ed. (Princeton, NJ: Princeton University Press, 2019); and Michael D. Bordo, Robert D. Dittmar, and William T. Gavin, "Gold, Fiat Money and Price Stability" (PDF), Working Paper Series, Federal Reserve Bank of St. Louis, Research Division (June 2003).

extremely deflationary assets like Bitcoin), but currencies that are either inflationary or deflationary are not useful.[17]

Limitations on economic growth.   It is generally accepted that regulated credit generates economic growth.[18] This requires two conditions: the credit must have oversight (or greed causes bad loans), and the credit should be offered to households of various income levels instead of public administrations or corporations (or no increase in consumer spending, so no economic growth). Deflationary economies punish debtors, because they end up paying back more value than they contracted for, which reduces the likelihood that people will want to use offered credit. Economic growth diminishes accordingly.

Monetary policy restrictions.   The worst problem, in my opinion, is that to have a currency tied to a specific thing, like a rare metal, means the monetary supply is limited to the availability and supply of that metal. When an economy grows, or even just a population grows, the amount of money available should grow as well. With a limited amount of metal, monetary policy can't be used to expand monetary supply, to address noneconomic concerns.[19] That alone should make it a nonstarter for any currency. Everyone thinks monetary policy should be sacred and used only for strict supply control—until something bad happens. Then forcing liquidity into a system or

---

17 In inflationary economies, too much currency is floating around chasing too few goods, so each unit is valued less. If you have a fixed dollar value in wages (making $50,000 per year, for example), inflation will make each dollar worth less than it was the prior year (or, in hyperinflationary economies, than it was the prior day), so your $50,000 of salary will now buy only $45,000 worth of goods. This perpetuates a cycle of merchants requiring more and more currency to make up the value of the goods and services offered, which further pushes down the value of the dollar. At an extreme point, people have to convert all their cash into real goods and services as soon as it is received, because any delay lowers the purchasing power of the cash received. This prevents any ability to save or experience long-term gains, and forces most into subsistence living.
On the other hand, deflationary economies have too little money chasing too many goods. This means each unit is worth more each day. So, your $50,000 salary is now worth $55,000 in goods and services. That sounds great, but what happens? People tend to save and hoard deflationary currencies to conserve any future gains. This removes money from circulation, creating more deflationary pressure, and so on. If people stop spending money, the economy comes to a screeching halt, and when that happens, the currency can quickly crash and fall to zero. Neither inflation nor deflation are great currency outcomes in the long run.

18 See, e.g., Bana (Butiuc), Ioana Madalena, "The Impact of Credit on Economic Growth in the Global Crisis Context," International Economic Conference of Sibiu 2013, Post Crisis Economy: Challenges and Opportunities, IECS 2013, *Procedia Economics and Finance* 6, Elsevier (2013).

19 For example, monetary policy was used during the 2020 pandemic to increase capital available to a large percentage of the population unable to access capital through employment (the spending relief package). While this did, in fact, help relieve some of the economic pressure, it also resulted in some inflationary gain, which had to be addressed in 2021. Unfortunately, countries that had been relying on the US for monetary stability (such as the economies that held US dollars in reserve for their own economies, or economies that substituted the US dollar for their own native currency) suffered a sudden 33%+ drop in value as the economic results of the relief package rippled through the global economy (e.g., El Salvador). This created a shock wave of varying proportions around the world.

---

introducing austerity seems not just reasonable, but necessary. When people are starving and angry, traditionally sound fiscal policy is a luxury.

As a result of these issues, nearly every currency has decoupled from commodity backing. Even Lebanon left the gold standard—but not until after it had already amassed debt over 100% of its gross domestic product (GDP), on which they have already defaulted. Backing clearly does not guarantee liquidity or austerity. Lebanon is considering using its gold reserves as collateral for financing, which is simply a securitized loan, not an asset-backed currency.

Backed by crypto

Here, *backed by crypto* means that one or more cryptocurrencies are being held in reserve to maintain the value of the stablecoin. is It's an interesting concept, because it depends on a derived value of an underlying asset that is highly volatile (as all cryptocurrencies are currently). It is unclear how a volatile asset (a cryptocurrency, like a stablecoin) can be stabilized by another volatile asset (another cryptocurrency). Backing volatility with volatility compounds risk.

The most popular crypto-backed stablecoin is the DAI, which is run by a decentralized group known as MakerDAO. This is a fascinating financial structure, but it gets a bit complicated. I'll simplify as much as possible to convey the main concepts. Hold your nose; we're diving in.

MakerDAO basically produces DAI as its product. DAI's main product feature is that it is worth exactly $1 and only $1, and that's all MakerDAO cares about (generally). How does this happen? To purchase DAI, you enter into a smart contract with MakerDAO in which you deposit one of the crypto coins it accepts as collateral (around 60% is the Circle coin [USDC], and about 30% is Ether [ETH]). Your deposit is kept in a personal vault, is not mixed with other collateral, and is custodial; you can't access it, but neither can MakerDAO unless you default. It's "locked up" in a personal, trackable vault. Then you are loaned an amount of DAI at the rate permitted for that collateral at that time (the *collateralization rate*).[20] You can then use that DAI to purchase other coins, including more collateral. You get your collateral back after you

---

20 The collateralization rate is set by MakerDAO members, is a percentage of the value of your collateral, and is never 100%. All DAI coins are overcollateralized, meaning you cannot get DAI worth the exact value you put in as collateral. This is because crypto is volatile (even stablecoins) and because MakerDAO has two priorities: (1) keep DAI at $1, and (2) see (1).

return the DAI and a stabilizing fee, if applicable,[21] and the DAI you minted is burned.

The stabilizing fees keep MakerDAO minting DAI in the event demand is too high or the value of the collateral increases too much. Otherwise, the price of DAI would be over $1. But what happens if the price of the collateral drops? In this event, they do what is done when any borrower fails to meet a margin call—they open the collateral locker and liquidates your collateral. But this one has a catch: they don't actually wait until the collateral drops low enough to impact the price. They have a minimum barrier that is above 100%. If the value of the collateral drops below the barrier, the collateral is automatically liquidated, and you are now the proud new owner of the DAI you borrowed.

What if the collateral sold was worth more than the value of the DAI you have? Do you get it back? Sadly, no. That's where the incentive to mint more DAI comes in; MakerDAO mints more DAI to bring the per unit price back down to $1.

What if the value of the collateral drops too much or too fast to recover 100% of the value of the DAI you borrowed? Then the MakerDAO community becomes a buyer of last resort and has to pony up the difference to make the value of the collateral held worth 100% of the outstanding DAI. They don't just throw in dollars or ETH. Instead, they have to use the asset that gives them a right to all those wonderful stabilization fees: their MakerDAO governance token (MKR). Ordinarily, this token is just a tiny digital genie, granting them rights over governance issues like setting fees and determining how the chain will grow over time, and, of course, giving them lots of crypto cash. But in this instance, they have to mint more of those wonderful MKR tokens, which reduces the value of the MKR tokens overall, and sell them on the open market. And they don't get to keep the proceeds—it all goes into the collateral pool to bring the value of each DAI up to $1.

OK, but what if a massive crash occurs, and all the collateral drops disastrously in value, or regulations are passed, or all the MKR holders sell their coins at one time and leave the system, any of which would make DAI as a whole unsustainable? Then a fail-safe mechanism kicks in: all DAI freezes, and anyone holding a DAI can cash it in to MakerDAO for a pro rata piece of the collateral pool, and all the collateralized DAI holders have their collateral returned to them automatically. All the DAI is then burned. This is called *global settlement*, and it is essentially the first time a crypto

---

21 The stabilization rate is complex to explain, but essentially it's a fee you pay when you repay your DAI to make sure the DAI is at $1. It's a rate that is set by an algorithm that varies extensively day to day and incentivizes MakerDAO members to create more DAI if the price of DAI exceeds $1, bringing it back down to $1. A high stabilization rate generally means high demand for DAI. Without it, the price of DAI would increase with increased demand, and there would be no incentive to mint more to stabilize the price of 1 DAI relative to all circulating DAI.

---

founding team actually considers a liquidation event and how to compensate the holders instead of just letting them take the loss and splitting the collateral and assets among the DAO (decentralized autonomous organization) members. It's incredible, and every crypto should have this sort of plan in place, at a minimum.

I mentioned DAI holders that *weren't* collateralized borrowers. Enough pre-minted DAI is circulating now that you can purchase it directly at any number of exchanges or swaps. This DAI is the DAI that was minted but the borrower failed to repay the loan for some reason, or the price of collateral dropped enough that the collateral was liquidated and the borrower was left with the borrowed DAI, or DAI that was minted by MakerDAO to bring the price back down to $1, etc. The DAI you buy on an exchange is the same rate as the DAI you borrow. However, you are not subject to the stabilization fee. Why wouldn't everyone just purchase DAI? Because if you really understand how to use DAI for leveraged purchases, you can borrow against your assets, use the DAI to purchase additional assets that at minimum offset the stabilization fee, pay back the DAI, and get your collateral back in its entirety. That transaction just gained you new assets—for free.

This seems like a pretty well-thought-out plan, and it is. It's fairly incredible. But they didn't really make a stablecoin here;[22] these are just collateralized loans that underpin a (likely) security instrument that has minimal volatility, but they are really just adjustable return collateralized debt instruments. This is a completely different analysis than the one most people in the crypto/blockchain community are aware of (the Howey test), but just as important and just as valid. Understanding the world of regulation beyond Howey is so important that we'll be going into a fair amount of detail on it in Chapter 4. For now, just know that this really isn't a stablecoin; it's DeFi. But it's a great entry into DeFi and one we'll return to again.

This type of backing doesn't have many other examples, but a few exist in the fiat world. This is analogous to the "basket of currencies" that back these types of currencies. The currency is based on a hypothetical, unreal value, and generally falls because

---

22 Stablecoins are generally nonvolatile coins backed by assets or algorithms to control flow. These are backed by debt, and DAI doesn't own the assets unless there is an event of default or a value drop in the collateral assets—and then it has ownership only for the express purpose of liquidation. But dollars are backed by debt, you say; it's debt on the federal government. Why can't DAI be backed by debt? Good question. It's because dollars aren't stablecoins. More than that, debt isn't the most important thing underpinning the dollar. It's actually two (related) things. First, the federal court system, because the federal courts can (and will) force any seller or creditor who is refusing to accept dollars to accept them in satisfaction of debt or payment for goods and services. The court can issue a court order to force acceptance, which is executed by duly authorized authority— generally a law enforcement official, like a sheriff. So the dollar really is backed by the federal government in its court power and police power. Second, the dollar is a dollar's worth (roughly) of all the economic activity generated by the US (the GDP), plus the value of all the dollars held in foreign reserves, plus the value of the assets held by the US, less the value of US debt. We'll call that total US Value. That's why supply expands and contracts—to keep the number of dollars in circulation such that each dollar represents one dollar's worth of US Value.

the view of each individual currency or the collective imaginary currency falls out of line with what perception or expectation had been. These break, also, and I encourage you to learn about what happened with the ECU (European Currency Unit), the European Monetary System's common currency before the euro. (Note: it did not end well.)

Algorithmic and seignorage coins

These stablecoins are similar but still distinct categories.

Algorithmic stablecoins. *Algorithmic stablecoins* are similar to the fiat-pegged coins discussed previously, because they are also pegged to a fiat currency. They hold a reserve of that currency on a blockchain and use a complex algorithm to maintain the peg. If the value of the stablecoin falls below the peg, the algorithm assumes too many coins are circulating, and it triggers a smart contract to release some of the reserves to purchase coins on the market. If the value rises above the peg, the algorithm assumes too few coins are circulating, and sells coins, placing the profits in the blockchain-based reserve. It essentially acts as a hidden buyer of last resort, because the smart contracts are automatically triggered by the algorithm.

The problem here is that, like bots, once the algorithm is perceived, it can be manipulated. This essentially has all the benefits and problems of the fiat-backed stablecoins. Like fiat-backed coins, the peg is impossible to maintain over any length of time. Worse, the ability to manipulate the price (forcing a purchase, which can drain reserves, or forcing an issuance and sale, which can drive the diluted value to nothing) will essentially force the stablecoin to break. In addition, if a black swan event occurs (a rare and disastrous occurrence), the algorithm cannot keep pace with the purchase or sell coins on the market, which just hurries the peg-breakage along.

Seigniorage stablecoins. *Seigniorage stablecoins* are far more interesting and complex, because they somewhat emulate the operations of a central bank. They are unbacked and have no reserves. Also, they factor in the cost of minting (which made sense for traditional fiat—minting isn't free—but doesn't quite make sense in the context of digital stablecoins).

I will say in advance that I am absolutely not a fan of this method, primarily because it serves to make money for both the central bank (here, the founding team and other rights holders) and large purchasers, generally high-net-worth investors and institutions. This is exactly the reason Bitcoin was created—to fight against this form of irresponsible enrichment. The fact that anyone wishes to emulate it in blockchain currency is unfortunate. My assumption is that most people in the blockchain community who support it don't really understand it, so let's figure this thing out. Maybe it's not so bad.

The procedure works something like this (we'll discuss it with fiat, as it's a bit clearer to understand where the profiteering comes in):

Central banks buy things like metal and paper to physically make fiat dollars. Usually, the cost to create a dollar is less than the face value of the dollar. So, if I sell you 500 one-dollar bills, and you send me $500 for them, but it cost me only $0.50 to make each one-dollar bill, I just made $250 profit on that sale. (Fiat is also a product—it costs a certain amount of money to mint, and if you sell it for an amount higher than that, you've just made a profit.) Then the central banks take that $500 and invest it in some interest-bearing financial tools, so they are earning profit *twice* on that minting. Minting money is *bank*.

The way this translates into monetary policy is the purchase and sale of instruments that keep the currency stable. We'll take a key financial instrument, the US dollar, and see how the seigniorage system works for the US's central bank, the Federal Reserve, or Fed (beyond its ability to make loads of profit for the government by ordering minting from the US Mint).

The Fed's goal, like all systems that create and monitor currency instruments, is generally to keep the value of the currency within a narrow band. Stablecoins, for example, try to keep their value at or near $1, and Hong Kong works to keep the HKD between $7.75 and $7.85. But you see the problem here, right? You can't peg a value to yourself, and there isn't another significantly sized economy that doesn't relate its value to the value of the US dollar, peg to the US dollar, or rely on the US dollar as the main or entire component of its own reserve.

So the Fed relies on a complex set of formulas to determine whether the supply of US dollars circulating both in the US and globally meet demand, or if there are too many US dollars for the current demand, or too few. Then it enacts a monetary policy to counteract that force to return the supply of US dollars to the exact amount meeting demand. How does the Fed find out if supply and demand are meeting? Glad you asked! Figuring this out requires an *enormous* amount of information. The list of data includes, but isn't limited to, the following:

- The economic activity of the US market
- The relative value of its imports and exports in key countries
- The relative value of the imports and exports of key US trading partners
- The amount of US dollar reserves held in foreign treasuries
- The political economy of those holding US dollar reserves
- The amount, type, and impact of foreign economic manipulation of the US dollar
- The amount, type, and impact of US economic manipulation of various key foreign economies

- The Consumer Price Index
- The Producer Price Index
- Predictions in particular industry growth or contraction
- Lots of other stuff

The Fed has to gather the data every day, then interpret it—and the Fed has only 130 or so people to do this. After that, they try to predict future expansions and contractions in various economies, including the US, and then, approximately every six weeks, decide what, if any, action is required for adjustment. This could be provisions to reduce the number of dollars in circulation, which is usually done either by buying dollars by offering Treasury bills or by dropping the federal funds rate, which is what the Fed is referring to when it talks about "interest rates."[23] Conversely, they can add dollars to circulation by buying back T-bills or by raising interest rates.[24]

As you can see, the entire system is incredibly complex, and it takes constant juggling and a deep understanding of the influences and results of economic activity—and not just in the US, but in economies around the world. If the crypto world is really thinking about making a currency with broad use and implications, this is what they have to address. It takes a strong understanding of political economics, economic theory, monetary policy, fiscal policy, financial history, psychology of spending, and more. I have doubts about many of these stablecoins from the outset because I just don't see teams with that kind of knowledge or depth, particularly when it comes to seigniorage or algorithmic systems. But hopefully, they'll be coming.

Let's talk about the Robert Sams paper.[25] This paper is fascinating in so many ways. It discusses the possibilities of elastic supply, rather than fixed, focusing more on money supply over interest rate policy. He discusses and dismisses rebasing coins, which will

---

23 *Treasury bills*, or *T-bills*, are debt instruments issued by the US government entitling the holder to the same amount of money at a set date in the future, along with a fixed amount of interest, called a *fixed-rate yield*. This is a classic financial tool, with the added security of being backed by the US government, so a negligible risk of default. By requiring purchase with dollars, buyers get to have an assured return, and the Treasury removes dollars from circulation. Because T-bills, and other major bonds, pay a fixed rate, when interest rates fall, the price of these bonds rises when the fixed-rate yield is higher than the interest rate. So, one way to encourage people to buy more notes is to drop interest rates, which removes dollars from circulation. Dropped rates also encourage spending, as the cost of borrowing money is cheaper, which can lead to inflationary pressure.

24 Buying back T-bills takes those bonds out of circulation and puts more dollars in circulation. The Fed can also raise interest rates, which makes fixed-rate bonds less desirable (once the interest rate passes the bond's already fixed interest rate, or yield), keeping dollars in circulation. The increased interest rate also makes the cost of borrowing (*cost of capital*) higher, which slows spending and the rate of economic growth, leading to strong deflationary pressure.

25 Robert Sams, "A Note on Cryptocurrency Stabilisation: Seigniorage Shares," April 28, 2015, *https://oreil.ly/ FnYhO*.

---

be discussed further in the next section. He argues that all coins have a monetary policy, including Bitcoin, but Bitcoin's policy is fundamentally flawed in that it is based on supply only, which isn't influenced at all by the value of Bitcoin. But the part that most people focus on is the use of a two-token model to power a decentralized monetary system. His base principle is "at the end of some predefined interval of time, if the change in coin price over the interval is $X\%$, change the coin supply by $X\%$." This is known as *elastic supply*.

He essentially creates two tokens, one called "coin" and one called "share." They are identical other than in title and in the fact that the price of shares is variable and offers the possibility of profit for its holders (coins do not). The coin token is the stablecoin, and it does not have a fixed supply, and both the shares and tokens are distributed.[26]

When coin supply needs to increase, coins are distributed to shareholders who are willing to trade their shares for coins, and the shares are destroyed. Assuming demand for the coin and shares continues to increase, the value of the coins decreases and the value of the shares increases. When the supply needs to decrease, the opposite happens. The swaps of coins and shares are voluntary and conducted by auction, through which holders of shares communicate the number of coins they wish to trade shares for, and the minimum coin-for-share price they are willing to accept. Winning bids are filled at whatever price clears the required quantity to be sold.

While Sams calls it a seigniorage system, it's really a rebase system—another stablecoin type, which will be discussed next. The only real examples of seigniorage systems have been Basis, Carbon, and NuBits, each of which were created with massive funding and experienced founders. None currently exist as stablecoins as of the date of this writing, two of them failing in fairly spectacular fashion.

The assumptions that market supply and demand is the only thing determining price, that demand is easily and accurately calculated by algorithm, and that the coin will have infinitely positive overall demand have all been proven false.

Rebasing

Rebasing itself is fairly complex, but we will try to break it down to its simplest concepts. Like a traditional stablecoin, it has a target price. However, it doesn't have a fixed reserve asset pool. Generally, rebase tokens have a target comparison or ratio. The coin uses an algorithm tied to an oracle to reprice at a set interval, often every 12 or 24 hours, but this may be much longer. The oracle goes off-chain to see the ratio of the rebase coin to the target coin on a market or series of markets. If it's not at the target price, it needs to adjust. But instead of adjusting the price by adjusting reserves

---

26 The method of initial distribution is unclear from the paper.

or collateral, it adjusts the supply of coins circulating, adding or subtracting coins automatically wherever they are—even in someone's wallet. These are also known as *elastic supply tokens.*

Let's look at Ampleforth (AMPL), a rebase token. AMPL has a target price of $1.009. Every 24 hours, the circulating supply amount and current price is checked by an oracle. If the price is over $1.009, the circulating supply will be expanded—new AMPL minted—so that the price goes back down to $1.009. If you are holding AMPL, you will find the number of AMPL in your wallet reduced, though the total value of the amount in your wallet will be unchanged. You are really buying market share, not a set number of tokens.

So, let's say you have four AMPL in your wallet, worth roughly $4. You go to bed, and a rebasing event occurs. It turns out demand for AMPL was higher than supply, and the market price has risen to $1.25. The AMPL protocol automatically added supply to all AMPL holders. The protocol didn't *sell* new supply—it literally just increased the supply proportionately to all current holders, so now the supply of AMPL meets the demand in the market, and the price returns to roughly $1. So you look in your wallet, and now you have 25% more tokens, or five tokens. The value of the tokens in your wallet, however, remains $4. The amount will change, but the value you hold will not. You still have $4 worth of market share. Because the supply shifts for every holder, no net gain or loss occurs.

Instead of the price increasing, you go to bed with four tokens, and the price goes the other way, maybe it drops to $0.75, meaning there was more supply than demand that day. You wake up the next morning, and you will find the supply contracted—you now have three tokens in your wallet, but still worth $4. This continues daily.

Benefits of this system are that it more closely matches the way actual currency works. The money supply expands and contracts with changing comparative valuations, and the supply adjustments ripple through the system accordingly.

However, several aspects present areas of concern. The price rebalancing is certainly faster than with physical money supply, but not instantaneous. The adjustment can contradict price indication in the market and could result in a toxic spiral. An example is the supply contracting to adjust price upward, but the market is selling and the price is adjusting downward with stronger pressure. You could end up with fewer shares that are worth less than they were before, which is particularly problematic if you are settling a short-duration loan without time for readjusting pricing before settlement. For this reason, rebasing tokens should not be used for flash loans or short-duration loans.

Other risks include contract issues, such as not locating every coin to adjust its supply. If any single coin is held in a manner inaccessible to the rebasing call function, the entire formula fails. There is also some risk of profit-taking when the market cap increases, but the rebase has not happened. This can result in improper rebasing and gains for some, with extreme loss for others. Pure rebasing tokens are not designed for gain or loss. However, the mechanism of expansion and contraction provides an opportunity for both.

Finally, there are issues with mixed application tokens, where rebasing coins have incrementally increasing pegged value, such as the ForeverFOMO token. These demand constant access to the call function, which may not be possible, and doesn't account for lag times, particularly with increasing supply. The Yam token mixed other DeFi applications into its rebasing and ended up with a smart contract bug that minted so many tokens, it was ungovernable. Others that have mixed rebasing in with riskier functions have ended up with failed tokens. Be cautious with these mixed-use tokens, and make sure you understand all the elements that affect price, use, and design/engineering risk before purchasing.

Backed by other assets

Backing by other assets one isn't used often, and it is very similar to backing by crypto. Here, a stablecoin is backed by assets like shares, profit streams, or other assets. These can be fluctuating in value, so the ability to maintain a set price is quite difficult.

A well-known example is actually the first stablecoin, developed in 2015 by Dan Larimer and Charles Hoskinson. Their project, BitUSD, was backed by BitShares, the cryptocurrency for a decentralized exchange (decentralized exchanges are discussed in Chapter 5). Though it sounds like crypto backing, it functioned generally more like an equity backing. Though BitUSD remains in existence, it hasn't been traded for years and rests well below its intended value of $1 for 1 BitUSD ($0.82 as of the time of this writing).[27]

Governance Tokens

We've mentioned governance tokens a few times in Chapter 1. Let's define them now, because they're an important part of DeFi. *Governance tokens* are tokens that give the holder some sort of voting and/or proposal right over the blockchain project or its protocol. In simpler terms, this means holders get to propose rules that govern the project, and/or vote on rules that are proposed. The "and/or" is because many projects have a minimum number of tokens you have to hold in order to propose, but any holder can vote.

---

27 Dan Larimer went on to found Block.one, EOS, and Tether, while Charles Hoskinson was one of the eight founders of Ethereum before he founded Cardano. Even powerhouse players have to start somewhere.

Many projects use the *one token/one vote* rule (each holder gets one vote), but I'm personally not a fan of that type of voting. Most governance tokens are purchased on the open market, and many use their general transactional token for voting as well. Because you buy these tokens, the people with the most money will always control the project or protocol. Other methods of offering governance capability exist, such as offering governance tokens to active members of the project or the project DAO, offering quadratic or other ranked voting models, or soul-bound governance tokens.[28] Choose the model that best promotes the goals of your project.

Keep voting and ownership clear. Is there a path to decentralization? Is that even a goal? Make sure your mission and goals are validated by your tokenomics. Where are benefits concentrated, and what may trigger any special votes or voting privileges? Votes and token rights should be clearly explained, and votes should always take place in a manner in which all voting parties can easily see the results of the vote as it happens. Blockchain votes are always tracked, so you won't need to audit the votes, but you will need to make certain that proposals, voting dates, voting rights, voting procedures, and outcomes are always clear to all the token holders.

There may be a tendency to "rig" or centralize voting rights with the founding team or a particular group of people. Always check the token distribution to see how voting rights are allocated and if rights are concentrated in a particular group. If investing, see if there is something forcing dilution into that concentration, like a public sale of those tokens on reaching a goal, or something that allows those tokens to move from the treasury into public hands (ideally without a windfall for an insider). If the voting deck is stacked against you, consider alternative investments.

These tokens have an advantage over the purely speculative transactional or securities tokens: they have a right that backs them. Rights are a type of asset, and that makes them fit right into DeFi, which relies on asset-backed tokens over purely speculative tokens.

This means NFTs are also going to be a tool of DeFi, because they are a token backed by a set of rights. They are not currently a fundamental tool, other than an occasional type of collateral, but they will be in the future. They are discussed in more detail in Chapter 3.

---

28 Quadratic voting gives a certain number of votes to each holder, and it allows them to use their votes individually (one vote yes or no for any proposal) or stack them (five votes yes or no, or even all votes yes or no) for proposals that are more important to them. This forces voters to choose where to exert power, instead of exercising it on every issue. Soul-bound tokens or wallet-based voting models focus on users instead of tokens, limiting voting per user to prevent larger holders from having outsized weight on the project. Of course, some say those who put their money into projects *should* have outsized say. It depends on what model you prefer when building or investing.

Now that I've discussed the building blocks of DeFi, let's look at some of the primary ways people have put these tools to use.

Lending

Lending provides some of the most interesting use cases we're seeing. This is what is getting most of the press, because this is the way people are making money. We'll briefly go over these types of DApps and platforms, because a great deal of the rest of this book will focus on the collateralized loans and financing part of DeFi.

Collateralized loans

Collateralized loans are the core of what is powering DeFi right now. As of November 1, 2021, the *total value locked* (TVL—the total value of the cryptocurrency held in DeFi applications) across the top platforms was $236 billion, an all-time high.[29] Compare that with November 2020 when the DeFi TVL was $12,612,200, and in May 2021 it was $66,356,150.[30] That's a nearly 19,000% increase in one year, and over 3,500% in six months. That is mind-boggling growth.

In the long bear market of 2022–2023, DeFi dropped as stablecoins broke. The US dollar pegged-coin on the Tron chain (USDD) broke its peg in 2022, and the Terra Luna crash (UST and LUNA), Anchor and Celsius failures, and prosecution of BlockFi and Voyager impacted nearly every exchange and investor.

What Happened to DeFi?

DeFi was riding high with enormous amounts of money in the system in 2020 and 2021. Then, it crashed. What happened?

First, we have the collapse of the crypto market. Most of the peak at this point was speculative trading and did not reflect true growth in the industry. Many investors, both accredited and retail, were unfamiliar with this type of investment finance—or finance overall. They simply saw high rates of return and put money in, without questioning how the returns were generated or even if the returns were actually generated.

When the market for crypto started to falter, the poor design of these products became impossible to hide. Terra Luna failed because the coins were fundamentally unsustainable, as discussed previously. However, many large parties were major holders in this token, including FTX's sister company, Alameda, which was intrinsically connected to FTX. The hole in value created by the Terra Luna loss was

---

29 FN Media Group, "DeFi Total Value Locked Hits All-Time High of $236 Billion," *PR Newswire*, November 1, 2021, *https://oreil.ly/O5W0B*.

30 "Amount of Cryptocurrency Held in Decentralized Finance, or DeFi, Total Value Locked, Worldwide from August 2017 to October 15, 2021," *Statista*, October 15, 2021.

irreparable—even purportedly using customer funds—and eventually toppled FTX. FTX, a major player and financier of crypto, then brought down other companies, particularly when its native token, FTT, was allegedly determined to be worthless.

Anchor, an investment protocol on Terra Luna that held 75% of the outstanding UST (Terra), was essentially a locked box that was somehow supposed to generate returns for investors (these are typically Ponzi schemes), making the fall of the entire chain much faster.[31] Celsius had an unknown, likely unregistered fund manager by the name of KeyFi make incredibly risky unhedged bets with customer funds. Voyager claimed it was a safe place for customer assets,[32] but when the market dropped, its dealings with failed financier Three Arrows Capital and FTX showed it had not acted responsibly with investor funds. The Federal Trade Commission (FTC) settled claims with Voyager by preventing it from ever handling customer assets again, and suing founder Stephen Ehrlich for falsely claiming funds were insured by the FDIC.[33]

BlockFi should have realized,[34] with any reasonable legal opinion, that it could not offer products with returns without dealing with regulation. Hex, PulseX, and Pulse-Chain are another group of products offering incredible rates of return on unclear premises and are now collectively facing a lawsuit by the Securities and Exchange Commission (SEC) along with its founder, Richard Schueler, aka Richard Heart, charging unregistered securities offering and fraud.[35]

The point here is that these are failings of these projects—major projects, with billions of dollars of invested funds—and their designers, not crypto, blockchain, or even DeFi. This is a clear failure of the founders to understand finance at best, or a willingness to commit fraud at worst. It is also a failure of all investors, including major venture capital funds, to conduct proper due diligence on these projects before endorsing them and encouraging retail investment.[36]

This is not a failure of the DeFi concept. It is a failure to design products that conceive of a down market, a failure to comply with existing regulations, a failure to safeguard assets of customers (while calling them "safe!"), and a failure of investors to ask questions about the operations of these protocols and the protections for their assets.

---

31 Antonio Briola, David Vidal-Tomás, Yuanrong Wang, and Tomaso Aste, "Anatomy of a Stablecoin's Failure: The Terra-Luna Case," *Finance Research Letters* 51 (January 2023) 103358, *https://oreil.ly/XNwFC*.

32 Dietrich Knauth, "Bankrupt Crypto Lender Voyager Digital Predicts 35% Customer Payout," *Reuters*, May 17, 2023, *https://oreil.ly/kczU-*.

33 "FTC Reaches Settlement with Crypto Company Voyager Digital," *Federal Trade Commission*, October 12, 2023, *https://oreil.ly/-5bRs*.

34 Cease and desist order against BlockFi, *https://oreil.ly/e-40c*.

35 The filing can be seen at *https://oreil.ly/Zf5kE*.

36 "Sequoia Named in Lawsuit for Adding Legitimacy to FTX," *PYMNTS*, February 15, 2023, *https://oreil.ly/Cb7fX*; Sequoia deletes its puff piece calling Sam Bankman-Fried the "crypto savior"; discussed in *https://oreil.ly/daDjI*.

Investors were more likely to attack those trying to elicit information that showed the risk and poor design of these products than reconsider their investment decisions.

Building better protocols and encouraging investor questioning and disclosure is the way to resolve this. Everyone needs more education and more restraint. Then the real financial impact of DeFi will be seen.

The TVL of DeFi currently sits at around $50 billion and has remained there since roughly April 2022. This is the demand for DeFi in a *drawn-out bear market*. The demand will be even more explosive in the next bull market.

And it should explode. In Chapter 1, we talked about how important financial tools are, and how they are restricted to those who can take large sums of money and lock them up for extended periods of time. The entry fee for access to these products is very high, and banks have no intention of lowering the bar so people with less money have a chance to create generational wealth. So, most people end up sitting with a smaller amount of funds in their bank accounts, earning no interest, and generally costing some amount of service fees.

Fortunately, that isn't the case in blockchain.

While it is possible to do peer-to-peer loans, using a lending protocol via a DApp such as Compound, Aave, or even MakerDAO is generally the preferred mechanism. Lenders are just people who have one of the permitted coins in their wallets who want to generate a return from them. Lenders first decide which coins to lend. Each DApp has a list of acceptable tokens that generally consists of the following:

- The primary incentivized governance tokens on that blockchain platform.
- Stablecoins available on that blockchain platform.
- The blockchain's primary utility token (ETH for Ethereum platforms and DApps, BNB for Binance platforms and DApps, etc.).
- Bitcoin (BTC). Note that Bitcoin, or even ETH, may be used as a *wrapped* version, which means that a coin native to the chain is pegged to the price of the underlying token (BTC or ETH), and used as a token that works on a non-BTC or non-ETH chain. Holders of wrapped BTC (WBTC) or wrapped ETH (WETH) hold those underlying tokens by proxy.

After deciding to lend the coins, the lender accesses the DApp and offers the coins to the protocol. This is done by sending the coins to a smart contract, which locks up those coins for a set period.[37] The coins go into a pool, and the lender receives not

---

37 This means the lender can't take those coins out of the protocol until they are released.

just an interest rate return on the loan but often a number of the platform's native tokens, which usually have a certain market value, should they be traded, which entitle the lender to a percentage of transaction fees for the period the coins are held. Some DApps even offer *borrowers*, as well as lenders, the right to a percentage of transaction fees. Compound famously started this in 2020 as part of a four-year plan to increase its user base, and it has been an incredible success. It's not hard to see why —where else can you *borrow* money and make a profit? This simply does not exist in traditional finance.

Interest rates are often, though not always, determined by a type of automated market maker (AMM) called a *bonding curve*. Bonding curves are algorithms that are generally governed by a relationship between supply and demand, but they have unique benefits and risks. Bonding curves are discussed more fully later in the discussion of AMMs, including the issue that an incorrect application of the curve leads to de facto implications of fraud. Because loan supply and demand is specific to each DApp, depending on use and user base, size of loan, etc., the interest rate on the coins loaned may vary significantly. Checking rates and accepted coins, as well as the value of the DApp tokens providing transaction fees, on each DApp is crucial to maximize return.

The borrower has to deposit collateral, which is generally one of the approved coins, and generally an amount far over the value of the loan. This is called *overcollateralization*, which is necessary because of the extremely volatile nature of cryptocurrency— even stablecoins. Collateral generally ranges from 150% to 200% of the loan amount. If the loan is not repaid, the collateral is transferred to the lender, which removes the risk of nonrepayment.

Now, why would you take out a loan and pay interest on what you borrow if you already have assets worth at least as much as you need? Quite a few reasons, actually, including that you don't want to sell the assets outright, you don't want to create a taxable event, or you want to generate value from your portfolio beyond asset appreciation by putting those assets to work. If the borrowed currency is gaining value faster than the value of the loaned asset, you can make a significant financial gain for only the price of the interest. However, note that liquidation can happen if the value of the collateral drops to 120% of the value of the loan. In traditional finance, the value of the collateral must drop below the value of the loan, and then a procedure must be followed to properly transfer the collateral. The *margin call* of these loans is earlier than those in traditional finance.

The benefits of the system are fairly clear. Anyone can obtain a loan. No credit score, application, or other system that contains significant historical bias will apply. Interest rates do not vary based upon things like ethnicity, formal educational background, address, or other discriminatory measures.[38] The timing of the loan is incredibly fast. It allows anyone the benefit of a key financial tool for far below the minimum entry amount of traditional financial tools. The borrower typically does not lose ownership of their coins unless there is an event of default, and the lender maintains ownership of either collateral or another asset-backed coin. And, most importantly, it allows the lender to use the DApp tokens, which are also asset-backed tokens, in a second investment, allowing a further potential return on the single investment of tokens to the pool. This concept, called *money Legos*, is described in more detail in the section "Playing with Money LEGOs" on page 158.

The disadvantages, however, do exist. You have to have assets to both partake of the system as a lender and as a borrower—and, in the case of borrowers, more than you would need to have if you were part of the traditional finance system. You are limited to the type of assets accepted by the DApp for the most part.[39] And, while initially most of these assets were inexpensive to purchase, they are becoming more and more expensive as the market price increases, which makes people with fewer resources priced out of the market because of a lack of assets or inability to accept risk of loss. Also, financial literacy and actual questioning or demand for disclosure from protocols is a real issue, as discussed in "What Happened to DeFi?" on page 63.

Additional risk includes the risk of the DApp failing and trapping collateralized or loaned assets within it. Lenders may face impermanent loss in the value of their tokens if the tokens contributed gain value in the market but are valued at a lower value (as of the time of contribution), so generate somewhat lower return. Periods of high volatility may result in a significant number of forced collateral conversions, even though neither party wishes conversion.

Legal risks are fairly extensive and generally unaddressed. Issues like the potential for failure of terms due to poorly written terms of service or failure to identify the parties, which will be required by most jurisdictions under the disclosure rules required

---

38 Raheem Hanifa, "High-Income Black Homeowners Receive Higher Interest Rates Than Low-Income White Homeowners," *Joint Center for Housing Studies Harvard University*, February 16, 2021, *https://oreil.ly/GRexd*; "2019 Hispanic Mortgage Lending Analysis," Hispanic Mortgage: National Community Reinvestment Coalition, 2019 HDMA Analysis (2019), *https://oreil.ly/BpZ5n*; "The Gender Gap: Women Pay More for Their Mortgages Than Men," *OwnUp*, August 15, 2023, *https://oreil.ly/69ZQi*; George Smaragdis, "FINRA Study Finds Most Women Pay [Higher Interest Rates] When Using Credit Cards," *FINRA Investor Education Foundation*, 2013, *https://oreil.ly/fvdK6*; Donn Feir and Laura Cattaneo, "The Higher Price of Mortgage Financing for Native Americans," *The Center for Indian Country Development*, Working Paper Series No. 1906, September 17, 2019, *https://oreil.ly/JkOOe*. Cf. Alexandra Dobre and Young Jo, "Challenging the Model Minority Myth: A Closer Look at Asian Americans and Pacific Islanders in the Mortgage Market," *Consumer Financial Protection Bureau*, July 1, 2021, *https://oreil.ly/qsOvk*.

39 Additional asset-backed tokens, such as NFTs and others, are beginning to be introduced to the system as permissible assets. However, they are certainly the exception rather than the rule. These additional assets are discussed in Chapter 3.

by FATF, discussed in Chapter 3, remain unaddressed. Privacy laws such as the California Consumer Privacy Act and the EU's General Data Protection Regulation may not be properly enforced by current protocols.

Liability waivers may be enforced or not, to the harm of one party. More significantly, most of the current DeFi platforms are likely offering unregistered securities, which could have significant negative impact—similar to the crackdown of 2017. This is not to say DeFi applications are per se illegal or offering unregistered securities—just that their most common incarnation is likely to face unpleasant inquiries from the SEC in the near future.[40]

Other collateralized lending protocols

Another field of loans deals with real-world assets, digital assets, and NFT collateralized loans. These operate similarly to traditional collateralized assets, but instead of cryptocurrency, traditional assets are used. The real-world asset loans work similarly to a mortgage, with the title to the asset being held on-chain until the loan is repaid. The digital asset loans are like traditional layaway finance programs, in which the assets are *purchased* with the loan, not preexisting, and remain with the lender until the loan is repaid. NFT loans use NFTs as collateral for loans, and they are likely to grow tremendously in the future as non-art NFTs become more common. These are discussed in detail in Chapters 5 and 6. None of these are widespread enough to give us an idea of default rates, liquidation amounts, or how popular they may be.

Examples of real-world asset loan protocols are OpenDAO and Centrifuge. Lendefi is an example of a digital asset loan protocol. And examples of NFT lending protocols include Aave, YouHodler, and Helio.

Uncollateralized loans

You may be surprised to find that uncollateralized loans are even considered a possibility in this space. Anonymity makes sense when you have overcollateralized loans. But anonymity when you have *no* collateral? How to assess creditworthiness? And was this bringing back the problems of biased and discriminatory practices common with banks? It was the "white whale" of DeFi. While the option of uncollateralized loans has been sought after since at least 2017, it wasn't until 2020 when this became a

---

40 The September 7, 2021, receipt by Coinbase's CEO, Brian Armstrong, of a "Wells notice" from the SEC regarding the likelihood of enforcement action based on its proposed Lend program gives us two areas of alarm. First, that the most common form of DeFi application is, in fact, a very likely securities violation. Many applications appear to be simply copying the structure of other existing applications, without confirming that illegality does not exist in those existing applications. Second, that a well-funded company with access to presumably well-informed, highly regarded counsel was "shocked" by the outcome. The fact that Coinbase even asked for a meeting shows a surprising lack of understanding of the SEC's operating procedures, as well as a poor understanding of long-existing securities regulations.

---

viable alternative. And now that it's here, it's brought its friends. Quite a few options are available. This segment has not been around for very long, so it will take a bit of time before we see if default rates climb in this segment.

Clear Chain Capital wrote an excellent overview of the space that is still applicable as of this writing. I will provide their organizational structure with my own additional information, but for a quick overview, I encourage you to read their article in its entirety.[41]

Flash loans

Flash loans are extremely short-term loans with essentially zero risk of default for lenders. These loans are used for a variety of purposes, from ensuring liquidity on a lending or liquidity platform to exploiting arbitrage opportunities. *Arbitrage* is the practice of exploiting small price differences of assets in two markets. In the DeFi market, the basic use case occurs when someone sees the price of something, for example DAI, on two exchanges, and notices a difference. An arbitrageur then decides to quickly buy an amount of DAI from the cheaper exchange and sell it to the more expensive marketplace. But the amounts are quite small—a 10-cent difference makes a small profit when only $100 worth of DAI is bought and sold. Most people wouldn't undertake this kind of risk for a $10 reward. But that same 10-cent difference on a $10,000,000 purchase and sale of DAI? That's $1,000,000 in the course of a few minutes—and there are many people who would take that risk.

Flash loans are unsecured, and they must be repaid with interest over the course of that *same transaction* (which is why we say essentially risk-free). This is generally said to be "instant," but really, it isn't instant. If it were, how could you do anything with the money? A time lag occurs in the period of settling the transaction—you have the length of one transaction block, which can be up to a few minutes, depending on the chain. If the borrower can't return the loan with interest, the transaction is simply undone, as if it never happened.

If the flash loan is just to exchange collateral in a MakerDAO vault, or something relatively risk free, the entire process is low risk. However, if the transaction is for something like arbitrage, and you have failed to make a profit because of slippage (the settlement price is lower than the price you thought was applicable to the transaction, resulting in a loss), undoing the loan can be disastrous. You still owe money for the transaction you've undertaken, and now you don't have it because the loan was magically undone. For the purpose of the arbitrage, you now owe the amount of your original purchase price. You've effectively bought $10,000,000 of DAI on margin and now you owe that amount.

---

41 Clear Chain Capital, "The Resurgence of Decentralized Prediction Markets—A Potentially New Form of Social Media," *Medium*, July 21, 2021, *https://oreil.ly/3NK9l*

Another risk is *flash loan attacks*, which are hacks that either exploit contract weakness of thinly traded markets to manipulate prices and/or steal assets from exchanges. Many examples of this exist, and people have lost tens to hundreds of thousands of dollars' worth of crypto as a result. This is a discussion too lengthy and detailed for this book, but I note it for those who wish to enter this space, as a reminder to explore this further. Existing protocols include Aave and dYdX.

Third-party risk assessment

These transactions are more typical DeFi loans, as described previously, but, as they are not collateralized, they use an outside group of anonymous risk assessors who are rewarded for their efforts. These risk assessors are given anonymized loan applications and determine whether the loan should be granted.[42] The outside assessors stake some of their own assets as part of the loan process—these assets are presumably either native DApp tokens or other chain-acceptable assets. If the loan is granted and the borrower repays the loan entirely, the outside assessors are rewarded with DApp tokens. If the loan is rejected, no one is rewarded or penalized. If the loan is granted and the borrower fails to repay, the assessors lose all or part of their stake.

Risks currently relate to the novel nature of this type of application. It's unclear whether a large enough pool of independent assessors exists for even one application to work with a high volume of loan requests, much less many applications with many requests. Also, it's unclear what, if any, rubric is being used to assess eligibility and how independence of the assessors is ascertained for every transaction. A personal relationship between the borrower and assessor would create a conflict of interest, and it's unclear if that is even being addressed, much less resolved. Finally, it is unclear if the amount of the loan must be matched in whole or in part by the assessors' stake or stakes.

It is a growing area, with protocols like TrueFi and Bloom in this space.

Crypto-native credit scores

This is exactly as it sounds—a credit score is derived from on-chain activities alone, using a combination of on-chain identity, staking and yield-farming activities (both described in detail in Chapter 5), and other financial activities. However, several problems arise. Who is determining what activities are reviewed? How is identity being determined—if more than wallet identity is used, what impact will that have? If wallet identity alone is used, what about activities conducted via different wallets and chains? How old or how new does data have to be to be determinative? Are these requirements known to borrowers? Are they reported to off-chain credit reports? What if the person is new to blockchain as a whole?

---

42 Ideally, the loan applications are anonymized. Protocols may vary, however.

This approach is too new and vague to be easily assessed here. Protocols using this type of methodology include Credmark and LedgerScore.

Off-chain credit score integration

This uses your traditional finance credit score to determine eligibility and interest rates, with all the inherent problems and biases. If you wanted to use this, you'd probably be better off with a bank in traditional finance. At least there you have clear legal recourse in the event of provable discrimination. Protocols using this include Teller.

Personal network bootstrap

In these are invitation-only applications, borrowers are approved directly by the lending pool. This seems to work a great deal like peer-to-peer lending, with all the attendant benefits and risks, but the risk is spread across a pool of lenders rather than with one individual lender. It's unclear how this will scale, or what percentage of the lenders must approve each borrower. If a high rate of approval is required, then it will be difficult to scale to borrowers outside the nucleus of the primary lending pool's acquaintance. If a low rate of approval is required, it is unclear how lenders can be assured of true knowledge, and how it will remain free of some sort of attack by collusion (one or more lenders work in conjunction with the borrower, approve a large loan, and take the proceeds off-chain and disappear).[43] It's an interesting area to watch, however, as proof-of-reputation consensus methods are taking hold, and reputation may be more scalable and manageable than appears at first glance. Protocols using this approach include Akropolis and Aave.

Derivatives and Synthetics

Derivatives are assets (tokens, in DeFi) that get their value from another underlying asset or index. This includes options, index tokens, and even the exchange-traded funds that were recently permitted by the SEC under very restricted circumstances. *Synthetics*, or *synths*, are assets that are tokenized derivatives or combinations of other underlying assets and derivatives. This area is complex, and generally speaking an area of great difficulty legally.

This area is regulated by the SEC and, depending on the asset, the Commodity Futures Trading Commission (CFTC). Most platforms trading these are likely to be subject to ongoing investigations, such as those faced by Binance and BlockFi. Most retail investors are not permitted in this field in the US because it tends to require a level of financial knowledge and risk not suitable to the extremely inadequate financial education given to US (and other countries') nonprofessional investors.

---

43 Attack by collusion is a risk faced by all the DeFi lending protocols. But, of course, it is also a risk faced by traditional lending protocols; scamming and fraud are not unknown in current lending practices.

The most reasonable way to deal with this, to provide some level of protection and still allow access to these financial tools, seems to be providing the financial education to safely undertake this area. Unfortunately, the preferred path of most regulators seems to be to simply close off the area to nonprofessional, nonwealthy investors. While certainly simpler, this doesn't provide the level of access to financial growth that is already denied these investors.

Insurance

Insurance is a fascinating new area. These are permissionless protocols and are typically backed by the community they serve. The community provides liquidity to the insurance protocol and determines the type and amount of payout, as well as the cost of premiums. They insure a range of risks including, but not limited to, smart contract failure, hacks and exploits, collateral loss, wallet breach, and more. They can also insure real-world assets from natural disasters like hurricanes and floods. The price is dictated by the value of the asset and the riskiness of the protocol.

Benefits include the ability to insure previously uninsurable risks and the ability to hedge risk in both digital and real assets, making it more likely people will enter into the purchase of assets. That is an enormous benefit, as many live on the edge of poverty, with one uninsured disaster having the ability to tip one into homelessness. If they enter the space of medical insurance for previously uninsurable or high-risk individuals, it may be a game-changer in terms of access to health care for the poor and/or uninsured.

This approach raises some concerns as well. It is unclear how the riskiness of platforms or real-life catastrophes is being assessed, if the risk is assessed dynamically, and by whom. These protocols are quite new, and it's unclear how effective they will be in the future. There is also a concern that community-funded insurance pools tend to be underfunded and overutilized, and community members have difficulty rating severity and eligibility for reimbursement, particularly if a large number of members are affected, as self-interest and the inability to equate one's own suffering to another's eventually seem to make this untenable. This is the reason that independent insurers, backed by large funds, have succeeded in this space. The determinations of payout and eligibility tend to be cold and unsympathetic—which is generally necessary when allocating limited funds to potentially unlimited liability and loss. Insurance protocols include Nexus Mutual and Etherisc.

Prediction and Betting

Prediction protocols and *betting protocols* are similar, in that they predict the outcome of both real-world and digital outcomes. This can include presidential elections, football game outcomes, post-offering pricing for particular protocols, and more. These are quite informative when the prediction is based on the outcome of something controlled by popular human action, such as elections, the newest flavor of a particular potato chip, or the most popular music site. They are considerably less predictive for things that are outside the control of popular vote or action, such as the high temperature of a city on a particular date, the date of the next SpaceX launch, or the outcome of a particular baseball game.

Some new protocols, such as Hedgehog, are no-risk. No-risk protocols place coins (generally stablecoins) that have been bet into a DeFi protocol, so they can earn interest immediately. If you guess correctly, you get back your stablecoins with the interest accrued. Top predictors may move on to a pool eligible for high payouts, depending on the protocol. If you guess incorrectly, you get back your stablecoins, but the interest goes to the protocol. This makes it seem much more a game than a predictive or betting site. Examples of prediction or betting protocols include Hedgehog, Augur, and Azuro.

Conclusion

In this chapter, we've covered the basic building blocks of DeFi. These include protocols, platforms, DApps, wallets, stablecoins, and governance tokens. Then we looked at the primary use cases for DeFi. We'll talk about all the ways you can make money in DeFi in Chapter 5—some of these aren't actually use cases, such as memecoins. But for now, let's move on to how DeFi works in Chapter 3.

The Tools of DeFi

Hopefully, the importance of DeFi is clear, even at this extremely early stage of development. If the entire blockchain industry is still an infant, DeFi is a newborn (once you have a child, you learn that's actually a distinction).

Think about the internet. It was developed in the 1960s, but it wasn't until 1998 that we figured out that (1) buying things (2) from home with (3) (very) easy returns was going to be the winning function. None of those things were accepted as either good practice or even possible in 1995. But those three years changed the business models of most industries, and gave birth to two of our most powerful industries: social media and software as a service (SaaS).

Internet platforms couldn't talk to each other until 1983, but we're just 15 years out from blockchain's "Hello World," in 2008, and we're already talking about interoperability. Blockchain is moving so much faster than the development of the modern internet. So when you think about what DeFi looks like now, remember that in three to five years, all this will look fairly quaint.

What Is DeFi Right Now?

Most of what we have in DeFi isn't really decentralized or finance. It's really quick, high-risk/high-yield money churn. In that regard, Sam Bankman-Fried is right: the DApps that currently exist are mostly just empty "magic boxes" that attract people's money by gaining increasing valuations—based almost entirely on the new money it attracts.[1]

---

1 Tracy Alloway and Joe Weisenthal, "Sam Bankman-Fried Described Yield Farming and Left Matt Levine Stunned," Bloomberg, April 25, 2022, *https://oreil.ly/OAuut*.

The returns are generated by new investment, not work done by the money invested. That means people aren't getting returns on investment based on money coming back in from paid loans or bonds; they are returns that were just assigned by the founders of the project, payable only because randomly assigned valuations keep increasing as the ongoing incoming money is added to the box. The "returns" are really just payments representing a promise of increased future valuations, and they are paid for by the newest investors to the older investors.

Keeping accusations to a minimum, I will say that I see his point, and that this structure is...well...not *not* a Ponzi scheme.

But that's the future of DeFi—decentralized, peer-to-peer (P2P) finance. If you have an asset and you need liquidity (aka cash), you will want to use this system. Also, it will be the least risky—though, of course, not risk-free—set of investments you can enter. But that's in the future. And since we can't predict the future any better than we could in 1965, let's wipe the newborn goo off this baby and see what we've got.

Smart Contracts

Whether it's a platform or a DApp, there's one thing we need to consider first: smart contracts. If we want our platform to do anything beyond a blank screen, we need to get these contracts in place. Remember, they are neither smart nor contracts. They are automated triggers that, when activated, automatically do a sequence of tasks—move this from here to there, add that column to this column and subtract the total from that column, mow the lawn, whatever. To do anything on its own, to promote the possibility of decentralization, to provide a reason for this DApp's existence—we need a smart contract.

Smart contracts are actually very complex. They are Turing complete programs that execute on a predetermined trigger and stop on their own after the action is completed. Making something start on command isn't hard; it's making something recognize when to stop, reset for the next start command, and turn itself off that's really hard.

What Is Turing Complete—and Can Something Be Turing Incomplete?

We mentioned Turing complete and Turing incomplete systems in Chapters 1 and 2. But what do they really mean? *Turing complete* and *Turing incomplete* are terms that are thrown around a lot in blockchain, but what do they really mean? Technically, Turing complete machines have three main properties.

First, Turing complete machines have *memory*. These machines have access to RAM (random access memory), can use memory to compute rather than relying strictly on input, and have access to infinite memory.

Second, Turing complete machines have full *simulation*. They can simulate any other Turing complete machine, and anything they can do. You see this in the fact that the languages used in one machine can be used identically in another (these are Turing complete languages, like Python and Solidity).

Finally, Turing complete machines can run *infinite loops*, or programs that don't end. This creates a halting problem: it isn't clear whether a program is going to end or will continue in an ongoing loop. Note that either stopping or looping isn't a problem—it's the uncertainty that makes it an issue. Ethereum was the first to solve this problem by creating smart contracts to execute actions, then tying them to a fee for execution. That fee is called *gas*, and the contract requires a set amount to start, spending the gas (more or less) as it executes. When the required gas is spent, execution ends. (Remaining gas is refunded.) So even looping actions are given a certain end: when the gas is expended. It's a pretty impressive solution.

Anything not meeting these criteria, like the Bitcoin blockchain, is Turing incomplete.

Wallets (Again!) and Oracles

So, remember that "predetermined trigger" requirement for smart contracts? Those are wallets and oracles.

We discussed wallets pretty extensively in Chapter 2. Let's just recall that they are the portals that allow us to interact with the blockchain. If you want to buy something, sell something, transfer something, or access something—you need a wallet. Different wallets work with different chains, so make sure you're working with a wallet that can recognize the token you need to work on whatever chain you're interested in. Hardware wallets are the only kind that cost money—both custodial and noncustodial internet-based wallets are free.[2]

Wallets trigger smart contracts when you activate the contract (click Buy, Trade, etc.), then initiate the contract by transferring the appropriate coin recognized by the contract using your private key. This is the chain's native token, like ETH if the contract is on the Ethereum chain, MATIC if it's on the Polygon chain, AVAX if it's on the Avalanche chain, and so on. The amount required is the cost of whatever you are purchasing or transferring, plus the cost of gas. See "What Is Turing Complete—and Can

---

2 Remember that custodial internet-based wallets are the hot wallets—ones you get on exchanges, like Coinbase or Kraken. These don't belong to you, and the exchange can access and claim your assets in multiple circumstances; leaving assets in these is not recommended. Noncustodial internet-based wallets are warm wallets like MetaMask, Phantom, and Trust Wallet. These are owned by you and cannot be accessed without a court order in the US. Both custodial and noncustodial internet-based wallets are quite accessible by hackers, so moving assets to a cold wallet (a hardware wallet) is highly recommended.

Something Be Turing Incomplete?" on page 76 to understand the use of gas in smart contracts.

Gas fees can vary significantly based on the size of the data transfer and the number of people waiting in line to complete transactions on that chain. People pay higher fees during busy periods in the same manner that Uber charges surge pricing during rush hour. More demand means more people are willing to pay higher fees to the limited supply, and those unwilling to pay those fees will wait until the price reduces. However, this price variance can create issues with being able to predict cost in the future, both for protocols and for users. Those operating on this margin will find themselves losing money instead of profiting if they don't plan carefully around gas fees.

The nodes set fee ranges, but the circumstances determine the exact fee to apply at any given time. If a highly anticipated offering or launch is happening on that chain, gas may be 10–15 times higher than average, or even more. But as soon as the bulk of the transactions have passed, gas prices go down pretty quickly. Note that proof-of-work chains, like Bitcoin blockchain and Ethereum, are significantly more expensive than chains offering other methods of consensus, such as proof of stake or proof of history. Ethereum moved to proof of stake in 2022,[3] and, while speeds increased substantially in line with other proof-of-stake chains, pricing did *not* reduce in line with other proof-of-stake chains. Although still popular, this forces reliance on cheaper protocols stacked on top of Ethereum (Layer 2 protocols, discussed in Chapter 4). Over time, this will likely make the Ethereum chain less competitive against other proof-of-stake chains.

So, one way to initiate these contracts is through tokens paid out of your wallet. The other way is by using oracles.

The fundamental problem of blockchain is that it is a navel-gazing technology. Chains can't communicate with one another or the outside world. They can analyze and track every aspect of themselves, but they can't include real-world events or other transactions off-chain on their own. This means chains are great at asking if the public key matches the private key, if the asset to be transferred exists within the account that will transfer it, if there is enough gas for the transaction—these kinds of questions.

---

3 "Proof-of-Stake (PoS)," *Ethereum*, *https://oreil.ly/0HDoL*.

Unfortunately, approximately 90% of the potential utility of smart contracts,[4] including all of DeFi,[5] require real-world interaction. Contracts need to know if someone has called them up, if a price on a market has changed, if the weather has impacted a route, if an account has been verified, etc. Smart contracts need to look outside themselves to find out information in order to act on it. So contracts (and chains) rely on oracles.

As you learned in the previous chapters, oracles are little bits of data that are sent out into the world to collect information, and an action is triggered or not based on what that information says.

The Origin of a Smart Contract, Alcoholic Version

Annie and Brenna are sitting at a bar, drinking shots of Jägermeister and contemplating the world at large. Out of nowhere, Annie yells, "Ryan Reynolds does everything right. He's going to be *People*'s sexiest man alive again."

Brenna, now way past buzzed and into her angry drunk phase, yells back, "You idiot! It's Kim Tae-Hyung—he's twenty times sexier! Fifty times! *He* is going to be sexiest man alive!"[6]

Annie responds, "People don't care about K-pop, and neither do I!" She sticks her finger into Brenna's left eyeball, screaming, "There! Now you're actually blind!"

Brenna then bites Annie's finger, leading Annie to punch her in the nose—and it's best we leave them there. Unfortunately, neither Brenna nor Annie appear to handle alcohol well.

The next day, as they nurse their hangovers and repair their friendship, they decide this is actually a good 1 ETH bet for them, so they open up their wallets and sketch out a smart contract with the following terms: Annie and Brenna each place 1 ETH from their wallets into a third wallet, which is an escrow wallet. They name the escrow wallet "Flaming Shot," because that's how Annie and Brenna roll. They connect their wallets and the Flaming Shot wallet to a contract that says on x day (whenever that year's Sexiest Man Alive issue is released), the contract will release an oracle to the People.com site, and find out who the sexiest man alive is that year. After retrieval, it does one of the following things:

- If Ryan Reynolds is listed as the number 1 "Sexiest Man Alive," take 2 ETH from the Flaming Shot wallet and transfer it to Annie's wallet.

---

4 "What Is the Oracle Problem?" *Chainlink*, November 29, 2023, *https://oreil.ly/IcbNU*

5 See the Gemini website (*https://www.gemini.com/*).

6 We do not endorse *People*'s ranking of shallow physical characteristics or Jägermeister. Please drink responsibly and choose your drinking companions wisely.

- If Kim Tae-Hyung is listed as the number 1 "Sexiest Man Alive," take 2 ETH from the Flaming Shot wallet and transfer it to Brenna's wallet.
- If any other person gets the number 1 spot, transfer 1 ETH to Brenna's wallet and 1 ETH to Annie's wallet.
- Stop.

Now they just wait for the issue to come out, and get paid.

Various types of oracles exist, and many excellent books cover oracles and how they work. For our purposes, I will just use the breakdown here:[7]

Listen
Monitor the blockchain network to check for any incoming user or smart contract requests for off-chain data.

Extract
Fetch data from one or multiple external systems such as off-chain APIs hosted on third-party web servers.

Format
Format data retrieved from external APIs into a blockchain-readable format (input) and/or make blockchain data compatible with an external API (output).

Validate
Generate a cryptographic proof attesting to the performance of an oracle service using any combination of data signing, blockchain transaction signing, Transport Layer Security signatures, trusted execution environment (TEE) attestations, or zero-knowledge proofs.

Compute
Perform some type of secure off-chain computation for the smart contract, such as calculating a median from multiple oracle submissions or generating a verifiable random number for a gaming application.

Broadcast
Sign and broadcast a transaction on the blockchain to send data and any corresponding proof on-chain for consumption by the smart contract.

Output (optional)
Send data to an external system upon the execution of a smart contract, such as relaying payment instructions to a traditional payment network or triggering actions from a cyber-physical system.

---

7 "The Blockchain Oracle Problem," *Chainlink*, November 29, 2023, *https://oreil.ly/yZ6m5*.

Oracles Sound Great—They Can't Possibly Have Problems, Can They?

Unfortunately, oracles do have a couple of problems. The first is that oracles can only trigger contracts only when something quantitative is involved. There are limitations on qualitative information an oracle can retrieve. For example, a person's written opinion could be searched ("Does *Architectural Digest* critic X consider that house ugly?" could send an oracle reading through a published review looking for the word "ugly."). However, related words like unattractive, ungainly, etc. would be missed. General qualitative searches ("Is it hot? "Is it big?" "Is it expensive?") require strict definitions and some sort of number metric to be even vaguely useful.

The second is the cleverly titled oracle problem, which was described briefly in Chapter 2 and is discussed next.

The Oracle Problem

The oracle problem has several parts:

Verification
> The blockchain relies on the information brought back from the oracle to execute a variety of smart contracts. However, it has no way of determining how good that information is or how likely that information is to be accurate. Chains cannot validate any information that is brought back by the oracle. Bad information will lead to incorrect results, which results in a cascade of errors. And no one wants an error cascade.

Validation
> Blockchain requires all nodes to have the same set of data—either complete, identical copies or access to complete, identical copies. Anything new has to be agreed on by whatever consensus method used and has to be replicated across everyone's copy of the chain. If this isn't done, some nodes will look like they are hosting fraudulent chains, and sorting through that mess of which is the correct chain is not anyone's idea of fun.

Scalability
> The need for verification and validation can add a lot of time and effort to closing blocks of transactions. Scalability is usually measured in terms of transactions per

second, or tps.[8] Practically speaking, scaling means having the ability to add masses of people or transactions with the current (or close to the current) infrastructure. Slowing down the closing of blocks and adding more effort creates major bottlenecks as more transactions are added to the line, and makes the chain unusable.

Hackability

Every time you add an access or exit point from a chain, you create a point of weakness—a place for hackers to attack. Adding oracles that come and go on chains can create multiple opportunities for attack. One easy form of attack is simply attaching a virus to a returning oracle and having that malware spread as other nodes add in the data. Others include injecting manipulated data into the external data source (data injection), manipulation during transmission of the data from the data source to the blockchain (data corruption), and creating multiple identities or nodes of the oracle network on the blockchain to disrupt the consensus mechanism and manipulate the data transmitted to the blockchain (a Sybil attack).

Centralization

One oracle providing information may make incorporating information easier, but it puts a lot of value on that one oracle. Remember all the types of centralization we discussed earlier. Even if it is verified as correct and validated, you've just created a concentration of power—one oracle essentially holds the key to initiating or confirming a set of transactions, and anyone who controls the oracle now controls all transactions that rely on whatever data the oracle brings back. Ideally, we will develop a vetted, highly trustworthy private or public data feed to use as a core source.

This doesn't mean we don't use oracles; we don't have a choice if we want to do more than count the lint in our blockchain's belly button. We need outside information to make the transaction processing *useful*. But we need to be careful about which oracles we use or rely on, and to plan for alternate resources if an oracle is compromised or risking control of the chain.

---

8 While Visa's stated global maximum capacity is 64,000 tps, its daily average is 1,700 tps. By contrast, PayPal's is 193 tps. Centralized processors typically process significantly faster than decentralized systems. Typical block confirmation speeds are as follows: Bitcoin 3–7 transactions in 10 min; Ethereum 15–25 transactions in 6 min; Solana 2,825 transactions in 0.4 sec; Polkadot 1,000 transactions in 4–5 sec; EOS 4,000 transactions in 0.5 sec; Cosmos 10,000 transactions in 2–3 min; Stellar 1,000 transactions in 2–5 sec; Dogecoin 30 transactions in 1 min; Litecoin 56 transactions in 30 min; Avalanche 5,000 transactions in 1–2 sec; Algorand 1,000 transactions in 45 sec; Ripple (XRP) 1,500 transactions in 4 sec; Bitcoin Cash 61 transactions in 60 min; Arbitrum 40,000 transactions in 15 sec; IOTA 1,500 transactions in 1–5 min; Dash 10–28 transactions in 15 min. Jeffrey Craig, "What Is Transactions Per Second (TPS): A Comparative Look At Networks," *Phemex*, November 2, 2021, *https://oreil.ly/ibJg2*.

Stablecoins Versus CBDCs

Now, we've talked fairly extensively about stablecoins and even a bit about central bank digital currencies (CBDCs), but we can recap quickly here.

Stablecoins, you may remember, are coins that are engineered to maintain a predictable value. The current stablecoins have short-term use, but all are extremely likely to break in the long term. However, that does not mean that stablecoins should not be used at all or that a functional stablecoin cannot exist. As with everything, understanding where the limitations exist allows us to plan well to avoid them or create solutions.

A truly functional stablecoin *can* exist but doesn't currently for multiple reasons. The primary one, in my opinion, is that most of the developers working on these coins don't understand that creating a functional stablecoin is essentially creating a full base economy. And yes, that's as major an undertaking as it sounds. But it's not impossible—after all, economies have been created thousands of times in history (with varying levels of success). Nevertheless, the current stablecoins can be used—and are used—in existing DeFi applications.

Incentivized Governance Tokens

Governance tokens are the other key tool for DeFi. They are also asset-backed tokens, but with rights, rather than money, backing the token. Governance tokens are a type of utility token—a token that "does something." Most utility tokens make things happen on chains, like paying gas fees, triggering smart contracts and oracles, converting to other tokens, and allowing purchase or allotment of goods and services such as storage or computing power.

When blockchain started, utility tokens were the only type of token. The early developers of blockchain used these tokens as the currency of the chain (this is still the role of most utility tokens). However, they gave tokens a perception of demand by giving the tokens limited supply, to make the chain more desirable. Unfortunately, scarcity in supply doesn't matter if there is no real demand.

If Everyone Is Supposed to Want Bitcoin in the Future, Why Are So Few Floating Around?

Bitcoin was the first real blockchain system to create this idea of scarcity-based demand. Originally, bitcoins were an odd type of utility token: it was the tool to transfer assets from one wallet to another on the Bitcoin blockchain, but also the asset itself. It's a strange concept, so take a minute to consider it. The blockchain is fairly simple: it *only* transfers bitcoin from one wallet to another. Whatever you bought or sold that resulted in the transfer of bitcoin (like pizza, an NFT, a sofa) is actually held

---

off-chain. The ownership of whatever you bought or sold doesn't exist on the Bitcoin blockchain.

So why even have it on blockchain? Why track half of the exchange of assets if you can't track all of it? Well, that's the other part of the Bitcoin utility—it is designed to actually *be* the other asset. The idea at this point in the evolution of blockchain was to replace a currency.

Since there is no innate utility for Bitcoin (you can't buy a burger or pay your rent with it, for example), the idea was to create value in two ways. The first was to create a secure record of transfers of value (bitcoin) from one wallet to another, guaranteeing no transfers were promised but not delivered. The second was to create demand by creating scarcity. Only 21 million bitcoins will ever be mined (created by computation). The thought was to create more demand for Bitcoin by limiting supply, which would, theoretically, build more demand for each bitcoin. Once all the bitcoins are mined, people who want to use Bitcoin will need to compete for any available coins, and the value of each bitcoin will go up.

Unfortunately, as with all great theories, they don't play out so neatly in reality. Scarcity works only as a floor for price, *provided there is sufficient demand at that floor*. What does that mean? It means scarcity (limited supply) keeps prices up only if demand exceeds that supply. If more than 21 million people want one bitcoin—or just want to use the Bitcoin blockchain—then each bitcoin has more demand than supply. They will bid against one another for each coin, and that will make the value of Bitcoin go up. That is generally how markets work. But it mistakes one key principle: it requires a minimum amount of demand.

Let's say I've magically limited all the dog poop in the world to 21 million pieces. Does that limitation on supply suddenly mean each individual piece of dog poop is more valuable? Nope. Why? Because there is (hopefully) no demand for dog poop. I could limit the supply of dog poop to 1,000 pieces or 1. The limitation does not increase the value of each piece when it has zero demand. *Scarcity matters only when there is more demand than supply*. If demand for Bitcoin goes to zero, either because no one wants the coins or no one wants to use the Bitcoin blockchain, the price of Bitcoin will fall to zero—even though it is limited in supply.

Now, all this is not to say there is no value to Bitcoin. There is.[9] But that value is not solely based on the concept of scarcity, or even the proof-of-work consensus method for that blockchain. These are two misconceptions often cited by those who believe in Bitcoin with nearly religious fervor. But Bitcoin is not magical. Nor is it a currency. It's a high-risk asset.

---

9 The value of Bitcoin is actually fairly complex but definitely real. It's beyond the scope of this book, but I encourage you to look at this as a part of economic modeling, and hopefully I can discuss this further in a different text.

Understanding the value of any token is called its *tokenomics*, and most chains are appallingly poor at understanding how tokenomics work, much less designing them properly. As a result, we have lots of chains with tokens based on useless scarcity and false market value. But that's for a different section.

Incentivized governance tokens primarily serve the third main purpose of tokens:[10] governance (clever, right?). Like any governance token, they typically give the holder rights such as voting, putting forward proposals, and nominating members for governing bodies. Incentivized governance tokens do more than that. They allow holders to do something to earn more tokens. Usually, this is something like staking, where the act of adding liquidity and stability to the chain or application is rewarded by additional tokens. We'll cover more of how this works in Chapter 4.

Usually, these reward tokens are more of the governance tokens, but they could be any type of reward. The point is these tokens are not strictly speculative; they have the ability to generate or be exchanged for another asset. So these would be another type of asset-backed token. And we know now that asset-backed tokens belong in DeFi.

Wallets Part III: Hosted Versus Unhosted and the Purpose of Knowing Customer Identity

I know, I know—back again with wallets? How much more is there to say?! Not too much, but we do need to discuss wallets that are hosted versus unhosted, especially as the risks to both have been overblown recently.

Hosted wallets are hot wallets. As you may recall from Chapter 2, these are connected to exchanges or, occasionally, other applications. These are the rented lockers you get when you open an account on Coinbase or Gemini, for example. You go through the Know Your Customer (KYC)/anti–money laundering (AML) process, connect it to your bank account, and can begin to buy and sell cryptocurrency. The host (e.g., the exchange) holds the seed phrase, so if you lose your password or it is compromised, you can always just let the exchange know and reset it.

Unhosted wallets are the warm and cold wallets—the internet-connected ones like MetaMask and Trust wallets, or hardware-based wallets, such as Trezor and Ledger. These are also called *self-hosted*: you are the only holder of the password, and if you lose access to your account and seed phrase, your access to that account is gone.

---

10 As you may recall, the three main purposes of tokens are to act as a utility or transactional tool, as a security to trade on markets, or as a governance tool to determine the direction of the project (generally via voting).

True or False?

If you listen to rooms, spaces, and events held by people in cryptocurrency for more than 10 minutes, you'll hear a few phrases repeated:

"Not your keys, not your wallet."

This is a rallying cry for people to "get thee to an unhosted wallet, immediately, if not sooner." This is because one of the core tenets of blockchain is self-banking. This means you are the sole holder of access and title to your assets, whether crypto or otherwise. It's an interesting concept, primarily since we've all been taught that banks are the safest place for your money.

This statement is true. Your funds are most at risk of phishing and direct hacks when held in wallets that are connected to the internet (hot and warm wallets). Cold wallets are safest from outside theft or attack.

Why Are We So Scared to Keep Money Out of Banks?

This is an interesting question. Historically, people who used banks typically used local community banks, with a chunk kept in an account to ensure that the bank could issue you a loan if you found yourself in a tight spot. Bankers and depositors knew one another by name, and this created the social pressure to permit lending in the time before it was easy to hire a private investigator, order a credit report, and download a full background check with one button. The funds were largely the bulk of crop sales or large orders, and needed to last the rest of the year.

The rest of the money was referred to as "pin money," available for immediate needs and purchases without the hassle of going to the banks, or having them know your business. Incidentally, this was a significant reason for unaccounted-for inflation: this money disappeared from the economy for all intents and purposes, resulting in the Fed needing to increase the number of dollars in circulation to account for missing currency.

During the Great Depression, the faith people had in the safety of their money in banks evaporated. Unfortunately, that resulted in even more depressed economic activity, as banks rely on deposits to fund loans, which return profit, which generates more financial activity. Money was being hoarded by the wealthy and the poor, and this resulted in drastically reduced economic activity. No one was buying or selling *anything.*

So banks and the government set up a major campaign to restore faith in banks. The Federal Deposit Insurance Company (FDIC) was formed and funded by banks to assure depositors that money lost or stolen would be returned to them. Banks stepped in to assure people that "the bank is the safest place to store money. Guaranteed." As a result, generations of ordinary citizens have grown up thinking they could not possibly carry the responsibility of holding and managing their own funds. It truly terrifies some people, and this can be reflected in their own deep reluctance to take on the task of self-banking with crypto. People literally no longer trust themselves with their own money.

"Not your keys, not your Bitcoin."

This is similar, though not identical, to the wallet statement. This refers to the idea that any tokens held in anything but an unhosted wallet don't actually belong to you.

This statement is true. Generally speaking, you have the right to the value of the profits or losses of the assets in your account, but not the assets themselves. So, when you buy Bitcoin, it's not actually Bitcoin that is transferred to your wallet. It's the value of the Bitcoin that is credited to your account. When you sell, the value of the sale is attributed to your account. It's only when you transfer crypto from the exchange wallet to your unhosted wallet that it is converted to actual bitcoin (or part of a bitcoin) or other cryptocurrency. Otherwise, in a hosted wallet, you typically just have the fluctuating value of Bitcoin (or other crypto), not the actual asset itself.

"Unhosted wallets, privacy coins, and crypto are used mostly by people who want to conduct scams or deal drugs."

This statement is false, although there was a time in our recent history (a funny statement considering our entire industry is less than 20 years old) when anonymity was used to conduct all sorts of illegal transactions, from unregistered securities offerings to the horrors of Silk Road.

However, crypto is used by institutional investors and for war relief efforts. Unhosted wallets are common, as they are considered the safest method of storing assets. Privacy coins, such as Monero and Zcash, are a different story. On one hand, they use mixers to further obscure not just the parties to a transaction but the transaction itself. This is fundamentally opposed to the core tenet of blockchain, which highlights transparency. And they are often the preferred payment of ransomware pirates and other actors with nefarious intent. But they also provide a level of security and protection that most cryptocurrency (and most general currency) cannot, and political dissidents use them for that reason.

In addition, Bitcoin took on some of the properties of privacy coins in the Taproot upgrade. This upgrade works to hide multisignature wallet transactions because these wallets tend to be owned by companies or projects and are ripe targets for hackers. Hiding the nature of these wallets protects the owners from theft. We aren't the same community we were before 2020 and the COVID pandemic. Although the original culture of tech-centric anti-institutionalist (mostly) males still exists, those in the blockchain space now include disenfranchised and underserved adults, progressive thinkers reimagining how payments and value are conveyed in economic systems, and individuals simply trying to access markets and communities in newer, more interactive ways. We are not simply tropes; we are as diverse as any modern group of people drawn to a technology, with many, often opposing, reasons for being in blockchain.

"Exchanges can steal your assets."

This statement, unfortunately, is *true*. When you leave assets (or rights to assets) on an exchange, exchanges have felt free to help themselves to your funds to shore up dwindling funds. Bitfinex did this to recover from a 120,000 bitcoin theft; it made itself whole by allocating Bitcoin from the accounts of its users to its own accounts. It was able to do this because it held the keys to both their wallets and the wallets of users. Coinbase and Kraken recently clarified that they will claim the assets held in their user accounts to satisfy debt if they go bankrupt. They use *your* money to pay off *their* bad debts. And Crypto.com stated that it will sell off your assets to cover your debts—even if you don't have any sort of agreement or margin loan with the company entitling it to do that. And FTX used customer funds to fund billions in bets by Alameda, a private, affiliated fund—almost 70% of its loans to Alameda were paid by FTX customer funds.[11] Going back to the earlier aphorism: not your keys, not your asset.

Anti-Money Laundering and Know Your Customer

People in the blockchain space tend to be a suspicious lot—partly by nature. A certain type of person would rally around a financial technology that evades detection or regulation. Conspiracy theorists, third- and fourth-party candidacies, and untethered libertarianism have found fertile ground among the discord servers.

Of course, not all of this is the working of the tinfoil hat society. The genesis of the entire movement was the 2007–2008 banking failure and the Global Financial Crisis, resulting in a $700 billion Emergency Economic Stimulus Plan in 2008 (the "bank

---

11 Vicky GeHuang, Alexander Osipovich, and Patricia Kowsmann, "FTX Tapped Into Customer Accounts to Fund Risky Bets, Setting Up Its Downfall," *Wall Street Journal*, November 11, 2022, *https://oreil.ly/rnyum*; Jahi, Assad, "SBF Trial—Forensic Accountant Reveals Almost 70% of Alameda's Loans Were Serviced with FTX Customer Funds," *CryptoSlate*, October 19, 2023, *https://oreil.ly/1JH7X*.

bailout" plan, later extended to General Motors and Chrysler) and another $780 billion stimulus package, the American Recovery Investment Act, in 2009. In the end, risky and poor lending practices ended up hurting everyone *but* the banks. People lost billions in assets, many even became homeless, because of predatory credit and lending activity or outright fraud, but when people actually needed loans, banks took their tax dollars and then decided to be conservative. Seeing your friends and family reduced to poverty or near poverty will change your perspective quite a bit.

Whatever the reason, the fact remains that if the majority of the pre-2020 community had their preference, the entire blockchain industry would be a mass of Bitcoin, privacy coins, and untraceable, Tor-based wallets that served as personal tax havens. Fortunately, the post-2020 crypto and blockchain are not so stringent ideologically—which is good, because KYC/AML rules are becoming mandatory across more and more jurisdictions. Getting access to these tools requires you comply with them in nearly everything that deals with money. So we should probably find out what they are and how they apply.

AML

Anti–money laundering rules started in the US in the 1970s with the Bank Secrecy Act, a set of rules broadly aimed at identifying the source of money flowing into banks and then entering commerce. These rules are designed to protect against criminals using banks to hide activities like money laundering, financing terrorism, human trafficking, prostitution, illegal gambling, and more.

These rules apply to corporations, banks, fintech companies, financial institutions, lenders, credit unions, lending platforms, private lenders, and broker-dealers. Basically, if it deals with money, AML applies.

What Is Money Laundering, and How Did It Start?

The term *money laundering* reportedly appeared in the 1920s, when US Mafia members were earning huge amounts of cash from illegal activities (including alcohol, prostitution, and gambling), and purchased laundromats to hide the origin of the money. In the 1970s, the US government targeted banks because the newly "clean" money would enter banks as legally earned revenue and then enter the stream of commerce. AML rules required banks to know a lot more about customers and sourcing, which limited the ability of the Mafia to create business fronts and pose as legitimate business moguls.

Before we get into what AML really is, let's talk about how and why we care about this in the crypto space. I mean, we just talked about "decentralized" and "anonymous" and other words that usually mean it's really hard to comply (if anyone intends to comply at all), and now we're talking about things that protect people from hiding assets. That means no hiding. Which means this anonymous, decentralized, "can't catch me" world is in conflict with governments trying to stop terrorists, criminals, and gangsters. Who do we think will win here? Hint: it's probably not the people who want to hide.

If this were limited only to the US, people would just set up exchanges and apps overseas and call it a day. But in October 2021, the Financial Action Task Force (more commonly known as FATF) revised its Recommendation 16 to clearly apply the Travel Rule to the crypto world. Say "Travel Rule" to anyone who has been in crypto for at least two years, and 90% of the time it's followed by a giant groaning eye roll. Get comfortable with that response. As soon as you finish this section, it will be coming out of you too.

Who is FATF, and why do we care?

First, we have to recognize that what FATF does is incredibly important. It is a global watchdog of financial crimes with the purpose of stopping the flow of money to fund terrorism, corruption, human trafficking, weapons of mass destruction, and other truly terrible things. Founded in 1989 because of the negative results of global economic flow, it now comprises 39 member countries and a series of observers and associates representing around 200 jurisdictions.

The way FATF works is that its members meet and come up with recommendations and rationales. Each member country is then expected to put laws in place to accomplish that recommendation's purpose over a "reasonably prompt" deadline. Technically, no member country is obligated to put these recommendations into legislation, but most comply in some form because the purpose of the recommendations is designed specifically to address an acknowledged harm faced by many, if not all, of the member, observer, and associate countries. They theoretically work to make people safer by cutting off the cash flow to fund criminals such as terrorists, drug cartels, and human traffickers—crimes that disproportionately impact women, citizens of poor countries, and underserved communities. When effective, this serves to save lives and prevent the endless ways humans find to exploit other humans. Such laws are necessary, and they need to exist until we find a way to be better to one another.

OK. That said, let's talk about how crypto got involved. As we mentioned before, crypto was once used primarily as a means to conduct illegal transactions, primarily the purchase of (then) illegal drugs, but also including ransomware payments, scams, hacking, theft, and human trafficking. FATF noticed. Unfortunately, once a governmental body of any sort notices you, it is extremely unlikely to un-notice you. It's not a coincidence that as knowledge of Bitcoin and cryptocurrency became more widespread, along with tax evasion and criminal connections, the beginnings of "digital asset" regulation began.

The (damn) Travel Rule

The Travel Rule was initiated in 1996 and applied to banks and other financial institutions (from the Bank Secrecy Act, so you know banks were involved in there somewhere). It's called the "Travel Rule" because it deals with money traveling between banks—the goal is to prevent money from hiding its origins.

It required these institutions to share information with one another about customers when they conducted transactions over at least $3,000. It required the institutions to collect the following:

- The name of the transmitter
- The account number of the transmitter, if used
- The address of the transmitter
- The identity of the transmitter's financial institution
- The amount of the transmittal order
- The execution date of the transmittal order
- The identity of the recipient's financial institution
- The name of the recipient
- The address of the recipient
- The account number of the recipient
- Any other specific identifier of the recipient

And right here, you can start to see the problem when it involved blockchain transactions, which occur between wallets with random letters and numbers. What exactly do you say about the transmitter? Or the recipient? And to whom? How useful are reports saying, "I sent 0.04 ETH to [bunch of letters and numbers], and I have no idea where that person is, but I think there was an NFT of a bunny in there..."?

The Travel Rule moved into crypto from an October 2018 recommendation that was incredibly contentious. It read, in part, that countries needed to adopt regulations requiring "countries and entities that engage in or provide virtual asset products or services" to "obtain and hold" information regarding senders of the assets and the transaction.[12] These recommendations were formally adopted in June 2019 as binding obligations, and countries were given 12 months to adopt regulations accordingly. Countries were slow to adopt, wanting clarity and unsure how much applicability "virtual assets" had in their jurisdiction. In June 2020, another 12-month adoption period was issued because only 58 of the 128 reporting jurisdictions (over 200

---

12 "Public Statement on Virtual Assets and Related Providers," *FATF*, June 21, 2019, *https://oreil.ly/g8qAw*.

jurisdictions, remember) had adopted some form of either regulation of virtual asset providers or banning these providers altogether. A new set of interpretive regulations was issued, and in October 2021, FATF issued a report reminding everyone that these recommendations were binding (not just "suggestions"), and illustrating the need for these providers and transactions to be tracked immediately, if not sooner.

For those who don't remember, the end of 2020 marked the start of a boom in crypto trading and investing. By 2021, a new group of investors flush with stimulus checks, bored with COVID quarantine, and terrified of both going to work and getting sick or staying home and losing a job, found the low entry fees and newly open access to crypto an irresistible spot of hope. This rush of cash into crypto and crypto trading brought the industry into the spotlight of the mainstream press, which fueled the growth of everything from NFTs to DeFi.

And with this surge of money and interest came a slew of hacks and scams. The first over-the-counter crypto trading platform was globally blacklisted (Russia's Suex). The Poly Network hack ($600 million), the Africrypt scam ($3.3 billion), the Colonial Pipeline ransom ($4.4 million)—altogether $14 billion in scams and theft occurred in one year. Scams increased 82%, and general crypto theft rose 516% in 2020 to $3.2 billion—and 72% of that was directly related to DeFi. A 516% increase in anything should make you perk up your ears to find out more. A 516% increase in crime in one type of asset? Well, that makes lawmakers notice. Because it makes those lawmakers' constituencies mad. Very mad. Voting mad. So it was understandable that FATF cracked down on their members—who cracked down on crypto. Thanks, hackers and scammers. You just made genuine project growth and adoption harder. Well done.

KYC Versus AML

As noted previously, KYC is Know Your Customer, while AML is anti–money laundering. Many people consider these identical or even just one thing. Neither is true. Generally speaking, KYC is the set of policies developed by a financial institution to protect against "bad actors." AML is the set of regulations designed to prevent corruption, financial crime, and subverting sanctions to prevent terrorism and nation-based crime.

As you can see in Figure 3-1, KYC is the "make sure your clients aren't bad people" scheme, while AML is the "don't let bad people use your products or services" scheme.

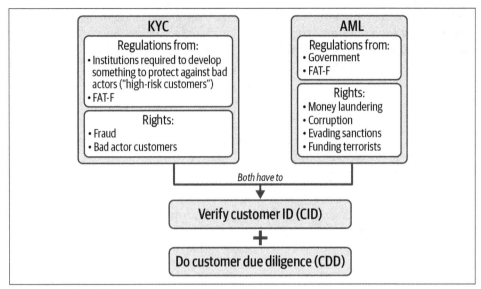

Figure 3-1. The difference between KYC and AML

What Is Required?

As shown in Figure 3-1, AML and KYC are completely different regimes that share one requirement: verify the identity of your customers. Beyond that, they are completely separate requirements.

KYC

KYC has several requirements. These include *customer identification* (CID): is the customer who they say they are? This requires checking government-issued identification, things like articles of incorporation, and possibly even financial records.

Also, KYC requires *customer due diligence* (CDD): how much risk of fraud or corruption does this customer present? Here, you're required to identify anyone who owns 25% or more of any customer company or entity. You also need to figure out the general type of transactions that customer will make so you can see what is "anomalous" for them. Then, you'll need to create a system to identify the risk of fraud and "bad actorhood" (it's a word; well, it's a word now) of every customer. Finally, you'll need to identify any politically exposed persons (PEPs) because they may be more at risk of fraud and money laundering.

Third, you'll need to do *continuous monitoring*, or checking for "gym memberships."[13] You need to have a monitoring program to check for suspicious activity, and submit Suspicious Activity Reports (SARs) to the Financial Crimes Enforcement Network (FinCEN, a bureau under the US Department of the Treasury) and any other relevant law enforcement agencies.

AML

AML requirements are similar but not identical. You'll need to do the CID and the CDD, as you do for the KYC.

You'll also have to create *internal controls* so employees will know how to be compliant. You'll need to designate a *Bank Secrecy Act compliance officer* to make sure people are following those internal controls. To no one's surprise, this is usually a lawyer. You need to have *ongoing training* to make sure everyone is following current regulations, and engage someone for *periodic independent testing* of the compliance system, ideally by an outside party.

What Is the Impact?

In October 2021, FATF issued an updated interpretation of Recommendation 16 that based the regulation of crypto on the use of VASPs. A *VASP* is a *virtual asset service provider* (but check out "Are We Even Talking About the Same Thing?" to see the incredible array of terms). They all have slightly different meanings and may have entirely different regulatory schemes. Don't blame the messenger.

Are We Even Talking About the Same Thing?

Several FAT-F terms *seem* identical but really aren't. Here's a little glossary to keep things from getting too confused.

Virtual assets are digital representations of value that can be digitally traded or transferred and can be used for payment or investment purposes.[14] *Financial assets* are digital representations of fiat currencies, securities, and other assets that are already covered elsewhere in the FATF recommendations. According to FATF, *everything representing value is either a financial asset or a virtual asset.* No escaping it. People have tried.

---

13 This is an uncredited meme quote: "I got a notice from my bank saying they noticed 'highly suspicious activity' on my account. It was for a gym membership."

14 From the Glossary of the FATF Recommendations.

Virtual asset service providers (VASPs)[15] are any natural or legal person (not covered elsewhere under the Recommendations)[16] that conducts one or more of the following activities or operations below. Note that it has to do this *as a business*, and for or *on behalf of another natural or legal person.*

The activities or operations are (1) conduct exchanges between virtual assets and fiat currencies, (2) conduct exchanges between one or more forms of virtual assets, (3) transfer virtual assets,[17] (4) conduct safekeeping and/or administration of virtual assets, (4) conduct safekeeping and/or administration of instruments enabling control over virtual assets, and/or (5) participate in and provide financial services related to an issuer's offer and/or sale of a virtual asset.

VASPs include many entities currently classified under different names under various agencies. These include "money transmitter business," "money service business," or "convertible virtual currency business" by FinCEN; "designated contract markets" by the CFTC; "digital asset trading platforms" by the SEC; and the succinctly named "providers engaged in exchange services between virtual currencies and fiat currencies" by the EU.

Digital asset entities (DAE) is the overarching term for any business built on cryptocurrency transactions, like Bitcoin ATMs or cryptocurrency gambling sites. These use crypto but are not financial institutions. VASPs are subsets of DAE. It can also be called a *virtual asset entity* or a *crypto asset entity.*

Digital asset customer is a DAE that uses the services of a bank or financial institution. Note that the Treasury's Office of the Comptroller of the Currency has already brought an enforcement action against M.Y. Safra Bank for deficient AML and ineffective monitoring.

A *money service business* is any entity doing business—*whether or not it's legally organized*—that does one of more of the following, *even if it doesn't do it on a regular basis*: (1) currency dealer or exchanger (over $1K per person per day), (2) check casher (over $1K per person per day), (3) issuer of traveler's checks, money orders, or stored value (over $1K per person per day), (4) seller or redeemer of traveler's checks, money orders, or stored value (over $1K per person per day), (5) money transmitter, and/or (6) US Postal Service. It doesn't include any entities that are banks and/or regulated by the CFTC or SEC.

---

15 From the Glossary of the FATF Recommendations.

16 A legal person is some sort of legal entity, like a corporation or LLC. Note that informal entities, like DAOs, that do not formalize as an LLC, etc., risk being viewed as a partnership, which has severe legal implications for members under US law. Also, there is the risk that each member of the DAO may separately be a VASP or other regulated entity.

17 In this context of virtual assets, *transfer* means to conduct a transaction on behalf of another natural or legal person that moves a virtual asset from one virtual asset address or account to another.

Since most jurisdiction regulations are going to incorporate these FAT-F recommendations, at least in some form, we'll focus on VASPs and what may be considered a VASP.

 Remember, VASPs (1) act as a business on behalf of another person, and (2) provide or actively facilitate virtual asset–related activities. So, if you handle your mom's crypto trading as a favor to her because no one uses vowels and the print on the phone screen is "so damn tiny," you're not likely to be considered a VASP.

VASPs include quite a lot of the entities and organizations that serve the crypto industry, but remember, the regulations don't focus on the type of entity per se but really on how the entity uses the virtual assets and for whose benefit. But, generally, they include centralized exchanges, decentralized exchanges, crypto ATM operators, wallet custodians, hedge funds, mining pool operators who also serve as digital wallet hosts, gambling sites that allow crypto, and more.

Let's talk about decentralized exchanges, and since we're in that section, a few other areas people working in or on DeFi will need to consider (if you aren't already).

Decentralized exchanges

According to FATF, DEXes aren't just VASPs but also are the developer(s), founder(s), or owner(s) who set up the DEX if they "facilitate or conduct the exchange or transfer of value, whether in virtual assets or in traditional fiat currency."

DApps

Now, technically, applications alone (strictly hardware and/or software) shouldn't fall under the FATF view of VASPs—but this is really just an exception for applications that do nothing but interact with protocols or other software. However, the DApp will be treated like a VASP under the following conditions:

- A group benefits from fees paid, and a party profits from the fees.
- Administrative "keys" restrict access.
- An ongoing business relationship exists between owners/operators and users, even if that relationship is just a smart contract.
- Any party profits from the service.
- Any party has the ability to set or change parameters to identify the owner/operator of the application.
- The application allows users to send virtual assets to other individuals (like P2P payments, personal remittances, payment of nonfinancial goods or services, or payment of wages).

- Creators, owners, and/or operators maintain "sufficient control or influence" over the "DeFi arrangement," *if* the application is providing or actively facilitating VASP service.

- Any developer(s), founder(s), or owner(s) who set up the DEX "facilitate or conduct the exchange or transfer of value, whether in virtual assets or in traditional fiat currency."

This list is neither clear nor exhaustive, so...hopefully we'll learn more in time.

Stablecoins

This one is going to hurt. First, the interpretive note on stablecoins by FATF is literally called "Virtual Assets—FATF Report to G20 on So-Called Stablecoins" (*https://oreil.ly/YF9Uy*). Second, Section 3 of this report has this sentence: "There should never be a situation where a so-called stablecoin is not covered by the revised FATF Standards." Please take the time to read these guidelines, because this is a very regulated area.

Generally, if a central governing body (which could just be the founding developer team) maintains control *or influence* over the administration or function of the stablecoin, the body is likely a VASP. What if this body is an ever-trendy DAO? As we've seen with decentralized exchanges and apps, decentralization doesn't protect against much. We could assume that DAOs also qualify as VASPs based on their influence and function regarding the stablecoin. This seems to depend on whether the body "carries out other functions in the stablecoin arrangement."

What if there isn't an easily identifiable body? Then FATF looks for oversight in the *pre-launch* phase. Yes, pre-launch. It is going to regulate whoever worked on the coin *before it was a coin*.

Wow—is there anyone not included in the FATF scheme to regulate the entire crypto industry? Fortunately, a few. These include the following:

- Validators, if your only function is validating transactions (no governance functions)

- Cloud service providers who are *only* providing cloud service for operations (not governance)

- Hardware wallet manufacturers who only make and sell the wallets (no exchanges, validation, staking, or any other operations)

- Unhosted wallet software providers who are only developing and/or selling the software and any hardware (no exchanges, validation, staking, or any other operations)

- Merchants who are *only* providing goods and/or services in exchange for stablecoins
- Software developers who don't do any VASP functions
- Individual users
- Miners who aren't doing any VASP functions

Nonfungible tokens

This is a tough area, primarily because so many people misunderstand what these are. NFTs are tokenized assets, but let's figure out that definition a little more clearly.

They are tokens (e.g., ERC-721 on the Ethereum chain) representing ownership of some sort (e.g., lease, license, sublease, full right and title) with a link to something digital (e.g., art, code, music, writing, a patent, an avatar) *or* a digital representation of something physical (e.g., provenance for a physical painting, a deed to land, a certificate of authenticity for a luxury bag).

NFTs just represent a set of rights held by owners, and they may include a royalty, or percentage of price on every future sale, back to whomever created the NFT. NFTs have a number of issues, including verification of IP rights, storage, transfer, flipping, and more—but a deeper discussion isn't the focus of this book. For our purposes, it's most important to look at NFTs as one of two things: either a financial asset, putting it squarely into the realm of virtual asset or digital asset—a tool of speculative financial investment—or a final product with no speculative aspect.

To see NFTs through the perspective of FATF, we have this incredibly clear guidance: it depends. While FATF doesn't generally consider NFTs to be virtual assets, they likely *are* virtual assets if the NFT is used for payment or investment purposes in practice. If, however, an asset tied to the NFT is a financial asset *already* covered by one of the FATF recommendations, then the NFT is likely not a virtual asset. Evaluation is generally on a case-by-case basis. (Much clearer now, right?) In any event, if the NFT is likely a virtual asset, the platform or application transacting the NFT would likely be considered a VASP.

Are we starting to see the issue here? If not, let's look at one other area, which should make this clear.

Unhosted wallets

Unhosted wallets aren't typically covered by VASP rules. However, if an unhosted wallet provider performs virtual asset activities or operations for or on behalf of another person, it would likely qualify as a VASP.

This is a problem because DEXes, staking, and liquidity pools all use unhosted wallets to conduct transactions. How these unhosted wallets are supposed to collect and convey the information required by KYC/AML is almost impossible to say. This would likely make unhosted wallets untenable, which would put these types of activities at risk—and these are the core of DeFi.

US Regulation

You'll see a lot of the FATF rules incorporated into the way US regulation is both written and interpreted by regulators. Right now, the securities part of the issue (FATF's "financial assets") are governed by the US SEC and the CFTC.[18] If any coin or token is offered that would be deemed a "security," it must be registered with the SEC or offered using an exemption to the regulations.[19]

Any securities offered to the public generally have to be conducted through some sort of registered platform. This could be a registered and otherwise compliant exchange (like the New York Stock Exchange), automated market maker (like Nasdaq), alternative trading system (like an accredited investor marketplace or dark pool), or even a crowdfunding platform (like Republic).

At this point, you can see the problem: nearly every crypto exchange and/or trading platform is not registered or otherwise compliant. So even if you do register your offering, where are you permitted to trade? Which platforms offer only registered coins or tokens? It's not Coinbase—in early 2022, it was hit with a potential class-action indicating that it was trading 79 unregistered securities on its platform.[20] Given the sheer number of regulatory questions and lawsuits that are still being issued even *after* the SEC and Internal Revenue Service (IRS) investigated Coinbase a few years ago, it would not qualify as a well-run, fully compliant, diligently monitored platform.[21]

It's hard to be too critical of project leaders for creating projects and thinking, "Why bother?" when considering whether to register, when there isn't a platform to legally offer the asset anyway. Of course, this doesn't make the unregistered nature better; you don't see more opaque disclosure than in the DeFi segment of the industry, and

---

18 The SEC regulates securities, both registered and exempt; the CFTC regulates commodities and securities futures offerings.

19 This concept alone is an entire field of law and beyond the scope of this book. Please contact a knowledgeable securities attorney in your area regarding your specific facts and circumstances.

20 See *Underwood, Oberlander and Rodriguez v. Coinbase Global Inc.* (2022).

21 See, e.g., *Bielski v. Coinbase* (2022), arguing that the poor compliance and organizational structure of Coinbase led to loss of recourse, in which Coinbase's request to move to arbitration was recently denied because the delegation and arbitration clauses were deemed unconscionable, and *Donovan v. Coinbase Global Inc.* (2022), in which the plaintiff sued for massively unstable "stablecoin" GYEN, among others.

lack of registration is not making this problem any easier. Nothing is preventing anyone from disclosing the identities of teams, the tokenomics, the percentage of ownership, amount of flipping, use of proceeds, and roadmap. Not offering information and/or holding themselves to standards of honesty and transparency is really just making everything worse.

Note that as of 2023, the SEC has finally approved INX, a platform to trade registered tokens as a registered exchange.[22] The SEC has also approved Prometheum to serve as a special-purpose broker to offer registered securities. So, as of the time of this writing, the pieces are all in place to conduct a fully registered offering and actually complete the sale to the public. But this does not help any of the projects released prior to the time when both of these were in place.

As an overview, the US regulatory structure as it impacts the crypto industry currently looks like this (you may want to sit down, as these aren't mutually exclusive):

- Coins or tokens that are designed or sold as a capital-raising asset or touting passive appreciation are generally governed by the SEC and/or state securities divisions. Enforcement can be from the Department of Justice, the SEC, and/or state attorneys general.

- Coins or tokens representing future interests in assets, or securities representing future pricing in cryptocurrency, are generally governed by the CFTC.

- Coins or tokens representing currency are governed by the Department of the Treasury, specifically the Office of the Comptroller of the Currency. Also, incidentally, Congress has the ability to make anything that is not legal US tender illegal.

- Platforms and applications that deal with currency or its substitutes (like coins or tokens), including but not limited to accepting deposits, making loans, and other money-related services, may be deemed banks and are governed by the Office of the Comptroller of the Currency.

- Platforms, applications, and wallets that require KYC/AML are governed by another Department of the Treasury division: FinCEN. Note that FinCEN tends to view crypto as a currency (for obvious reasons).

- Users, creators, platforms, applications, wallets, coins, tokens—pretty much anything in the world—that has been bought or sold for value is governed by state tax departments and yet another division of the Department of the Treasury: the IRS. Interestingly, the IRS tends to view crypto as property (again, for obvious reasons). Curiously, the enforcement division for FinCEN is...the IRS. Accordingly, FinCEN has had some issues with enforcement.

---

22 The author is an advisor to INX.

- Marketers, platforms, influencers, projects, and project leads that use false or misleading statements or fail to disclose paid connections or personal interest in items they are promoting are governed by the Federal Trade Commission and state attorneys general and consumer product bureaus.
- Platforms, applications, and tokens related to gambling are governed by state gaming authorities and the Department of Justice.
- And, of course, every person, platform, and application is always subject to both state and federal criminal and civil laws.

As of this writing, none of these agencies or FATF have publicly stated they have any desire to end either crypto or DeFi. In fact, there is significant tolerance within agencies for support of the blockchain and crypto industry. For example, Janet Yellen (the Secretary of the Treasury) is admittedly not a fan of crypto, but she has publicly indicated that overly restrictive provisions for prospective and signed bills would not apply to most members of the industry.[23] She has vocal supporters of crypto and blockchain in her department, and, as far as can be discerned, their open statements of support have never led to censure, repercussion, or dismissal.

Custodians and Intermediaries

According to the SEC, a *custodian* is a third party who has or maintains control of any assets. "Custody" means when any advisor or intermediary, "directly or indirectly, controls client funds or securities, or has the authority to possess them."[24] These can be advisors, banks, or other entities, and they are strongly regulated. Unfortunately, it's not entirely clear what the full impact of these custodians and intermediaries will be—this topic has been a priority for the SEC, but changing markets and shifting priorities has delayed more significant rollouts to the technology. Until then, we can only go on the guidance we have.

---

23 When the 2021 infrastructure bill was in the process of being passed, the blockchain community was understandably concerned that a particular definition of the term "broker," and all the obligations that entails, would apply to miners, software developers, validators, and others who had no ability to supply the information required by those deemed brokers. Secretary Yellen stated that "broker" would not apply to those parties.

24 Release no. IA-2176; File No. S7-28-02.

What Type of Transactions Count As Custody?

Here are examples the SEC has provided to illustrate the kinds of situations that result in custody:[25]

The first example clarifies that an adviser has custody when it has possession of client funds or securities, even briefly. An adviser that holds clients' stock certificates or cash, even temporarily, puts those assets at risk of misuse or loss. The amendments, however, expressly exclude inadvertent receipt by the adviser of client funds or securities, so long as the adviser returns them to the sender within three business days of receiving them. The rule does not permit advisers to forward clients' funds and securities without having "custody," although advisers may certainly assist clients in such matters. In addition, the amendments clarify that an adviser's possession of a check drawn by the client and made payable to a third party is not possession of client funds for purposes of the custody definition.

The second example clarifies that an adviser has custody if it has the authority to withdraw funds or securities from a client's account. An adviser with power of attorney to sign checks on a client's behalf, to withdraw funds or securities from a client's account, or to dispose of client funds or securities for any purpose other than authorized trading has access to the client's assets. Similarly, an adviser authorized to deduct advisory fees or other expenses directly from a client's account has access to, and therefore has custody of, the client funds and securities in that account. These advisers might not have possession of client assets, but they have the authority to obtain possession.

Several commenters suggested that we change the definition of "custody" to exclude advisers' access to client funds through fee deductions. We are not adopting this suggestion. Removing this form of custody from the definition would mean that clients would not receive the quarterly account statements that are required under the rule, and which are needed so that clients may confirm that the adviser has not improperly withdrawn amounts in excess of its fees. We are, however, amending Form ADV so advisers that have custody only because they deduct fees will not need to amend their registration statements.

The last example clarifies that an adviser has custody if it acts in any capacity that gives the adviser legal ownership of, or access to, the client funds or securities. One common instance is a firm that acts as both general partner and investment adviser to a limited partnership. By virtue of its position as general partner, the adviser generally has authority to dispose of funds and securities in the limited partnership's account and thus has custody of client assets.

---

25 Ibid.

Conclusion

In this chapter, we have discussed the tools of DeFi, including the potential risks and regulations of the various aspects of the blockchain tools that are currently operational. In the next chapter, we will discuss how to put these tools together to make money, and the risks of operating in various parts of the DeFi space.

CHAPTER 4

How to Build a DeFi Application or Protocol

DeFi apps are blooming all over, and it seems every chain has a collection of return-generating and yield-farming apps ready to circulate funds. You should take a look at "Anti-Money Laundering and Know Your Customer" on page 88 before you start your build, because it's important to see what you need to avoid when building your application.[1]

Now, let's talk about the order of operations in developing your DApp. Remember, they all deal with the same basic principles of finance.

Basic Principles of Financial Tools

Let's review the basic principles of financial tools. First, you have to put your money to work. Sitting in a box or piggy bank isn't going to do it (I've tried). You have to make your money go do something to come back with more; everyone needs a job to get money, and money is no exception. Generally, you'll be loaning out your money, and this amount of money that comes from your wallet to theirs is the *principal*.

Next, you have to loan that money to another person or entity—someone who isn't related to you or your company. Make sure it's a genuine third party, not one you control or in common control with you. Otherwise, you're just shuffling money around or, worse, pretending to have revenue you don't really have. This is called *cooking the books*, or *fraud*. It's not great. Don't do that.

---

1 I'm assuming, of course, that you don't plan to scam anyone or hack accounts. If that's your goal, please put this book down immediately and do one of the following: (1) read one or more books on ethics, (2) volunteer to help someone in dire need, (3) find a therapist, (4) join a cult, preferably on an island. That last one is mostly just to keep you away from the rest of us.

Now, how does this money generate more money? Because you've rented out your cash (you need to get that back), now you also get a rental fee because someone else is using your money and you can't use it while the borrower has it. Think of it like this: your money is a truck. You rent out your truck (your money), and your whole truck has to come back, and you get a rental fee for using that truck. That rental fee is revenue to you, and we call it *interest*. That rental fee would be high for someone with a bad driving record or for someone who couldn't be trusted to return the truck in one piece (or at all).

That's how credit scores make interest rates vary. A credit score accounts for your history of paying things back and your current liquidity, converted into a three-digit number. This number signifies the risk in lending to particular borrowers. If you have a great score, everyone will want to lend to you, you're low risk, and your interest rate will be low because lenders are competing for your business. If your credit score is low, you are a high-risk borrower, and some (or many) lenders won't want to do business with you. As a result, the ones who will lend to you will demand you pay a very high interest rate to account for the risk you won't pay the loan back, and because they know they can—you are unlikely to get a better deal elsewhere. Brutal, right?

But what happens to determining the riskiness of a borrower when you don't have a credit score? Blockchain is conducted with anonymized wallets (for now), and there is no history of repayment or liquidity to attach to these transactions. For the most part, blockchain protocols resolve this by requiring collateral of some sort, usually valued significantly more than the amount of the loan. Collateralization will be discussed further, but both methods of reducing risk have problems.

Finally, you need to consider the length of time the money is loaned out. Lenders generally lower the interest rate for a longer lending period, because it guarantees revenue without having to spend time and money to look for a new borrower. Sometimes, however, lenders charge more, because the item is in high demand, and it is being taken out of circulation for a longer period, which means the opportunity to charge more for increased demand is reduced. Either way, longer periods usually mean a greater total amount paid in interest, because interest adds up quickly—especially when it is compounded instead of simple.[2]

---

2 *Simple interest* is calculated on the principal per period. So, if it's 10% simple interest per year on $1,000, the amount owed at the end of the year is the $1,000 + (10% of 1,000), or $1,100. *Compound interest* is calculated on the principal *plus accumulated interest* per period. So, if it's 10% interest compounded quarterly per year, the amount owed at the end of the year is calculated using the formula CI = P[1 + R100T -- 1], where P = principal, R = annual interest, T = annual period, or $1,103.81. The more compounding periods and the longer the period the principal is rolled over, the more extreme this difference between simple and compound interest.

Developing Your Application

This section is for readers who will be building decentralized financial protocols on blockchain. The temptation is apparently very high to merely copy something that already exists and put it on another blockchain—or even the same chain, under a different name. I urge you not to do this. Most of the products currently developed for the DeFi market are either illegal or impossible to maintain under basic business principles. Start from first principles and build cleanly.

Don't worry about what anyone else is building, or how much money they've raised, or from whom. If you are solving a major problem for your market, applying business principles and legal constraints, you'll be miles ahead of any of your competitors.

Rule 1: Which Market?

Ask yourself the following question: who are you building for?

First we have to think about who your application is for. Which market are you targeting as customers? Every financial market has three general categories:

Institutional market
> This market includes large banks or funds that move huge amounts of money around every day. They regularly borrow and loan money to one another, often using stealth markets like dark pools to manage market price.[3] These include hedge funds, venture funds, investment banks, and similar entities. They have strong use of financial tools, but not novel ones; they are precluded from taking on more than a certain amount of risk, and new financial tools, such as DeFi, are quite risky. These investors have the benefit of being qualified institutional buyers (QIBs), which have additional advantages like early release from trading restrictions. Large, publicly traded companies (other than those driven primarily by a single person) should be considered part of this category.

Enterprise market
> This category includes large and small businesses, or even high-net-worth individuals. It can include smaller banks, small and medium enterprises (SMEs), collectives, DAOs, and other entity types. Large, publicly traded companies (e.g.,

---

3 *Dark pools* are financial markets that allow large buyers and sellers to move huge amounts of cash or security interests without moving the market price until after the entire deal is closed and registered. Without these pools, the price would change significantly with each chunk of securities bought or sold. Not only does this impact the potential profit or loss of any party, but knowledge of these movements can result in retail investor panic or poorly executed greed, such as attempting a short squeeze without knowing how or when to move in or out of it. Poorly executed greed also makes retail investors subject to a wide variety of low-level scams, which can destroy livelihoods.

Apple) tend to be what people think of in this group, but in financial tools (and lots of other things), they act much more like institutional investors.

This group has the largest contingent of novel financial tool use. They have enough money available to generate real returns using financial tools and are not too afraid of risk to try novel approaches. Actually, this entire group tends to be the least risk averse out there but is generally not considered a source of early adoption. They are more nimble than institutions and able to adjust quickly to new conditions. Realizing liquidity is their biggest concern. Investments that don't lock up assets for years are incredibly appealing.

Retail market

This group includes general consumers and people who generally aren't accredited investors. They don't have access to the most important source of wealth building—investing in private companies—so they have to make do with the pieces they get access to. Overall, they tend not to understand the level of risk suitable for their investments and tend to crowdsource investment picks and strategies.[4] The lack of information, experience, and expertise available to this group makes them highly susceptible to fraud and scams, which they exercise by creating mildly viral negative social media posts and groups. They are vulnerable and often suffer unbearable loss simply because they do not understand risk or risk management. Both livelihoods and lives have been lost as a result of "novel investment opportunities"—including in DeFi—with risks and consequences neither the founders nor the investors fully understood.

If you want to pursue the retail market, please make sure you are completely aware of the following facts, which make the general industry resistance to the protection of regulation dangerous. This is the group the regulations were designed to protect, and the more we design for this group yet refuse to acknowledge the reason the regulations exist (they don't know what questions to ask, they are susceptible to emotional investing, they don't have access to skilled and reliable sources, etc.), the more we seem like the wolves in sheep's clothing the regulators accuse us of being. To fight this, please take note of the following:

- Retail investors are *highly* susceptible to abuse and trickery. You have an active responsibility to keep either scams or retail investors out of your space, even if you want to be decentralized.

---

4 Crowdsourced investment picks are found in various subreddits, through social audio and traditional social media, and similar places. They are productive places for scams, and great long-term investment strategies rarely come from these sources. They are not the place for thoroughly (and properly) researched and vetted information.

- Retail investors are also, as mentioned, the group most regulation is designed to protect. More regulation is coming, and you will have significant legal expenses in both hiring counsel and paying for them while they learn how to deal with the new rules and uncertainty.

- Retail investors tend to take losses hard. Because access to investment is an all-or-nothing enterprise in most Western countries (either you have access or you don't, but there is no path to progressing from no access to access), they don't have training in risk management. Many have harmed themselves or others as a result. Consider how you will create stop-loss opportunities or other breakfalls to prevent this type of catastrophic loss. Also, consider how you handle leverage and credit. Many retail investors have no idea how to use these tools, much less how to manage the risk. Quite a large percentage have ended up in significant debt after bad trading calls and have taken drastic measures as a result.

If managing these risks is not appealing or possible for you, please do not create for this space.

Consider carefully which market you want to address. Though you may eventually get overlap in markets (Great for you! More use = more money for you!), basic business principles still apply. Let's take a look at those now.

Rule 2: Did You Apply Basic Business Principles and Process?

Next, we need to apply our business principles and processes. I'm assuming this is a revenue-generating, for-profit entity that is being created, not a nonprofit entity or a money-losing entity. For those who say we don't need to run a profit, I would just like to point out that money-losing operations don't last. Even patrons run out of patience for operational black holes. If you can't build something that at least pays for itself (doesn't require volunteers to continue running, or continued token offerings to gain value), you don't have a business, you have a charity. And charities are more work than businesses.

Let's look at those processes, to make sure you're running something that *can* last.

Find a problem

First, you need to find a problem. Note that this is a problem, not an annoyance, not something you'd like to see addressed, or anything that starts with "Wouldn't it be cool if…?" The problem with most projects, particularly in blockchain, is building something because you can, not because you should. If there isn't a real pain you can alleviate, or a real benefit (10 times better than whatever people are currently doing to resolve it), don't build it.

Build your community

Who is going to be in your community? Primarily two types of people: those with the problem you're investigating, and other developers who either have the problem or want to help resolve it. Both are wonderful and will form the core of your platform. Finding them is your first hack and can be done in many ways, depending on what you are addressing.

Examine the problem

Third, make sure you have taken the time to fully examine the problem. This is where you talk to all those people you've been creating community conversations for. "Find a problem" and "build your community" occur repeatedly. Ask everything you can about the problem: what are they doing now, how important is the activity that underlies the problem, what have they already tried, what were the results, etc.

Do not ask about potential solutions, your solution, or features to add.

Design

Fourth, think about the design. Keeping the problem first in your mind, you need to develop two things: the base of your solution beta, and your revenue model. This is where you figure out what you're going to build and *how you'll make money*.

Truism No. 3

Revenue is generated from *what you produce*. You make money by selling an awesome solution to a problem, and people are so happy with your solution they *pay you for it*. Your revenue model is based on the repeated sales of that thing you are offering.

Unless you are solving the problem of not enough tokens, selling tokens is *not* a revenue model. At best, you are selling access to whatever your solution is—your protocol, etc. But your recurring revenue is based on the demand of your protocol—the *use* of those tokens, *not the token market price. Again, selling tokens is not a revenue model.*

Release the beta

Then, you release the beta. This goes to your community and those with direct access to your community. Get feedback, refine, and repeat until you are ready for public launch. Done well, this will make your community your chief evangelists, which is how you gain users both cheaply and quickly. Make sure you have your revenue model in place and that your community accepts it. Everyone likes things when they're free. When cash has to change hands, people start telling you what they *really* think.

Truism No. 4

What people really think is never, "This is so incredibly awesome! Here, take my money now!" Don't expect it.

Public launch

Finally! We're at the public launch. You will need to engage with your community continuously following launch. One of the biggest mistakes protocols make is having very intense engagement for the months leading up to launch, then assuming the product will autopilot after it launches.

Your product will falter on launch, and you will need to continuously adapt, manage, repair, and engage. You will need to keep lines of communication with your community open on both Discord and Twitter to make sure people are always aware of what is happening and how you are addressing it. You want to avoid the worst of all responses: avoidance. In the event of avoidance, your community *will* find shortfalls (even if they don't exist), blame you for personal losses, make up a reason that will become a surprisingly intricate conspiracy theory, and crash both your protocol and your TVL. Don't assume it won't happen to you. You exist only because people use your protocol. Make sure they know you see them.

Truism No. 5

See truism no. 3. If you sold tokens, you're going to see a lot of flipping now. Your price may rise. It may plummet. This is normal degen activity—don't let it distract you.[5] Don't look. Don't address it. Don't think about your own tokens. Heads down, keep getting feedback on your product and building.

If you are selling a token (and have determined that it is not a security), be cautious in releasing founding tokens to the market. Have a lockup or other agreement for tokens held by the founding team, or strictly limit the amount that can be sold to under 10% total. Flooding the market causes users and traders to worry that you've created a honeypot (even when the protocol is in active use), or the core team or main developers are taking the opportunity to leave the protocol. Wait, and publish your liquidity strategy so people know when to expect a downward surge on price— and that it doesn't mean someone is on the way out.

Now what? Well, you *iterate and grow*. Just like any company.

Rule 3: Where Do You Build?

You can build on a variety of platforms or even create your own. In 2021, the choice was fairly straightforward: you built on Ethereum, or you had no chance of building a community or being used.

The industry has broadened considerably since then. Not only are there cheaper alternatives to Ethereum within the Ethereum system, but there are also a number of platforms that are compatible with Ethereum by bridge (a link between base platforms), backward compatibility (they usually evolved from an Ethereum standard, and the platform token is a derivative of an ERC-20 token), and/or the EVM (the

---

5 *Degen* is a community term of endearment for *degenerate*. Degens populate most speculative areas within the blockchain space, particularly the NFT and DeFi communities, often combining the two when possible. They flip and trade, with short-term strategies (or no strategy) designed solely to maximize gain. They hold no allegiance to chains, tokens, communities, or projects, but cluster into tightly held "alpha" communities to pass along information about which tokens/projects/memecoins—even memestocks—will start to rise in price. *They are not value investors.* They generally do not orchestrate illegal activity (to my knowledge), such as actively promoting pump-and-dump or honeypot scams. They are welcome in most communities as a way to spread news and generate activity in any particular token, and they were among the first to promote and use Compound when it offered transaction benefits for borrowers.

Ethereum Virtual Machine, essentially a code compressor that some people think is a magic device that creates the blockchain version of HTTP. It does not.).

Ethereum is still the largest, most prolific, most used, and most mature ecosystem in the blockchain universe. In addition, the US SEC currently considers Ethereum a commodity, not a security, and therefore not in violation of state or federal securities laws. So, assuming you want to build something compliantly, it is possible to stay completely clear of US regulatory issues, either not being subject to regulatory agencies or, more likely, building in compliance with them. Most other ecosystems have violations baked into the system, making building on them more complex because you are just adding violations on top of preexisting violations.

Accordingly, we're going to take a more detailed look at Ethereum, including what types of platforms people are building on and connecting to Ethereum.

Platforms and DApps offering DeFi capability are growing every day. We'll just add some examples of each kind, so you have an idea of what to look for and why.

> ## Scaling Ethereum—Child Chains, Sidechains, and Main Chains
>
> We're still focusing on the Ethereum and Ethereum-compatible ecosystems, because they are so far ahead of other ecosystems in development and use. However, Ethereum had a pretty well-known problem regarding scalability—prior to the 2022 merge and modification of Ethereum from a labor-intensive, sluggish proof-of-work chain to a faster, cheaper proof-of-stake chain. For example, prior to the merge, it could run only 7–15 transactions per second.
>
> People really wanted to use Ethereum, so developers came up with a whole host of solutions to solve this. The primary groups of solutions, and examples of each, are described next.

Option 1: Layer 2 options

Layer 2 protocols are sort of child chains to the Layer 1 parent (here, it's Ethereum). I think of them as umbilically attached: they aren't designed to be compatible with other chains and stay nestled within the Layer 1 universe.

Layer 2 options include state channels, rollups, and plasma. Let's look at each.

Layer 1? Layer 2? Sidechain? What?!

Ethereum is a Layer 1 solution, meaning it is a foundational chain. It is a base protocol, complete with its own consensus, security, governance, and token-based operational system. Layer 2 solutions are protocols and platforms built within the Ethereum ecosystem that take some of the transactional weight off that base chain but don't do anything independently. They don't have their own security or consensus; they rely entirely on the base chain (Ethereum) for that. They are strictly performance boosting. Think of this like being an accountant at a company, and your division does taxes for other companies. But your company grew a lot over the last year, and the annual reports are due. The 10 people in your group just aren't enough. So your boss starts asking for accountants who are free in other groups, then anyone who can help, including the bottled water delivery guy who thinks "numbers are cool." You're boosting the amount of work you can produce but keeping it all within the same structure.

Sidechains, on the other hand, are completely separate protocols or platforms, and they have their own security, governance, operations, consensus—and often their own token. They work by a two-peg system, and Ethereum has a particular protocol, the EVM, that assures that smart contracts and code are recognized between the Ethereum main chain and all the Ethereum sidechains. You are working with an entirely different chain when you use a sidechain. You lose your ETH when you use a sidechain because you "buy" into the separate chain; you have to trade your ETH for the sidechain token to engage in that chain's operations and smart contracts, and you don't get ETH back unless and until you sell whatever tokens you have when you have completed your sidechain transactions and convert them back into ETH.

Option 1A: State channels

State channels are platforms or protocols between two parties that basically conduct their transactions off the main chain, then transfer the results of those transactions in batches to the main chain to settle. These transactions *could* take place on-chain but don't; they take place off-chain because it is (presumably) faster. This works only if they don't add significant additional risk. State channels work very well for transactions that have simple state changes between parties and require speed to be useful, and the only cost is the cost to open and close the channel.

A few drawbacks are that even when transactions are sent and settled on the main chain, they aren't final until the channel is closed, which usually requires both parties to cosign closure (but not always). Also, state channels require a lockup of payment to secure liquidity to the channel, which may make this less desirable. Finally, settlement back to the main chain introduces vulnerability in the security of the chain.

Payment systems, for example, are ideal use cases for state channel systems. Let's look at how this works.

Hustler's Paradise: A State Channel Love Story

Ann and Bob are crypto traders. They trade large amounts of crypto on behalf of other parties, and they need those transactions to happen quickly to reduce the risk of loss due to rapidly changing prices. They discover that by setting up accounts on a state channel within Ethereum, they can trade between each other and settle the accounts at the end of the trading day by pushing the results of the transactions down to the main Ethereum chain.

Ann is ready to get started, but Bob, being Bob, is naturally suspicious. He begins to pepper her with questions. "How do we know the correct amounts get settled at the end of the trading day? What if something happens before then in the account—how will the channel know? What if someone (*cough* Ann *cough*) decides to erase transactions when I'm away or offline? What—"

Ann cuts him off, ignoring his jibe about theft and trading out his fifth double espresso for soothing green tea. "Bob, state channels have to address these problems in order to operate." She hands him a paper with an image (Figure 4-1) on it.

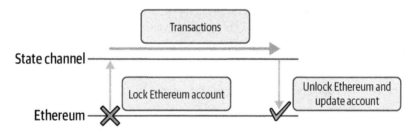

Figure 4-1. How a state channel works over time

"See, look—when the state channel is attached, the state of our accounts on the main chain is locked. Then we conduct our transactions. When we batch the transactions and send it to the main chain, the channel unlocks our accounts on the chain and updates with our new account states."

"How will it know to send the lump of batched transactions at the end of the trading day?"

"We send it, or we can program it. We can send it anytime we want. It's just that the more often we send the information, the slower we go, and the more expensive it is."

Bob rubbed his forehead. "If we update it more often, what happens if the transactions get clogged up? How does it know what the most recent update is?"

Ann looked up, surprised. "Wow—have you been studying blockchain, Bob? You're right, timing could be an issue. Especially if one of us decides to do something sneaky like unlock the account before a big spend, or something like that. We have to attach a sort of judge smart contract to it—something that attaches a timer, or a penalty, or even just something that we agree to abide by to close out the state channel and settle everything on the main chain. It's a fairly complex set of procedures that we put into place to make sure neither one of us decides to trick the other by pretending a transaction didn't exist, or trying not to close out the account, or whatever. The good thing is, once we have one we put into place, we probably never need to use it. We just know it's there and there are strict penalties if we don't comply with the terms of the smart contract."

"A tiny little Securities and Exchange Commission, right?"

"Sort of," Ann laughed.

"So can everyone see what we're doing?"

"Nope. That's the best part. All of our trades are separate and offline, and just the settlement amounts are updated to our public accounts."

Bob sat back. "Whoa. Did we just create a blockchain dark pool? I think I need a drink."

Ann smiled. "I could use one. We can save a lot of money and time on this one, and our institutional buyers will see the benefits pretty easily once we explain it."

Bob looked at Ann. "I think O'Malley's is still serving. Can I buy you a celebratory drink?"

Ann grabbed her coat, and they headed for the door.

Option 1B: Rollups

Rollups are very similar to state channels, in that they have multiple transactions that occur off-chain, then are batched back to the main chain (they "roll up" a bunch of transactions into one, so you have to pay for only one transaction). However, rollups use proofs to verify accuracy and settle on the main chain, instead of closing transaction signatures. They are controlled by operators, who are node operators, or validators, and often require a stake in the system to ensure they contest incorrect decisions and pay a penalty for contributing to false data.

There are two main types of rollups: optimistic and zero-knowledge (or zk).

Optimistic. Optimistic rollups are a bit surprising, mostly because they require withholding a certain amount of skepticism that is innate to most of us in the space. Here, parties stake a certain amount of ETH to engage with Layer 2. All transactions are assumed to be correct when transferred to the main chain (hence, optimistic), and no judge smart contract or other device is used to ascertain the truth of transfer. Instead, if one of the parties believes the transfer or any of the underlying transactions to be fake, that party then gets to contest the fake transaction(s) by submitting it or them directly to the Ethereum network. The defending party must prove the transactions are correct and not forged, or the staked ETH is turned over to the other party.

Transaction data and state node updates are compressed and stored in a separate off-chain virtual machine (not the EVM) that is not controlled by the child chain operator. They have their own consensus method and governance, but use the main chain for security.

Rollups can take advantage of the EVM, which adds a lot to their arsenal. The EVM provides code, libraries, programming languages, testing tools and toolkits, and a host of other supplies that have been extensively vetted and debugged, all available for use and easily compatible.

Optimistic rollups commit their status at set periods to the main chain, like a state channel, only it is committed automatically. When transactions are finalized, the child chain assets are burned, and the proof of that burn is submitted to the parent chain, where they are minted as new assets for the holder.

They don't produce immediate final validations, because of the fraud--proof option. You have to wait around seven days before you close to exhaust the fraud-proof period; then transactions are settled finally. If users don't want to wait this period (and most don't), they can use a liquidity provider to cash out, less a fee. Liquidity providers can always check the chain for proof by becoming an operator and executing the chain.

There are some censorship risks with bad actors, in that malicious node operators can go offline or refuse to produce blocks or particular transactions within them, can attempt to place their transactions ahead of others' transactions (front run), or can withhold transactions to prevent final withdrawal. However, most of these are managed by the structure of the rollup. Another operator can take over as a node and produce the next block or execute transactions. Asset owners can use their own transaction data to produce a Merkle tree and prove ownership of the particular asset. And transaction parties can always write their transactions directly to the main chain, circumventing the operator altogether.

A Quick Word on Merkle Trees and Blockchain

A big part of closing any block on any type of blockchain is the encryption process that compresses all the transactions and anonymizes them, which is what makes the chain immutable (you can't easily identify, much less separate out, any particular transaction and alter it). The compression also turns all those transactions into a block, so each computer node is just processing one block at a time, rather than all those individual transactions—which is less secure and would take much longer.

How does this happen? Generally, once a block is ready to close, an algorithm takes pairs of transactions and mixes (*hashes*) them together into one, which then combines with the hashed result of another pair. Think of it like an NCAA bracket (Figure 4-2 is from the men's basketball tournament in 2023).

Figure 4-2. 2023 NCAA Division 1 Men's Basketball Championship bracket © NCAA 2023

Going from the outside in, imagine the teams on the outer edge are individual transactions in a block. Instead of two teams playing a game to determine a winner, pairs of transactions are hashed together to get a new transaction identifier. Just as the winner of each game plays the winner of another match in each subsequent round, each transaction identifier then gets hashed with the new identifier of another pair to get a new identifier. Eventually, you end up with one winner (in 2023, it was the University of Connecticut), or a single transaction identifier that we call the *root*. That identifier is then used to connect with the opening of the next block, linking the prior set of transactions to a new set of transactions.

Nearly every chain uses some form of a Merkle tree, regardless of consensus method. Chains just modify the process according to their network ability and consensus method.[6]

Zero-knowledge. Zero-knowledge (zk) rollups are the opposite of optimistic rollups: you have to submit the proof to have the transactions submitted to the Layer 1 chain for settlement. Zk proofs are usually done using a zk-SNARK system, although a few protocols using zk-STARKs are beginning to appear.

Zk proofs allow the person providing the proof (e.g., a password) to confirm the accuracy of the transactions without having to reveal what the proof actually is. This is what we mean by "zero-knowledge"—instead of asking for a password, which could accidentally reveal the password to someone trying to steal it, we ask to reveal proof that you know what the password is, without actually revealing the password itself.

SNARKs and STARKs are fairly similar but have some fundamental differences; see Table 4-1. One major difference is that the genesis, or creation, event for SNARKs requires a hidden parameter that creates the core of that zk proof. If the initial creators don't destroy this parameter, anyone who knows it could create a "false validation" of any transaction. This means they could get fraudulent transactions approved, or create tokens out of thin air, or any other bad action. This is an enormous risk—you have to trust that the initial creators destroyed access to this parameter. In my opinion, that presents significant risk.

STARKs, on the other hand, hash from the outset, and they do not require any users to trust that the original developers did or did not do anything that can't be seen in the code on-chain. While STARKs are more expensive to use and take longer, Layer 2 STARK chains are more likely to alleviate these problems while still providing the protection of the STARK system. However, SNARKs are far outpacing STARKs in adoption, likely due entirely to cost and speed.

Zk rollups attach to the main chain via a root contract, and they publish automatic state updates to Ethereum after every transaction. They also send a batch of transactions on a regular basis to Ethereum as a Merkle tree, which includes the validity

---

6 For example, Solana uses a "concurrent Merkle tree," while Hedera uses a "Hedera-optimized virtual Merkle tree."

proof of every transaction. This is the batch of transactions that is settled on Ethereum, and closed immediately.

Table 4-1. A quick comparison of STARKs and SNARKs

	STARKs	SNARKs
Name	Scalable Transparent Argument of Knowledge	Succinct Noninteractive Argument of Knowledge
Cheaper		✓
Less susceptible to quantum computer attack	✓	
Does not require trust in genesis block	✓	

How Does Zero-Knowledge Work? What Does a ZK Proof Show You?

Zk proofs solve the problem of how to show that you know the solution to something, without revealing what that solution is. Imagine you have a password to a secret room with a box of treasure, and the only people who have seen the room are those who have proper access to the code.

Imagine that a guard is standing at the door. He's new, though—you haven't seen him before. The guard demands the code. But you don't know whether this is a legitimate guard or a guy who is trying to rob the room by waiting for someone to give up the passcode. He hasn't seen you before and doesn't know whether you're a crook either. You don't want to give up the password. So you ask the guard if he has been inside the room. The guard says yes. You've also been in the room and know the treasure box is under a large red chair.

You tell the guard, "The box is under the chair." The guard then lets you pass. Why? Because you have proven you have been inside the room and therefore know the password. He has also proven he has been inside the room and knows the password. It is a way to reveal that you have access to information without revealing you know what that information is.

Zk rollups are able to produce final transactions without delay, because each transaction is written to the main chain with a validity proof. Transaction data and state node updates are compressed and stored in a separate off-chain virtual machine (not the EVM) that is not controlled by the child chain operator. They have their own consensus method and governance but use the main chain for security.

There is an interesting censorship prevention option for zk rollups. While they can be controlled by "supernodes" to increase efficiency, if anyone suspects the supernode operator to be censoring them, they can write their transactions directly to the main chain, forcing an exit from the child chain and bypassing the supernode operator.

Alternatively, child chains can rotate this supernode role to reduce the likelihood of abuse.

Zk rollups tend to cost more than optimistic rollups (500,000 gas as compared to 40,000 gas, respectively) because they include the proofs. However, many more transactions can fit into a zk block than an optimistic block,[7] making the per transaction price much lower.

Option 1C: Plasma

Plasma chains are the native child chains of Ethereum. The plasma chain has to tell the parent chain what it's doing regularly, to keep the parent updated and have a constant state of "settlement." Otherwise, the plasma chain can't take advantage of the security of the parent chain.

Ethereum plasma chains use Merkle trees just like Ethereum, and they regularly commit a state update (just like a state channel, but it's automated) to the main chain. It's attached to Ethereum by a smart contract bridge called a *root contract*. Originally, all assets had to be created on the main chain to move to the plasma child chain through the root contract. Now, the root contract allows assets created on the child chain to be as valid as those created on the main chain. Assets are transferred to and from the main chain via bridges. Like optimistic rollups, assets generally aren't directly transferred across these bridges. They are burned, and the proof of burn is submitted across the bridge. Then the asset is re-created on the main chain.

Like optimistic rollups, plasma bridges have the restriction of requiring 7–14 days of delay before withdrawal of the plasma chain token from the main token. This is because there is a challenge period in submitting the final state to the main chain. People originally had to stake funds to operate on a plasma chain, and they had a period of time to submit a fraud proof if they disputed a transfer. However, many people prefer immediate withdrawal, so platforms like Polygon created a separate bridge (the PoS [Proof of Stake] bridge) that provides immediate transfer of funds or assets but no ability to refute.

The data unavailability problem.   Plasma has one major problem: data availability. Data is not stored on the main chain, other than the periodic state commits. It rests entirely on the plasma chain. That means that the plasma chain operator has to provide data for any fraud proofs. But what if the operator is acting maliciously? The operator might decide to hide real data and offer invalid data to let co-conspirators exit the plasma chain with assets that aren't theirs.

---

7   This is mitigated in part by using BLS (Boneh-Lynn-Shacham) signatures, which save significant space by aggregating multiple signatures on an elliptic curve. The cost per transaction would then be nearly equal to zk rollups, per Vitalik Buterin.

One solution is to try to create a mass exit: get everyone else off the chain first, so the bad actors can't front run everyone and exit with funds that aren't theirs. But, aside from creating total chaos, that would also clog up the slow-running Ethereum system (which is why we have these child chains in the first place), and could break the whole system.

This means we have to trust the operators of these plasma chains. And we hate that in general. As a result, few plasma chains are being used, and none are being created.

Sidechains. Sidechains, on the other hand, live completely outside the primary chain. They have their own consensus, tokens, governance, and security. They connect with Ethereum by sidechain bridges, which pose a risk—every bridge point is a potential access point for a hacker. They typically use the same mint-and-burn system as the child chains discussed previously.

Sidechains may or may not be EVM compatible. Those that are not compatible may have a difficult time creating compatible assets on their own systems, as they may not be able to recognize asset innovations newer than the bridge installation. Sidechain bridges typically do not have constant update and development like the connection with child chains, as internal developers are overseeing all the child chain infrastructure, but neither the sidechain nor the main chain is deployed particularly to maintain and update the bridge.

All these options are summarized in Table 4-2.

Table 4-2. Ethereum child chains versus sidechains

	State channel	Optimistic rollup	Zk rollup	Plasma	Sidechain
Not limited to two parties only		✓	✓	✓	✓
Parties don't have to be identified to one another prior to transactions		✓	✓	✓	✓
Does not require trust in operator/validator		✓	✓	✓	?
Lowest gas cost per transaction	✓				
No data storage problem	✓	✓	✓		?
Transactions are final when entered/ appended to on Ethereum				✓	✓
Transactions can be refuted		✓			
Censorship can be avoided [a]		✓	✓		?
Can use EVM		✓	✓	✓	?
Fastest/most transactions per block				✓	?

	State channel	Optimistic rollup	Zk rollup	Plasma	Sidechain
Seamless interaction with Ethereum	✓	✓	✓	✓	?
Public can't see transactions	✓			✓	?
Don't need to lock up funds to secure liquidity				✓	?
Examples	Connext, KChannels	Optimism, Arbitrum	Loopring, Immutable X	Originally Polygon, but now most are not plasma	SKALE, Gnosis

[a] One party can't really censor the other, but the party can harass the other in a griefing attack, for example.

Post-merge Ethereum. Ethereum 2.0 (post-merge) is vastly more streamlined with its unique sharding technique, called *danksharding*, and switching from proof of work to proof of stake.

This created an interesting problem: with Ethereum now running proof of stake, a faster and cheaper form of transaction processing, wouldn't protocols all want to run directly on Ethereum, rather than on a secondary chain that then has to settle on Ethereum? This is exactly what the Layer 2 protocols were concerned about, and one of the reasons they were so reluctant to have Ethereum pivot to proof of stake.

In the end, the Layer 2 protocols (and the miners)[8] reached a compromise. Ethereum would gain significant speed but would not reduce its transaction fees. That was understandable, but a shame—a mature ecosystem operating at a fast and cheap scale would have opened up opportunities for general adoption much quicker.

Option 2: Wallets!

The most recent innovation in the DeFi world has been to build a DeFi DApp inside a wallet, particularly an exchange, accepting as many tokens as possible within the ecosystem. It allows the holder of the wallet to avoid the fees of transferring to and from the wallet, and you can stake directly within the wallet.

Wallets have evolved from the MetaMask or nothing days, but they seem to be going in a few specific directions. The first is general use, or wallets that are user-friendly for easy onboarding into blockchain. As blockchain properties gain national

---

8 The Ethereum miners were also reluctant to pivot, for a different reason. Proof of stake does not use mining, so their source of income (relatively free Ethereum gained by mining) would no longer be possible. They could move to becoming validators on the chain, but they had a new problem: as miners, they set the gas fees for transactions and took a share of those massive costs. With much lower transaction costs, and no say in the transaction fees, this revenue stream would also be reduced or cut off.

attention, ease of onboarding people entirely new to the ecosystem will be mandatory. Some of these are even centralized, with centrally held passwords for easy retrieval. DeFi seems to be too complex an application for these entry-level wallets, but the UI/UX is truly delightful.

The second direction is the broad holding, basic DeFi wallets. They hold as many coins as possible within a particular ecosystem, and some in adjacent, compatible ecosystems (for example, Ethereum assets and some main Binance tokens and NFTs). They tend to have basic DeFi applications such as a swap exchange and basic staking, but nothing more complex like yield aggregation or flash loan protocols.

The third is the more advanced wallets, and there have been relatively few of those. Those have manual staking and locked staking, yield aggregation, and a variety of loans and vault functions. Options and other derivatives and forward contracts may be available, but those are not possible for tokenized assets in the US without using a registered token exchange like INX.[9]

Ideally, more wallets will be added with better capabilities that include advanced DeFi applications, and built in a compliant manner using a registered exchange. The great UI/UX of the introductory wallets would be very appreciated in complex wallets—I'm not sure where the desire for complicated functions to look like early 1990s DOS comes from, but I wish it would just die already. A great interface would allow for easy walk-through of functions, including a summary and highlight of risks so new users would be alerted to the risks of particular transactions before starting.

All the ecosystems discussed here have DeFi wallets already built as an option or are wallet-accessible.

Option 3: Non-Ethereum ecosystems

There are a number of alternative systems, though they are significantly smaller than Ethereum. Here are the most popular of the alternatives.

Option 3A: Binance

Binance is a Cayman-based chain that was originally a Layer 2 of Ethereum, which gained enough traction to branch off on its own. It is still easily compatible with the Ethereum ecosystem and uses much of the same naming and terminology (e.g., Ethereum's ERC-20 token is renamed the BRC-20 token, etc.).

Binance grew enormously after its launch in 2019 because it used proof of stake, a much cheaper and faster consensus method. As interest in blockchain grew, gas prices rose dramatically for Ethereum, which limited the ability of people to take part in

---

9 In the interest of disclosing all potential conflicts, note that the author is an advisor to INX.

the crazy price surges and even bull runs that seemed to keep popping up overnight. Binance was optimized for fast, cheap trading—but couldn't run smart contracts.

Binance then launched the Binance Smart Chain (BSC) as a parallel chain in 2020 to fix the shortcomings of the main chain (the main chain was renamed the BNB Beacon Chain in 2022). The BSC was able to provide fast, cheap transactions, and permitted the use of smart contracts, which immediately set it up to be a challenger to Ethereum. The Binance ecosystem is the largest ecosystem in the world, transacting more cryptocurrency than any other ecosystem. It is an excellent system for the demands of DeFi.

However, it operates now nearly entirely offshore (not in the US). It is fully centralized, in that the entire system is controlled directly or indirectly by one person: Changpeng Zhao, also known as CZ. Binance has had multiple regulatory issues in nearly every primary jurisdiction, and it operates primarily in Africa, South Asia, the Middle East, and parts of Europe. Binance prefers to leave jurisdictions rather than revise operations and comply with regulations. Most recently, Binance is subject to a regulatory action by the CFTC in the US.

These violations make it more challenging to build on Binance and be clear of violations in the US. US builders will already be subject to US law, and may not be able to build on the Binance system without considerable difficulty and challenges by the Binance founding team and/or the US regulatory system. As of this writing, Binance has halted US dollar withdrawals, which is a major issue for even non-US-based users.

Other regulatory jurisdictions also have issues with Binance, so please be aware of any legal challenges you face in building on that chain.

Option 3B: Tron

Tron is a Singapore-based chain founded by Justin Sun, in conjunction with Samsung, Poloniex, and a few companies that he also owns or controls, like BitTorrent. It was originally designed as a peer-to-peer system that would allow content creators to directly transfer content to their consumers, under the title "Decentralizing the Web." Content providers did not pay a fee to the Tron network. Instead, its users paid the network and the providers to access the providers' content or applications.

Tron is extremely compatible with Ethereum, given that it uses the same base language, Solidity, the same types of smart contract, and the interchangeable token protocols. It has two key differences from Ethereum, however: it processes 2,000 transactions per second, and it costs nearly nothing. In fact, its fees have run as low as $0.000005. That is hard to beat in terms of value.

As a result, it hasn't really developed a killer app as much as a reputation as a solid payment platform, particularly in dollar-denominated payment coins such as Tether (USDT) and Circle (USDC). This makes Tron extremely popular in countries that don't have easy electronic payment transfer in peer-to-peer form, such as PayPal or even Venmo, and have a local currency that is less stable than the US dollar.

It is considered fairly centralized, given the ownership of the chain itself and its corporate nature. However, non-US builders may find Tron to be a particularly desirable ecosystem on which to build. DeFi DApps would place little strain on the system, and the cost of transactions would likely be negligible. Tron isn't easily available in the US, but the US may not be the desired market.

Option 3C: Solana

Solana is a 2017 Swiss-based chain that came to prominence in the US in 2019. It was promoted as the Ethereum killer, and it looked as though that may have been possible, particularly when the cost of gas soared in 2020 and 2021. It operates using the Rust language.

Solana had a revolutionary concept, combining proof of stake with proof of history to end the bottleneck presented by software in scaling up transaction speed. In attempting to scale up to Visa's maximum of 65,000 transactions per second, founder Anatoly Yakovenko realized putting a trusted clock to record a timestamp on transactions would greatly speed up the ability to prove or disprove transactions. Using the clock on each independent node, messages that were accepted or rejected by timestamps could be automatically synchronized across the network instantly.

The combination of proof of stake and proof of history has a theoretical upper limit of 710,000 transactions per second on a 1 gigabit network. However, it seems to average 5,000 transactions per second, with a peak of 65,000 transactions per second on a test net.[10] Its average cost per transaction is $0.00025, compared to $1.68 per transaction for Ethereum.

Solana has a few problems, unfortunately. It hasn't reached its projected pinnacle of speed, largely because of insufficient transaction demand. It suffered outages due to major attacks (one in 2021 and one in 2022), and there is no real evidence to assume it is any safer from major attacks than it was before. It also has an unfortunate connection with Sam Bankman-Fried, the owner of the fraudulent FTX platform and Alameda fund. Bankman-Fried was a prominent supporter of Solana and held a huge number of Solana coins, which are now being held in the bankruptcy proceedings. He

---

10 Peter Wind, "Solana TPS–Will Solana Handle 600,000 Transactions per Second Soon?" *CoinCodex*, March 20, 2023, *https://oreil.ly/AWUcn*.

was also the primary proponent of Serum, the popular Solana DeFi exchange, which further dropped the value and utility of the chain.

This doesn't mean that Solana isn't a good candidate for a great DeFi application. The success of Serum shows that demand is certainly there in the ecosystem, and a significant amount of community support remains for the project. It's unclear whether it can reach anywhere near the speed promised. If it can, it will exceed any known payment system speed and become the default of both centralized and decentralized networks. Provided it can become more attack- and failure-resistant, of course.

Option 3D: Tezos

Tezos is a 2014 Swiss chain that went live in 2018. It was designed to make creating DApps faster and easier for the digital community. It runs on a unique bilingual system: an imperative language (Michelson) for designing its smart contracts, and a functional language (OCaml) to build security in the blockchain. Imperative languages, like Solidity and Michelson, are designed to create flexible smart contracts, while functional languages, like Ocaml, are strictly mathematical, and designed to be extremely robust and secure. This maximizes the strengths of both, while offsetting the weaknesses.

Tezos averages around 40 transactions per second on its main chain, but 1,000 transactions per second including scaling with rollups.[11] The 1,000 tps limit is set by the maximum amount of allowable gas. This could be adjusted by governance or off-chain use, if the community wanted. It is well designed for DeFi applications.

Tezos is focused on decentralization and community cohesion, in that it avoids the possibility of forks. Votes require an incredibly high 81% approval in order to assure community acceptance and prevent hard forks. The network also passively amends constantly in order to maintain a constantly updated status, also preventing the need for a fork.

It uses a consensus method called liquid *proof of stake*, which allows anyone with one tez (listed as XTZ) to participate in electing a delegator.[12] Holders who wish to participate stake their tez in a process called *baking* and hope to be selected as one of 32 random delegates for the next block. If selected, they are rewarded by being able to charge transaction fees for all transactions within that block.

Tezos is still a fairly small system, however, and is not compatible with Ethereum directly or via EVM.

---

11 "We're Doing 1 Million TPS on Tezos! Here's How," *Nomadic Labs*, August 24, 2023, *https://oreil.ly/Os07I*.

12 In the older model of delegated proof of stake, only those holding high numbers of tokens were able to participate in electing delegates, removing large chunks of holders from the governance process.

Option 3E: Avalanche

Avalanche is a Singapore-based chain that launched in 2020. It is a proof-of-stake chain that is designed to be cheaper, faster, and more secure than Ethereum. It has a unique feature of having three distinct, interconnected chains:

The X-Chain (Exchange Chain)
> This is a DAG. DAGs have traditionally had faster processing speeds, but at the expense of security. This particular one was built before a number of innovations in security were developed in this area (which is 2022–2023), so is unlikely to have any of the most recent advancements in security. This layer is the exchange layer, where users' assets are held and transferred.

The C-Chain (Contract Chain)
> This is the smart contract chain. It is EVM compatible and can work with any Ethereum or Ethereum-compatible DApps.

The P-Chain (Platform Chain)
> This is the base chain that coordinates all the nodes and creates the subnets that create expansion in the Avalanche network. Each subnet can create its own consensus, governance, economic model, etc. It can be public or private. These are like the internal child chains of Avalanche that rely on the platform's security, but otherwise function fairly independently.

Avalanche uses a particularly complex consensus method called *random subsampling*. It's a proof-of-stake chain, but instead of the traditional voting and staking mechanism, a random sampling of volunteer validators are asked to vote on a group of transactions for validation, then revote and revote, sharing information, until consensus is achieved within a specific time frame.

Generally, Avalanche is given good marks for speed and cost, processing approximately 4,500 transactions per second with an average cost of $0.13 per second.[13]

However, though it is supposed to be immune to attack below 80%, a network bug shut down the network in March 2023. More concerning was the insistence of the team that the network was not, in fact, shut down, despite evidence to the contrary. This lack of opacity and confusion made the Avalanche token, AVAX, stumble along with its reputation. It seems to have recovered, but people are still watching to see if it falters again.

---

13 Salomon Kisters, "Avalanche Versus Solana—Which One Is Better?" *OriginStamp*, March 24, 2023, *https://oreil.ly/LjkZP*.

Option 3F: Cardano

Cardano is a 2014 Swiss chain that still is not in its full public release. It is a proof-of-stake chain that has shown quite a lot of promise, but the build is so excruciatingly slow that what was cutting-edge at the time of starting the build (proof of stake) is nearly as outdated as the proof of work Charles Hoskinson was improving upon. It isn't cheap, fast, or well-known, so it's not likely to be a leading contender. However, it is a leading force in Africa, so for those building there, it may be a solid start.

Option 3G: Polkadot

Polkadot is a 2016 proof-of-stake chain that is based in Switzerland and was launched in 2020. Polkadot is an interesting development in the blockchain world; it and Cosmos (discussed next) had a new take on how to build infrastructure. Instead of building a platform and then trying to connect it with other chains, both of these chains are Layer 0 platforms. They sit beneath Layer 1 chains and are essentially a network of bridges to other chains. They provide interoperability and allow developers to create Layer 1 platforms in minutes to sit within these Layer 0 networks.

The Polkadot layer is called the *relay chain*, and it provides core security, consensus, validation, and interoperability for all the Layer 1s. You also stake the native Polkadot token, DOT, on the relay chain.

The Layer 1s are called *parachains*, and they are auctioned off to developers and users who wish to build within the Polkadot ecosystem. Layer 1s are built within a structured protocol called Substrate, which makes building the parachain more standardized and easier to integrate. All the parachains are proof of stake, but any applications, programs, conditions, etc. the parachain wants to add can be put into the parachain easily.

Polkadot also offers a *parathread*, which is a "pay as you go" blockchain model for those who don't need continuously operating blockchains.

Polkadot averages approximately 1,000 transactions per second,[14] and the average market price is approximately $0.54.

One major event in Polkadot's history occurred in 2022, when a major hack tanked the primary stablecoin in the Polkadot ecosystem, Acala. This is particularly problematic because Polkadot provides the security for all the parachains and parathreads. The system works only if the relay chain keeps everything moving. However, Acala never recovered. The primary concern is no clear upgrades or updates in security were released. As with Avalanche, we keep an eye on this and keep moving.

---

14 Ningwei Qin, "Polkadot Eyes Increasing Transaction Speed by 100 to 1,000 Times," *Yahoo! Finance*, September 27, 2022, *https://oreil.ly/Mscug*.

Option 3H: Cosmos

Cosmos is a Swiss-based project that launched in 2019. At first glance, it seems very similar to Polkadot, in that it is a Layer 0 and provides a method for developers to easily create new blockchains. But, other than those two items, they are quite different. What's really remarkable about Cosmos is it allows blockchains to use and trade assets from other, unrelated blockchains—even if they aren't compatible.

These assets don't have to be locked and wrapped or burned and reminted. They can travel freely from one chain to another as though they were native. This, in my opinion, is true interoperability.

The Cosmos network consists of three main layers:

Application layer
> This processes transactions and updates the state of the network.

Networking layer
> This allows the transactions and blockchains to communicate with one another.

Communication layer
> This allows all the nodes to agree on the state of the network.

Cosmos runs through a central hub, which connects all the developer-created chains, called *zones*. Cosmos provides a free set of tools for developers (an SDK) that runs a protocol called Tendermint Byzantine fault tolerance (TBFT). This allows developers to build blockchains without coding them from scratch, and the application blockchain interface connects the completed zone to the hub.

Unlike Polkadot, Cosmos isn't there to provide security—though the TBFT assures a certain amount of security. It is basically an air traffic controller, making sure the validators in the zones all work together as a network, even though they are fundamentally working on completely different chains. The validators on the chains are all tied together by the native Cosmos token, ATOM. The ATOM token is staked by validators and locked up indefinitely. The top 100 stakers are validator nodes,[15] though smaller holders can delegate their staked ATOM to receive rewards. Users can switch validators to delegate to as often as they want, which does give a measure of community trust to those validators with significant holdings of delegated ATOM.

---

15 This, unfortunately, does mean the wealthiest are always making the decisions. Moreover, this is a weakness in the system, as being able to identify the wallets that are most likely to be validators limits who must be attacked to control the system. That is a fundamental weakness in rich validator systems.

The Validator Weakness

The only drawback is the one described in "The Validator Weakness" in this section.

Beyond this, all the blockchain developers can develop whatever they want. They can have their own token or use ATOM. They can be public or private, have whatever consensus or security measure they wish, have whatever governance they want, choose validators however they want. The Inter-Blockchain Communication Protocol allows these disparate chains to communicate, and everything is recorded three times: to each zone and to the hub.

Building a DeFi application in the Cosmos system would be straightforward and would allow a vast array of assets to be staked or pooled. The ability to use nonnative assets as though they were native opens up an enormous avenue of opportunity in the range of assets that can be used in a particular application as staking or as collateral. The SDKs have been extremely popular, and the use of the Cosmos protocol has been exploding.[16]

Option 3l: Algorand

Algorand is the sleeper here. It is a Boston-based project released in 2019. It had initial buzz as a much cheaper, faster Ethereum alternative that allowed you to create any tokens or applications easily.

It uses a consensus method called *pure proof of stake*. In this method, instead of a few people with the most tokens (often the wealthiest network users) becoming the validators, Algorand puts every Algorand token holder into a pool of potential validators. You must hold only a single ALGO to be part of this pool. One holder is randomly selected by Algorand's Verifiable Random Function to open the next block.[17] Then 1,000 other ALGO holders are randomly selected to form a temporary committee. The committee members are unknown to one another. The members then vote on whether to accept the block proposed. Once this is approved or rejected, all the members go back into the pool, and the process restarts with the next block.

This creates more security, as any attacker does not need to focus on wallets with the most tokens. It must focus on *all* wallets at *each* block opening, as it has no idea which wallets are the validators at any given time. And that means a 100% attack requirement, which makes it significantly more secure than Ethereum.

---

16 Over 20 blockchains use Cosmos, including Binance, the permissioned Chinese blockchains, Cosmos Hub, and Crypto.org.

17 As randomly as is possible without quantum computing.

In addition, all transactions are final once the block closes. There will not be any forking, and there is no waiting 6–12 blocks for finality. Once the next block opens, all sales are final, and the opportunity to contest or revise, such as it may have been, is over forever. It produces 6,000 finalized transactions per second.

Finally, there are no gas fees on Algorand. It has a flat fee of 0.001 ALGO, which is $0.000165 as of this writing.

It's not the fastest or the cheapest, but it is one of the strongest in terms of security and transparency, and it seems easily fast enough and cheap enough to attract winning applications. The main reasons Algorand isn't discussed as often or considered in the top potential ecosystems are likely the concentration of its tokens in the hands of founders (over 50%) and the inability to attract successful DApps to date. It is a vicious or virtuous cycle, and Algorand needs to figure out where it sits in this battle.

Option 3J: Sui and Aptos

Sui and *Aptos* included were released in 2023, both from teams that were part of the failed Facebook/Meta blockchain/metaverse project. These chains are fascinating innovations on the DAG and modularity, using object-oriented or modular architecture to process transactions much more quickly. They both rely on parallel execution, or processing multiple transactions simultaneously, rather than one at a time like traditional blockchain. This is the "quantum-like" computing we see developing in the future until actual quantum computing becomes available for commercial use.

Unfortunately, we haven't seen enough beyond early purchased hype to know how good these systems are and how hardy their networks and communities will be. It's really quite early for both of them. We can keep an eye on these to see how they grow, but they have some excellent potential.

Rule 4: What's Your Token, and Did You Apply Proper Tokenomics?

Tokenomics, as noted previously, are the economics of tokens—what makes a token valuable. Before creating complex tokenomics, first make sure you understand the difference between revenue models and tokenomics. Tokenomics are more like your stock structure, or bus tokens, or loyalty points, or money substitutes, or game tokens, or even an envelope of rights. None of these are revenue models—they are not what brings money in your door day after day, and they don't represent the key to growing value in your company. They may represent *captured* value in your company, but not the value of what you put into the marketplace. If they do, you are doing this wrong, just like so many others in the industry, and will, at some point, fail disastrously.

So, your business does something. It's on a blockchain. It's a DeFi protocol (that's why we're here, right?). And you generate revenue. You are likely selling access to earn or borrow money in some context.

But you decide you *must* (not might—must. You must.) offer tokens. They are required for a certain purpose. First, you need to figure out that purpose. There are a few key purposes.

Types of tokens

The primary purposes are utility, currency, securities (the fundraising kind), governance, and nonfungibility. A single token can do one or more of these roles, sequentially or simultaneously. It's one of the unique things about tokens, and one of the strongest arguments for a new form of regulation.

You'll likely be developing them for the first four purposes, but may use all five in your protocol, depending on what you develop. Let's look at each of them.

Utility tokens

Utility tokens are the bus tokens. They are ETH when used as gas fees, and tokens that make transactions move through and across chains. They are the easiest to justify, the least regulated, and also the least likely reason to create a token. Unless you are building a new Layer 1, your platform will need to connect with the Layer 1 of your ecosystem—Ethereum, Binance, Cosmos, etc. So you could just use the base token of that system. You are not required to create a new token, and you are making the Layer 1 ecosystem more valuable if you use the base token of that Layer 1 system. It should also make your token more interactive with other applications, and grant finality to your transactions easier and faster.

This is the only type of token sale you can really call revenue. If these tokens are being created and sold in response to demand and represent actual use of the protocol, they may be a whole or partial substitute for revenue.

Why wouldn't you want to use the Layer 1 token? Good and bad reasons here: a good reason is there is not enough supply of the Layer 1 for your protocol. You anticipate heavy use, and all the Layer 1 has been issued and is being hoarded or not recirculated in large quantities. You'll need to create a new token to avoid making your transactions very expensive. You could also be playing a game in your protocol, and the base token doesn't have enough technology to manage the DeFi protocol and the game dynamics.

On the other hand, a bad reason would be just wanting to raise capital. That's making your token stock, and you're now in the securities field—and you need to treat your token like it's a security, and your buyers like the investors they are (with the protections they deserve).

Currency tokens

Currency tokens are tokens or coins that are used like money. These are generally stablecoins (discussed extensively earlier) or other tokens that are used for payment. They may or may not be exchanged directly for goods and services, or they may just be a means of exchanging different fiat currencies or a fiat and cryptocurrency.

These are regulated by the Treasury and FinCEN, among other agencies, and regulations can vary from state to state. You will likely be required to register as a money services business and/or a money services transmitter. These regulations will be changing significantly under FATF, as discussed previously, and three pieces of legislation currently regulate these tokens. If this is what you're offering, you'll need to stay abreast of current legislation, because it will impact your business significantly.

How Much Does the SEC Even Matter to DeFi, Anyway?

The SEC's impact on DeFi is, not surprisingly, unclear. Gary Gensler, the current head of the SEC, stated in August 2021 that the SEC would need more congressional authority to govern DeFi, which has not occurred as of this writing. However, he was clear in stating that the SEC will govern to the extent securities are involved. That makes sense—if your tokens are securities, running them through a decentralized exchange (DEX) shouldn't save you from regulation.

Depending on the type of security your token is, you'll likely be looking at either the Howey or Reves test (discussed in this chapter). If you're using a DEX, you've got a problem if you've got a security—but a weird no-man's-land if you don't. In my opinion, DEXes should be permissible as an alternative to over-the-counter markets, which I discuss in the final chapter.

Securities tokens

Securities tokens are the ones that most people are pretending don't exist, but we all know they dominate the tokens that currently circulate. When buyers are more interested in the market price of the token than the use of the token, you're looking at a security.

Many people have been relying on "the Howey test" or "the orange grove test" to determine if their token is a security. This refers to a 1946 case that resulted in a four-factor test to determine if something is a security because it is an investment contract.[18] The four factors are: (1) an investment of money, which is interpreted as an investment of value, (2) in a common enterprise, (3) with the expectation of profits, and (4) solely or primarily from the efforts of others. Essentially, it requires invest-

---

18 SEC versus W.J. Howey Co., 328 U.S. 293 (1946).

ment in something, with the hopes that other people doing their jobs will make your investment gain value.

SEC Analysis of the Howey Test

The SEC has put out a paper discussing their analysis of the Howey test as it relates to tokens. You should definitely review this document, which can be accessed at *https://oreil.ly/ud4Xa*.

There are a few important notes. First, the analysis does not outright say all tokens are securities. This means you have to use a good securities attorney to complete an analysis—but also that you can design your token to *not* be a security. Second, the SEC indicates not just how they interpret each of these elements, but also how to make your token more or less likely to be considered a security (*use this wisely!*). Third, you will do better looking at this before you design your token and tokenomics, rather than after. It's hard to undo things on blockchain after they've been initiated. Finally, note that this may not be the test used for DeFi. As I discuss in this chapter, Reves is the one you should likely be focusing on, though you should keep Howey in mind for non-DeFi aspects. As always, confirm your analysis with your own counsel.

So, even if the primary test in DeFi is Reves[19] (which is discussed in "So, What's This Reves Test?" on page 136), let's go ahead and clarify one thing: if your blockchain isn't even functioning, or your protocol doesn't work, and you're trying to sell tokens, you likely have a security.

If this is what you have, find some great securities lawyers who understand crypto (there aren't many, unfortunately, but the number is growing), and look at your registration and exemption options. Registration options are likely to fall under Regulations A/A+ or a traditional Form S-1 offering, or an exemption under Regulations D, S, or CF. Be certain you're dealing with registered brokers, dealers, alternative trading systems, and/or exchanges if you use them, and file all documents if exempt!

---

19 The primary test in DeFi will likely be *Reves v. Ernst & Young*, 494 US 59 (1990) (the "family resemblance" test).

So, What's This Reves Test?

The *Reves test* is fundamentally different from the Howey test. Howey is looking at whether something is a security simply based on the sales offering. Reves is determining whether a debt instrument is a security by seeing if it's more like a security or a bank loan, in a test called the "family resemblance" test.

It has four factors: (1) what are the motivations prompting a "reasonable" buyer and seller (not necessarily your buyer and seller) into entering into the transaction—is it more likely it's for a commercial or investment purpose, (2) what is the plan of distribution of the token—does it look like a speculative investment, (3) what is the reasonable expectation of the investing public, and (4) does another regulatory scheme exist (like banking law, etc.) that makes application of securities law unnecessary.

It also requires *horizontal commonality*, which means not only does each buyer rely on the seller's efforts to gain profit (vertical commonality, which exists in Howey)—but the buyers' interests have to be tied together, or pooled, as well. Usually this is by the assets being combined and profits distributed pro rata to buyers. This is usually interpreted as something like "more buyers = bigger profits for everyone."

This is where chain staking tends to fall apart. Staking, discussed earlier in the chapter, is paid by a set number of tokens locked up and distributed in small, set chunks automatically to correct validators after each block. The more validators there are, the fewer tokens each validator gets—though, ideally, each token is worth more because of increased use and activity. With additional staking, these token allotments are subdivided further. Thus, the stakers are working competitively, not in collaboration. It is difficult to say how there would be horizontal commonality among them.

Governance tokens

Governance tokens give holders the right to propose and vote to approve or reject other proposals on the platform or DApp. These can deal with fees, development, audits, hiring, firing, forking, launching, burning, or any other item related to the underlying protocol. These tokens generally don't have any sort of regulatory issues related to them other than, possibly, shareholder vote issues under the securities rules. However, this has not been established as of the date of this writing.

Nonfungible tokens

Nonfungible tokens (NFTs) are not interchangeable with other tokens of the same type. These NFTs are essentially ownership rights with a digital link that connects to an asset. This asset could be a digital asset (music, digital art, code, a digital document of provenance) or a digital representation of a physical asset (a deed to land, a rental agreement, a car title, a title to a specific collectible).

These asset-backed tokens are issued in a set amount that links holders with either full ownership or a defined set of rights, and the owner of the original asset can still retain interest in the original asset (like offering a private limited license in an art asset, but holding the remaining title for themselves). These assets can be traded between owners, but the rights remain the same unless changed on the blockchain for that holder or all holders.

These *may be* securities, depending on the type of asset, the type of NFT, and the nature of the offering—so please be mindful!

Applying Tokenomics

Tokenomics typically apply to securities tokens—how the token gains value in the market. But that's really too narrow an application. You need to apply tokenomics to *every type of token* you employ. And looking at your tokenomics will show you if your multiple uses (e.g., a utility token, a security token, and a governance token) have tokenomics that work against one another, and require different tokens or changes in structure. Remember that unless these represent actual use of your underlying protocol, any tokenomics do *not* represent revenue. They are one-time income.

Your tokenomic model will vary based on the token's goals and what you are creating, but here are some of the factors you will need to consider.

Supply

Supply has two parts: maximum supply and circulating supply. For maximum supply, you need to determine whether you will have a hard cap. The argument for a hard cap is that tokens with a limited total number of tokens issued (whatever that number is) will gain value because a certain amount of scarcity exists. However, we must remember that scarcity is not, in and of itself, useful. Scarcity creates a floor below which price can't fall, and that floor is based on the amount of *demand*.

Scarcity matters only when people want that particular token or asset. After all, if only 21 million pieces of dog poop are in the world, that doesn't make each individual piece of dog poop suddenly more valuable. Why? Because there is zero demand for dog poop. If you tell people there are only 21 million pieces, they won't rush to grab what's available; they will walk over what they see and say "good."

So make sure you base your maximum supply on how much you think you will need to create to have enough to meet the requirements of whatever you are building. If there is more demand than supply, the price will increase. If not, the price will fall. But if there isn't enough, people can't use it. If you are not trying to limit price or availability, you may not need a maximum supply.

Circulating supply refers to the number of tokens actually available to purchase, rather than created and held in treasury or in a locked account. These are the tokens you've issued. You need to have enough to meet the minimum amount of use the token is designed for. Circulating supply and maximum supply are important for securities tokens, where price and availability are key factors in demand, and every increase in circulating supply will likely drop the price. When circulating supply is low because most of the maximum supply is committed to founders and "partners," particularly when those insiders have little or no lockup period, this is a signal that may harm your price and keep away serious investors.

Distribution

How are you offering the tokens? If a security, it has to be compliant with securities regulations. If not, are you dumping them all on the market? Giving some people a right to purchase first? Giving everyone a fair shot (called a *fair launch*) to purchase, whether they are an insider or not? Are you matching demand for the token, or hoping demand meets the supply you offer?

Moderation

Do you need a method of moderating supply or use? Is it possible to use up all the tokens, or do you need to maintain a specific value? If so, is there a method of adding tokens to inflate value or simply increase supply? Do you have a method to deflate value or decrease supply, like rebasing, buybacks, or burning? How are those determined and conducted? What is the purpose—to maintain or manipulate value? To ensure available supply? Something else?

Backing

What is the core value underpinning your token? How are you assuring it maintains its value? Do you require collateral? How much, and how is it stored? When do you liquidate? On what terms? When do you pay out? On what terms? How does the market (such as interest rate changes or inflation of fiat) impact your economic modeling? If you hold a token that represents collateral held on another protocol, how do you fall in terms of liquidation rights?

Also, how do you approach the specific issues of your token type? For example, if governance, for example, are you ensuring an easy governance participation and communication structure, and active community participation for more proposals and voting? If it's a currency, are you actively maintaining whatever supports the liquidity of the coin? If a utility, is the underlying protocol gaining users? Are you constantly upgrading and iterating to ensure more onboarding and use of the protocol, and that it is solving a real-world need? If a security, are you providing a real asset value for investors? If an NFT, is the underlying asset worth investment, and is it maintaining its value? These are vital to ensure long-term viability and limit concerns with fraud and scams.

Cash-in/cash-out

How are people onboarding and offboarding to and from your token? Is there a method for both? If there is only one direction (in + utility or in + game), is that clearly indicated? Is there concern about how to exit your protocol? Can you address or correct it?

Incentivization

Are you incentivizing the right people—the ones who actually generate value for your protocol? Make sure you align any incentives with the people who are putting in value—that may not always be the people who put in cash. For example, in the Axie Infinity game, all the incentives were directed toward NFT holders, when, in fact, it was the NFT renters who were driving adoption and value for the game. Know who is making your DApp work, and drive as much value as possible toward them. Anything else causes eventual collapse.

Many more issues arise when it comes to developing your particular tokenomic model for your token(s), but these comments identify some of the main issues in creating tokenomic models. They are quite complex and need to be created with care. Please don't just copy someone else's model; it is probably a copy of someone else's, also—and a bad one, at that. Create your own.

Know how the value flows in your system. If you don't, you're going to either scam others or get scammed yourself. Hopefully, neither is what you want.

Rule 5: Did You Audit Your Tech?

Please, please, please—audit your tech before your public launch! And after your public launch. And at least every six months. Get an independent auditor to make sure your smart contracts work as intended without breaches or holes and that there are not clear security breaches in the user journey of your DApp. Check access to bridges and wallets in particular.

Every time anything you connect with updates, conduct a new audit for everything relating to that updated connection. Publish your results, and switch auditors every year, or two years at the outside. Have an active bug bounty program, and pay those who find bugs. It's a constant battle to keep the crypto streets clean, and every protocol, platform, and DApp of any type has to do its part.

Rule 6: How Do You Launch?

There are many ways to launch now, any of which are fine as long as you are not offering a security. These include launching via a centralized exchange in an initial exchange offering (IEO), via a decentralized exchange in an initial DEX offering (IDO), from your website in an initial token offering (ITO), as an airdrop, and a few other formats. If you are offering a security token, you will need to conduct either an exempt or registered offering and stay strictly within the regulations (just as nearly every other stock offering does).

There are so many variations depending on the nature of your market and the size of your community, whether you attach to another community or draw from your own, whether you have a beta test that offers useful tokens or dummies, or a wide variety of other issues. Here, again, you need to speak with counsel who is seasoned in doing these offerings to understand the options available to you and the cost.

Conclusion

We've covered a lot here, including a good look at what you'll need to know to build a financially viable product and the basic business principles and processes (or why and how to build). We took a deep dive into the Ethereum ecosystem and all its key concepts, and a more tailored look at other ecosystems you may want to consider. There's a lot to think about! But don't quit now—we're about to get to the best part: how to make money in DeFi.

CHAPTER 5

Making Money with DeFi

This is the big kahuna, the one everyone is asking about: how to make money. In fact, I'll bet a decent percentage of you reading right now just skipped directly to this chapter. Good. My kind of people.

Investing with a DeFi Protocol on Blockchain

A word of warning: the current incarnation of DeFi does not really reflect the potential of DeFi, or what it will be in the future (we hope). That version of DeFi we'll discuss in Chapter 6, and you will see that it will involve significantly less risk than the current type of DeFi and will be more along the lines of secured peer-to-peer finance, or lending directly between individuals and/or companies without using banks, secured by some sort of asset as collateral.[1]

Right now, it's basically a very speculative set of ungoverned, noncompliant DApps that offer great potential gain—but with commensurate risk. There is no real risk mitigation in DeFi currently, despite what anyone claims. Most of crypto is collateralized with other crypto, which tends to move in a pack in the market, not opposite one another. Crypto is viewed as one category of *risk-on* (or high-risk) asset, and there aren't other asset classes yet within crypto to offset that risk. So, unless fiat or another asset class (like a real-world asset) is involved, there is no real risk mitigation.

Now that you understand that *a lot of risk is involved in the current selection of DeFi DApps*, let's get started on how to use these DApps!

---

1 This asset may or may not be crypto—in fact, it will most likely *not* be crypto, but a real-world asset that is recorded to the blockchain using a token.

Is It Really "Investing"?

No, not really. There are two primary types of investing most investors do:[2] equity investing and financial tool investing. Equity investment, remember, is investing in a company or project for an undetermined period (generally at least more than six months). Your money buys a set amount of stock of some kind, which represents a percentage of ownership in the underlying company. You invest because you think the percentage you are buying now is cheap relative to the cost of the same percentage in the future. You bought a slice of a tiny pie, say 1/10 of the tiny pie, but you think that tiny pie is going to grow to be a huge pie, and your 1/10 slice of the company is going to be a gigantic slab in the future.

Alternatively, there are financial tools, which I've discussed in Chapter 4. Financial tools loan your money out (like a truck), which has to be returned entirely along with interest (the truck's rental fee).

DeFi is more like financial tool investing than anything else, but with a very important difference. In most financial tools,[3] the loans are generally used to pay for revenue generation (like an operating business) or to purchase an asset that will (hopefully) increase in value and make a profit when sold (like real estate). This is how people can pay back the money borrowed with interest—otherwise, the loan doesn't make sense.

In the current iteration of DeFi, however, the loans that are made often don't end up in an enterprise that increases in value or generates real revenue. They tend to be extremely short-term loans, ranging from minutes to weeks. People gain returns by putting money into a variety of applications, each promising a yield, or interest rate, of some sort. Sometimes they also promise a portion of the transaction fees gained during a set period on the platform. The yield is supposed to be in exchange for locking up (promising not to sell) particular tokens, making tokens available for a protocol's use, conducting particular transactions with the token, or other specific actions. Some of these yield promises make sense, like getting a return in exchange for staking, which secures the chain, or making tokens available for lending protocols, which allows a protocol to have inventory.

---

2 Here I'm using "investor" to mean an individual who is a long-term holder of assets, as opposed to "trader," which is an individual who moves in and out of positions quickly to take advantage of short-term price changes. Investors hold assets to receive benefits from holding (such as dividends or other payments), or in anticipation of selling them after an undetermined period, hopefully at a higher value than was paid. The undetermined period is typically longer than six months.

3 Not all loans are financial tools. You can get a personal loan for any reason, like paying off medical or gambling debts, but financial tools are about people lending and borrowing money as business or investment decisions.

Other yield promises don't make much sense. These tend to be unsustainable and collapse. If the requirement driving the yield (locking up, making tokens available, etc.) isn't part of the fundamental thing that drives value or revenue in the protocol, that protocol is not going to succeed. If you make people lock their tokens up in a box and then promise them a yield just for those tokens to sit there so you can say you have X amount of tokens locked up—but not generating any revenue—you have a failed application. How are you going to keep paying that yield? What are you doing to make revenue? The requirement for those tokens isn't driving revenue or value, so ultimately, the ability to make those yield payments will fail. And it will be painful to be on that DApp when that happens.

If the founding team of the protocol is able to access the tokens, collateral, or any of the funds related to the DApp rather than an unhosted community wallet,[4] this is not DeFi. This is centralized, because an intervening party controls the flow of assets between the lender and the borrower. This is also a red flag for a scam known as a *rug pull*, because the temptation is strong to take the wallet full of assets and run instead of using the assets to run the protocol. Many appear unable to avoid that temptation.[5]

With all the DeFi protocol types, and with blockchain protocols in general, note that *if you do not see a way to exit the protocol, or cash out of the protocol, without a significant financial penalty or going through a third party—be careful. This may be a scam.*

DeFi Protocol Types

DeFi protocols are just the procedures and rules for lending and borrowing, and you can use a few different ones in any DApp or platform in which you want to create a DeFi application. I'm going to go over the main types of protocols and discuss in each type: (1) how it works, (2) reasons you would get a return, (3) the procedure, and (4) any quirks or red flags on the protocol.

Protocol 1: Staking a Token

This is one of the easiest, simplest types of DeFi DApps. You deposit a token into an account on a platform, where it then is used to supplement chain validator accounts or nodes. It gains a certain amount based on the APY (defined in the following sidebar).

---

4 An unhosted wallet is a wallet to which no party holds the private keys, so no one can spend the assets. It can operate only according to smart contracts attached to the wallet, and those contracts require governance agreement to modify. The private keys are "lost" by sending them to a "burn" wallet, or a general-use wallet that is unhosted, so no one can send them to another party.

5 This just happened to $PEPE, where four of five multisig wallet holders drained the main community asset wallet of three-quarters of its assets and changed all the codes, leaving the remaining one to deal with the project and unhappy holders.

This type generally merits a token, because you are supporting the stability and liquidity of proof-of-stake chains, and adding to the staked validator nodes. When the validator node to which your tokens are attached is selected to validate, and is subsequently rewarded, your tokens are rewarded, as well. Your payment of additional tokens is then deposited to your account.

Staking can be done to any proof-of-stake chain, and it is a core requirement and benefit of those chains. You can stake from centralized exchanges, like Coinbase, decentralized exchanges, like Uniswap, or directly from wallets, like Trust Wallet.

APY Versus APR

You'll see APY on everything DeFi instead of APR, which you usually see on everything from loans to credit cards. People get confused, and they have some pretty incredible, entirely untrue, guesses about what this means. What's the difference?

APR is based on the amount you *owe*. It means *annual percentage rate*, and it is the yearly interest rate on the money you borrow, including fees, but not including any compounding on the interest (also known as *straight interest*).

APY, or *annual percentage yield*, is based on the amount you *earn*. This is the yearly rate you earn on the money you loan, and it includes compounding.

And that's it.

The procedure for staking a token (from the user standpoint) is fairly straightforward. First, find a token that lists an APY. *Check the token contract and confirm that this is the correct token. Fake tokens are often added to get people to accidentally buy them instead of the real token.* Next, purchase it, and select "staking." That's it. There are more steps if you have a specific validator pool you wish to be part of, but that is not the case for the vast majority of staking users, so this is it. Staking rewards show up automatically in your account for as long as you hold that token and it remains staked.

This process has a few quirks. For example, when you want to sell a staked token, make sure you select "unstaking" if it isn't automatically done for you. If not, you may transfer your staking profits. Also, check for detailed instructions in the specific application—buying and selling may vary by application, but the core process is always the same. Finally, be certain you know whether your token is in a custodial or noncustodial wallet or protocol. Custodial wallets and protocols require you to move your token into a location where you no longer control access to ensure the token is locked up for a minimum period of time. You cannot sell or move the token if your token is in a custodial or locked protocol or wallet.

Staking Versus Lockup

Sometimes you'll see a protocol that looks like a staking protocol ("Deposit token here, get paid X%!"), but it's not to secure a chain. Instead, it's to lock up tokens. On one hand, this can make sense—locking up a certain number of tokens can prevent a mass sale of the token and shore up a flagging price without forcing someone to lose value altogether by burning the asset to reduce supply. It also ensures people don't "cheat" by saying they won't sell tokens but then selling tokens when others are prevented from selling and taking advantage of the limited supply.

What's interesting about this is that these protocols are often billed as accounts that are similar to bank accounts but offer significantly higher-than-market returns. Generally, they are quite different from interest-bearing bank accounts, which are typical financial tools.[6] As discussed previously, financial tools convert your money (or tokens) to loans or other financial resources, and your return is based on the interest earned on the tool created.

Here, however, while you're basically getting paid to lock up, or refrain from selling, your token, it's unclear how the money you are locking up is generating revenue to pay your return. This is a huge problem in most of the DApps using this protocol. They are unclear about how the locked-up token converts to an activity that generates revenue that pays out that increased yield.

Accordingly, you have to be extremely cautious about anything using a lockup protocol instead of straight staking. You need to know how they are generating the money to pay you, because *merely locking your tokens up doesn't generate any revenue.*

If the yield is being paid from money paid in from new investors, it's most likely a Ponzi scheme (e.g., Anchor protocol). If there is a revenue source, it may be from a highly risky scheme with unhedged risk (see Celsius) or another complex or unsustainable scheme (e.g., Hex). It is difficult to generate higher-than-market-rate returns without a revenue source for any length of time, which is why you see so many of these protocols crash.

Protocol 2: Lending Protocols

Here, you are doing the basic financial tool function: loaning out your money for it to be returned with interest. This is different from staking to the chain. You aren't

---

6 When you create a bank account, the bank has the right to use the money you deposit for investments, as long as it maintains a certain amount of liquid cash on hand at all times in case you want to withdraw funds. The more money you deposit and promise not to remove, or lock up into an account, the higher the return you get from a bank, because the bank now knows it has more money to use for investment and isn't going to be required to maintain liquid cash on hand to pay you because you can't withdraw funds. The promise not to withdraw gives you the right to higher returns.

earning a return in exchange for supporting a chain. You are earning a return in exchange for loaning out your money to a specific borrower. You don't know who the borrower is; the protocol matches your loan with a borrower. But you are earning a return for regular lending services.

Generally, you just have to deposit your funds with a lending protocol. A wide variety of lending protocols exist, so I'm going to break down the major categories in this protocol into what I'll call *subprotocols*. To make it a little easier to understand, each category will discuss (1) what the subprotocol is, (2) the subprotocol procedure, (3) how to determine pricing for the assets on the subprotocol, (4) the average returns a lender should expect on that subprotocol, and (5) primary risks for that subprotocol so you can manage them.

Remember that the average return is just an average. However, if you see something offering significantly higher returns, you should expect to see significantly more restrictions than average. If you don't, expect a scam. If you see significantly lower returns, it should offer significantly more freedom—or perhaps it's a very conservative (or maybe not very good) protocol.

You can use these discussions to benchmark against any particular protocol you're evaluating. If it looks very different, be careful. It could be an intriguing innovation—or it could be a scam.

Subprotocol 2A: Liquidity Provider on a Swap or Decentralized Exchange

A *swap exchange* is a decentralized exchange that is an *automated market maker* (*AMM*), a type of exchange that runs on a matching algorithm instead of matching by brokers.[7] These AMMs are open 24/7, and, as the swap name indicates, offer a trading desk that exchanges one cryptocurrency for another.

This is common, and is one of the earliest financial innovations in blockchain. Ordinarily, if you want to trade one token for another, you'd have to find someplace, like an exchange, to trade. Exchanges generally are like stores: you have someone who wants to open one up, so they get a bunch of cash together and buy a bunch of inventory to sell. If you want to exchange tokens (and get a transaction fee on each trade), you need to have a stockpile of tokens to trade. But that takes a pool of cash. And a central person or group to contribute that cash, buy the tokens, and orchestrate the sales.

---

7 NASDAQ is another type of AMM. AMMs, along with automated trading systems (ATS), are fully regulated exchanges in the US.

Instead, we had Uniswap, the first decentralized exchange, that went a totally different way. Its developers said, "We want this to exist, but we don't want to raise a bunch of money and buy tokens—we have no idea what people have or what people will want. And we don't want to run this. And we have no idea how to price any token anyway." Normally, most people would stop here, decide startup life wasn't for them, and grab a beer and a bunch of lottery tickets.

But not our intrepid Uniswappers. They looked around and saw a bunch of wallets with tokens sitting quietly, bothering no one but earning no money. So they came up with a cool plan: send us your tokens, and we'll loan them out to others and you'll earn interest on them.

Procedure

Everything has rules,of course, and this is no different. First, users can contribute only tokens that are established assets (Bitcoin or ETH), stablecoins (Tether, Circle, DAI, or other tokens convertible to a set or stable US dollar exchange value), or governance tokens (tokens you can stake that grant you additional tokens and/or rights, like MATIC and Gnosis).

Second, users have to contribute tokens in pairs—an equal number of any two tokens the exchange allows in pools. This makes sense because people using the exchange are swapping in pairs—trading one token for another. So, you can contribute one DAI and one ETH, or 10,000 DAI and 10,000 ETH, or whatever amount you want, as long as the number of tokens is equal. Those tokens are then submitted to an existing liquidity pool (here, the DAI/ETH pool) or used to start a new liquidity pool.

Then, in exchange for the tokens, you get a token that represents your interest in the pool and entitles you to earn a portion of the transaction fees from that pool. For Uniswap, that token is UNI. So, if your tokens make up 50% of the DAI/ETH Uniswap transaction pool, you get 50% of the transaction fees for anyone using Uniswap to exchange DAI for ETH, or ETH for DAI, for as long as you leave your tokens in the pool.

Ta da! You now have a way of earning money on the tokens that were just sitting in your wallet, and Uniswap has access to thousands of tokens without any cash outlay. This part is brilliant, honestly, regardless of whether any current or future regulation decides to reduce or eliminate these pools. The idea of creating communal inventory with communal, tracked profits was revolutionary then and remains so.

In addition, you can use that UNI token as collateral for additional financing applications, something called "money LEGOs," which will be described later in this chapter.

Pretty cool, right? Now you are earning a return for loaning out your coins. There is an incentive to loan out tokens that people want, because those pools earn the highest fees. As a result, many other decentralized exchanges formed, copying exactly this formula but basing them on different chains. These include SushiSwap, PancakeSwap, and many, many others.

And it is a loan—whenever you want, you can reclaim your coins, as long the exchange is noncustodial. Noncustodial accounts, if you recall, never own your assets. You remain the owner the entire time. But, of course, that means the exchange could lose some or all of its supply of coins at any given time.

As a result, some exchanges also offer custodial accounts, in which you lock up your coins for a longer period of time. In exchange for locking up your coins, you earn a higher return (often significantly higher), because the exchange is assured you won't be pulling your coins off the exchange for a minimum period of time.

Pricing

Pricing is interesting, and this is where arbitrage and bots are not only common, but encouraged. Liquidity pools use dynamic pool pricing. This means the price of any coin in a liquidity pair is based on the coin's value relative to the other coin in the pool. That made perfect sense, didn't it? An example is probably easier and is given in the following sidebar.

Pricing is occasionally done by bonding curve (which will be discussed in "Subprotocol 2B: Borrower-Lender Platforms" on page 153) where we see them much more frequently.

Pricing Some (Ridiculously Cheap) ETH

Suzy wants to buy some ETH, and she wants to buy it with DAI. This sort of looks like trading DAI for ETH, but it actually is buying ETH with DAI, since both have monetary value.

Suzy pulls up Uniswap and checks the price of the DAI/ETH pool. There are 100 DAI and 100 ETH in the pool. (Note: this never happens—in this scenario ETH has plummeted to levels it will never see again, except in hypotheticals. Lucky Suzy.) The exchange rate is 100 DAI to 100 ETH, or each ETH is worth one DAI. The price of ETH on Unswap will be written as ETH = 1 DAI (1 ETH costs 1 DAI).

Note that other pools have DAI and ETH, paired with other tokens. Their prices are based on the value of that token as compared with the other token in the pool, so 1 DAI could be worth 1 ETH, 7 GNO, 0.5 USDT, etc.

Suzy decides to buy 10 ETH, which costs her 10 DAI.

(Later that day…)

Tommy also decides to buy some ETH and has some DAI to spend. He checks the Uniswap price. Were you expecting 1 ETH = 1 DAI? That's not what he sees. Let's take a look.

Suzy's trade went through, and there's now 90 ETH and 110 DAI in the pool. The exchange is 90 ETH to 110 DAI now, or 1 ETH to 1.22 DAI.

What?! Tommy is paying 1.22 DAI for his ETH, but Suzy paid 1 DAI?! Welcome to *dynamic pool pricing*, another interesting innovation in the space. Each pool customer will pay an incrementally higher or lower price for their token based on what the prior customer did with the pool.

That means you will have different pricing for specific tokens in different pools, and on different chains. Arbitrageurs (and their bots) take advantage of these differentials to make profits on the differences. They hunt these discrepancies (for example, buying ETH for 1 DAI on one chain, selling ETH for 1.22 DAI on another chain—but in very large quantities, so they make a large profit), which brings the prices more predictably in line across chains.

There are risks with this, however, which will be discussed shortly.

Average returns

The average return for a liquidity provider is around 1%–6% APY. That's significantly better than 0% just sitting in a wallet, and likely better than a standard interest-bearing bank account (depending on the Federal Reserve's overnight rate at the time).

Risks

Well, we knew risks existed, right? Liquidity pools carry multiple risks. We're going to discuss them in some detail here, but you'll see them pop up in other methods as well. These definitions apply to all the instances in which they occur:

Slippage
> This is the one that results from the dynamic pool pricing model discussed previously. Slippage is what happens when you think you know the price of your transaction, whether it's in a token, coin, or fiat, and hit Send or Go or Swap or Enter or whatever button your app requires to trigger the smart contract. Except—you're in line. Remember, all transactions on blockchain process in a chain, or sequentially. This means you may not be the next transaction in line for that pool or protocol. If one or more transactions in front of you skew the price of your pool or the coin in your chosen protocol, then your price may be slightly or very different than you thought it would be on execution of your transaction. This could work to your favor or, as so often happens, result in you losing money or a more expensive transaction. Arbitrage trading is a gut-churning, antacid-popping, ulcer-producing career for a reason: you're betting huge money on slight differentials, hoping no one gets to them first after you enter your trade.

> For those of us just trying to enter trades and get the best deal, good rules of thumb are to try to execute in low-transaction periods (when Western and far

Asian markets are closed) and add 2%–3% to allow for slippage when scheduling transactions to assure your transactions will close.

Other than that, we can just wait for the broader adoption of crypto, as thinly traded, highly volatile markets are the type slippage loves to camp out in. And the new trend toward directed acyclic graphs (DAGs) and, eventually, quantum computing-assisted chains will allow parallel transaction flow. This means less waiting in line, which means less likelihood of slippage. (And other cool stuff that doesn't relate to pricing.)

Impermanent loss

While your tokens are held in a liquidity pool, they take on the value of the pool—the pool's pricing. So even though the price of ETH may be skyrocketing, your ETH that's pooled with DAI is still worth however many DAI the pool is pricing at, which may be significantly lower than the market price.

This is called *impermanent* because it's not permanent. It's more an accounting issue. As soon as you remove your tokens from the liquidity pool, they immediately regain market value.

Problems arise when you have tokens stuck in the pool, either because you've locked up the tokens or the pool doesn't have enough tokens and has to wait for more to come in to refund you. If, for some reason, the token decreases rapidly in value ("tanks"), you won't be able to sell quickly. If you remember the Terra Luna disaster, watching the price plummet to zero while your coins are trapped is not the way anyone intends to experience any aspect of blockchain.

Remember that everything involves risk (not just in crypto), and never to invest more than you can afford to lose.

Securities risk

This is a major risk, and descriptions of the regulations and tests that likely govern these particular securities are discussed in Chapter 3. Many of these token offerings are actually securities in the US. This is currently a hotly contested issue, and the crypto industry and SEC seem to have dug their heels in against each other.

A bit of background: without going into the details of securities law, which is beyond the purview of this book, the US has long held that anything speculative offered for value with the expectation that it will increase in value is likely a security. This means it is subject to a host of regulations, most of which come down to two main requirements.

First, the tokens can be offered to accredited investors only;[8] certain disclosures need to be made, but only a simple Form D filing needs to be made (or Form S if the investors are overseas).

If, however, you want to offer the tokens to the public (which most projects do), you need to go through a much more significant procedure. You need to disclose everything about your project and the founding parties, as well as get audited financial statements. Then you have to go through a full review by the SEC staff, who will make sure you've fully complied with the securities rules.

Alternatively, you can do a crowdfunding campaign, but you still need to do a significant amount of disclosure and either attested or audited financials (depending on how much money you want to raise).

Either way, you're looking at a lengthy, expensive process. It requires lawyers and auditors (CPAs qualified and registered with the SEC), and that alone is enough to make anyone think twice (or 10 times) about starting anything that deals with securities.

However, it's honestly nothing more than what every other industry has dealt with in offering securities. Every company in every industry has had the exact same problem: needing money to build. But for some reason, people in crypto have desperately clung to a completely false notion that somehow, for some reason, our tokens were magical and excluded from registration even when we sold them speculatively. For value. With the expectation that they would increase in value.

This was wrong. This industry is now, and always has been, fully regulated.[9] It has simply not been compliant.

Now, there is a lot to say about the state of our regulations and the viability of some of these laws with respect to a technology that allows anonymous transactions, but, again, not part of this book. The crypto industry has chosen to largely ignore regulations and either move offshore (with limited ability to prevent US jurisdiction, which will disappear as we move to the new regime of

---

8 Accredited investors are generally defined by the SEC as individuals (i) with a net income over $200,000 for each of the past two fiscal years or $300,000 for a married couple, (ii) with $1 million net worth minimum, excluding principal residence, or (iii) have a qualifying certification, which right now means passing the Series 7, 65, or 82 exams. Series 7 and 82 require a sponsoring brokerage, but Series 65 does not. Generally, "accredited investors" are wealthy investors.

9 There is a possibility that DeFi itself is not regulated by the SEC, as stated by Chairman Gensler in 2021 and discussed in Chapter 4. However, tokens that are securities are undoubtedly governed by the SEC, so this may not be as much of a safe haven as hoped. More about the regulatory issues and tests for these securities tokens are discussed in Chapter 4.

multijurisdictional regulation[10]) or act in spite of regulations. The SEC, for its part, and even the CFTC, which governs commodities, Bitcoin, and Ethereum (for the moment), have shown their reluctance to destroy the industry in that they have only induced fines for the many (many!) regulatory violations. They could have taken other actions, such as force a rescission or even criminal charges, either of which would kill any project. But they have not done so, for the most part.

However, the situation has recently taken a much more antagonistic turn. Coinbase, the largest US exchange, has chosen a path that may be considered antagonistic toward the SEC. Many have cheered this. I do not. This should be resolved with more discussion between the industry and the public sector. Congress is trying to enact laws without understanding the industry. The US Department of Treasury and other federal agencies have been enforcing regulations that tend to harm useful projects but not ones that are actual scams; these agencies are not timely in their notice and don't always seem to understand how the industry and technology work.

It's important for this industry to survive. Most of the regulations are designed to provide access to the most reliable source of opportunities for wealth—private companies and projects—to the wealthy. This lack of access to opportunity is one of two things that create the bulk of the wealth divide in the US and many other countries.[11] It's true that the poor and middle class are the ones driving the growth in crypto, especially in DeFi. But why? Because they don't qualify as accredited investors, and it's one of the few ways most can generate any return on their assets at all.

While regulators must learn more about the technology and function of blockchain, we also need to come to terms with regulation.

We must take seriously the fact that the bulk of our users are not financially educated or financially skilled, and that gives us more obligation to disclose and inform about our offerings, not less.

We must ensure that we root out proven bad actors and prevent them from rejoining our ranks. We must add education to every facet of our operations, without cost or benefit.

---

10 Two hundred countries are bound to a new regulatory regime that will change the way that many of the laws regarding crypto are interpreted, as discussed in detail in Chapter 3. These laws will fundamentally mirror one another, and there will be cross-border enforcement of these rules. The European Union's Markets in Crypto-Assets law (MiCA), passed in May 2023, is the first major implementation of these new rules.

11 The other is access to financial education. It is not required in school and generally not taught, leaving the understanding of wealth building to those whose families have already gained it.

Unfortunately, we cannot antagonize established institutions and regulators in the process. Too many people rely on us to continue our existence. There is a way forward, but it involves less rhetoric and noncompliance, and more diplomacy and compromise.

Not FDIC insured
There is no insurance at all on anything in DeFi.

Subprotocol 2B: Borrower-Lender Platforms

Borrower-lender platforms are more like traditional finance tools: one side loans assets to the protocol, and the other side borrows those assets. The parties are anonymous to one another. Borrowers don't need a credit score or other identifying information. Instead, they offer collateral. This collateral may be in the form of a few accepted tokens (generally ETH, Bitcoin, or stablecoins) or an NFT.[12] These NFTs are usually only a select few with consistent, high market value (*blue chips*). These include collections like the Bored Ape Yacht Club, Mutant Ape Yacht Club, Doodles, Meebits, and CryptoPunks.

Just like a bank loan, borrowers have to submit more collateral than they are allowed to borrow—usually around 150% of the amount they borrow. This seems pretty high, until you realize how volatile most cryptocurrencies are. If the value of the collateral drops, there is usually a condition that it is force liquidated (sold) when it reaches somewhere around 100%–115% of the value of the outstanding loan (these percentages all vary by protocol, of course). When NFTs are force liquidated, they are usually auctioned on an affiliated site to the best offer if over the value of the NFT, or at least 90% of the market value of the NFT. However, as interest rates have risen, it has become harder for borrowers to meet loan repayment terms, and NFTs have been liquidated at 75% or less of the value of the NFT, which has reduced the popularity of NFT-backed loan protocols.

You may wonder why someone would take out a loan in crypto when they have to offer collateral in crypto. Usually, this is because they think another currency will shoot up in value, leaving them with a profit after repaying the principal amount and interest, and then they still get to reclaim their original crypto collateral. Alternatively, they may want to put the loaned amount into an investment vehicle that

---

12 An NFT is a nonfungible token. These took hold of the industry in late 2020 and early 2021 with the sale of noted digital artist Beeple's piece, *Everydays: The First 5000 Days*, which sold for $69.3 million via Sotheby's auction. NFTs are tokens representing some form of ownership (rental/lease/purchase/exclusive right/temporary right/etc.), with a digital link to either the asset represented (digital art/code/spoken content/music/etc.) or a digital representation of something physical (provenance to physical art/digitalization of a deed to land/ digitalization of a patent/a link to a government database file of title/etc.). Many people think these are just cartoon art pieces, but this is false. There are many, many types of NFTs. The ones you see most are actually community access tokens. Whatever the type, NFTs represent one key asset: rights.

returns a higher rate than the interest on the loan, without selling their original crypto to get into that investment vehicle.

Uncollateralized loans are starting to make their way into the space, but, unsurprisingly, they are looking more like centralized bank loans. They need some kind of identity and history, and more legal documents are required. These kinds of loans may gain favor if they accept aspects of credit that traditional banks don't, such as consistent bill and rent payment, focusing exclusively or weighting the most recent 6–12 months of payments instead of all payments over 7 years, including prior crypto loan repayments, consistent school tuition, tutor, or assistant (e.g., therapist or aide) payment for children, and the like.

Procedure

To access one of these protocols, first you look for a lending protocol, such as Aave, MakerDAO, or Compound. There are dozens—across chains, likely hundreds. Choose the chain or ecosystem you want to focus on; then pick the protocol that offers the best return for the assets you want to lend.

Then, upload and launch the protocol or Web2 app with the protocol, and connect your wallet. Make sure this is not your primary wallet, but just a wallet with only the assets you want to lend.

Next, click "lend" or "deposit" or "supply" to get into the lending side of the protocol. (The other option is "borrow" or "withdraw" or something like that.) Then choose the asset (cryptocurrency) you want to lend. Indicate how much you want to lend, and decide the minimum length of time if it requires a lockup period (you generally agree to terms with the lockup, or you pick one of several lockup options with additional terms attached). Then, submit the transaction.

Voilà! You are now a lender, and the returns will be automatically deposited in your wallet.

Pricing

Pricing of the loan and interest rate is generally done by use of a bonding curve, which changes the price and rate based on supply.

Bonding Curves

Bonding curves are curious things. When executed correctly, they can be useful to AMMs. But, of course, how often are they executed correctly? Not nearly often enough. Unfortunately, when executed incorrectly, they result in a de facto scam. Many protocols don't mean to do this, but they don't understand bonding curves or how they are supposed to work. But we're going to talk about them now, so you'll be

---

able to see right away whether the bonding curve in the protocol you're looking at works or marks the protocol for failure.

Bonding curves are literally graph curves. The basic theory is every time someone buys something, the next purchase should cost more. Every time someone sells, the next buy should cost less.

They usually look like Figure 5-1. In this example, when the 40th item of whatever we're selling is bought, it costs 6. And the price keeps increasing with every one sold so that by the time we sell the 50th thing, the price for that one is now 7. Similarly, though, when someone sells, the price goes back down incrementally toward 6.

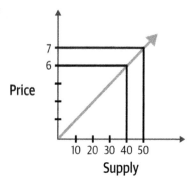

Figure 5-1. Price versus supply

Bonding curves could also look like Figure 5-2. You can make the ratio of price to supply whatever you want. The point is that the price fluctuates formulaically with each purchase and sale. You can see in the figure, though, that buying ends up having a rapid effect on pricing, pushing market price up quickly. Selling also has a network effect, dropping the price quickly.

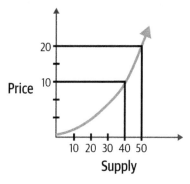

Figure 5-2. Price versus supply

You can also build in a bid-ask function, creating a *spread* (the difference between demand curve and supply curve). That spread can be placed in the collateral pool to cover gas fees, be used for community benefit, be used for a foundation, or any other communal purpose.

Bonding curves have multiple benefits. They remove the need for secondary markets and exchanges, which can make an asset functionally illiquid if it is thinly traded. They mitigate pump and dumps by encouraging early adopters to hold, because bonding curves work as price multipliers. They allow mass curation of assets and are difficult to price manipulate if they are done correctly. They allow a method for automatically funding community development. And they immediately record the price impact of each holder's decision, which can rapidly increase price for early holders.

Of course, as mentioned, if done incorrectly, they can be an easy way to scam investors. They can also have unintended consequences of a complete sell-off if one big holder sells and the market perceives it as a collapsing asset.

Bonding curves have four key principles, and we're going to put them in terms of crypto markets. *All* of them must be met for the bonding curve to be legitimate and avoid being a scam:

- The market must be automated (some type of AMM), and minting must be automatic and at the time of purchase. This does not work for future mints.
- Price must change automatically with supply. Whatever moves the price should be completely transparent.
- When a purchaser buys, the money goes into a pool balance or pool reserve—*not a privately held wallet*. It then becomes collateral given in exchange for tokens purchased, like a liquidity pool.
- Purchasers must be able to liquidate their assets by selling at any time. This means they must be able to burn the token and get the collateral returned to them at the current price automatically. If this step is not possible, the bond curve is compromised.

Some projects that have used or currently use bonding curves are Bancor, 1Hive, Meme Factory, and Molecule.io.

Average returns

Average returns range from 2% to 10% APY. Outrageous returns are often offered in these protocols. Most of these have failed. *Always make sure you know how your return is being made.*

A shocking number of people have no idea if their funds are being loaned out, sitting in a locked protocol, trapped in an improper bonding curve (usually a private wallet), improperly hedged (or not hedged at all), or sitting in a box under someone's bed. I'm always surprised at how few questions people ask before sending someone money. Don't be like that. Ask, ask, ask, and ask some more. Don't trust social media or your best friend or an article you just read. Do the research yourself. The smartest investor in a bankrupt or seized fund is still dumber than the investor who asked questions and realized they shouldn't put money in.

Risks

These risks are similar to the liquidity provider risks and include the following:

Scams or poor design
> Most of this is mentioned in pricing, and it includes improper use of bonding curves, Ponzi schemes, inappropriate risk-taking and failure to hedge against risk, and use of unlicensed money managers. Make sure you know how the platform works.

Impermanent loss
> Discussed previously.

Securities risk
> Discussed previously.

Not FDIC insured
> Discussed previously.

Subprotocol 2C: Borrowing Platforms

I'll bet you didn't know you could earn a return from *borrowing*, did you? One lending platform, Compound, has rocketed to the top of protocol lists because of its innovative promotion. It has a four-year program offering incentives to both lenders and borrowers, who both get a share of daily transaction fees. It's unusual but popular, and certainly worth mentioning.

The protocol, price, return, and risks are all the same as for subprotocol 2B (the borrower-lender platforms). An additional risk, however, is that if you do not repay the loan, you will lose your collateral up to the amount of the outstanding loan.

Subprotocol 2D: Yield Farming

Yield farming, also known as *liquidity mining*, is a method of maximizing returns from the various lending protocols. Either through your own research or using an automated aggregator, you use several strategies to increase your returns. This is a risky practice and not suitable for beginners. Accordingly, I'm not going to detail the procedure here, just generally how this protocol works, the average returns, and the risks. Once you've worked through the lending platforms yourself, the procedure will become self-evident.

Going through your favorite platforms, you continually move your assets from one interest-bearing protocol to another. The interest rates can fluctuate daily or more frequently, so this can entail some work. You need to account for gas fees, as well, as every move will have some loss to gas.

Another option is using an automated aggregator tool, such as Beefy Finance or Yearn, which goes through the search for you and automatically moves your assets. Many other people also use these aggregators, however—the more people use them, the lower the benefit to any individual.

Alternatively, you can stack returns, which is also called "money Legos." This is where you take those tokens you receive from earlier investments and turn them into new investments.

Playing with Money LEGOs

How does stacking returns work? Let's walk through an example.

Let's say you loaned 10 DAI and 10 ETH to Uniswap. You got a Uniswap token that represents your interest in the DAI/ETH liquidity pool and entitles you to a share in the transactional fees of that pool. Now you have an asset-backed token.

Remember that asset-backed tokens can be staked in lots of protocols. What about that Uniswap token? It turns out that can be used as an asset you can stake.

So now you take that Uniswap token to Curve, and you get a Curve token representing your interest, which you then take to Balance.

You can stack these returns by just taking these tokens to new protocols. But is this really safe?

No. It's built on a fallacy: that each of these new tokens is fully backed. But they aren't. Remember that original Uniswap token? It represents 10 DAI and 10 ETH and a share of transactional fees. But what about that Curve token? It represents…your Uniswap token. Which is the 10 DAI and the 10 ETH and the share of transactional fees. What about the Balance token? It represents your Curve token. Which goes back to…your Uniswap token.

It looks like a series of fully backed transactions, but in fact it's a series of transactions that aren't backed—only *one* of them is backed! The theory that they could collect on a core asset is wrong, because superior right rests with the Uniswap token (under US law). The rest have no remaining right to the DAI and ETH or the transactional fees.

It is true that those are governance tokens and have rights to assets if staked to the protocol (if that is permitted) and, generally, some form of voting rights. But in terms of assets you can cash out and collect on, only the Uniswap token has that right. The rest have the right subject to the prior token's right. So they probably get nothing if there is a failure to repay.

This is one of the reasons that regulators are beginning to scrutinize the space, in my opinion. I'm not a fan of money Legos, because the risk is high not just to the person doing it but to the space overall.

Average returns

Here's where people lose all caution. Average returns are 60%–80%, but they have been known to be much higher. But, again, the risks match the return. Know what you're getting into. This isn't for beginners or for those who don't know how to manage risk.

Risks

I can't overstate the risks here. Many hear about the massive returns on aggregators, but you don't hear about the losses as often because those people don't discuss them or leave conversations about crypto altogether. These risks are the same as with all lending platforms, but multiplied—by a very, very large number:

Simply shutting down
Some can't maintain the return, or they were scams, or they mysteriously disappear. If your money is in the protocol or aggregator when this happens, your money disappears too.

Impermanent loss
Discussed previously.

Securities risk
Discussed previously.

Not FDIC insured
Discussed previously.

Protocol 3: Memecoins

Memecoins represent a somewhat unusual category, particularly given that this book discusses finance. However, memecoins are now classed with DeFi in the world of crypto, so we'll add these in and dive in.

What's the Difference Between Investing and Trading?

I will preface this by saying I am not a trader; I am a long-term investor. Long-term investors use fundamentals for most investments. *Fundamentals* include financial statements, key ratios, core value, revenue, and growth potential as a basis for investment, and largely disregard price (other than to determine whether the asset is a value or growth asset). Traders, on the other hand, focus on maximizing short-term differentials in price, and could care less about the underlying value of the asset they are trading. Consequently, traders often use leverage, or borrowed money, to increase gains, and long-term investors do not.

Leverage has enormous risks—if you bet on price direction and are wrong, you not only lose the money you bet, but also have to pay back the money you borrowed, with interest. This is how people become bankrupt on "one big trade." Leave the drama for the movies, and don't borrow if you don't need to.

Memecoins are tokens without any function or purpose, usually based on a pop culture or crypto culture meme or joke. The first memecoin, DOGE, began as a joke based on a shiba inu meme that was floating around the internet. (It was the "doggy" coin.) However, it quickly became an important experiment in decentralization. Could a token be created and function entirely without input from any founding team member? It turns out it could—it grew a huge community supporting this shocking development. Every other token has had a founding that was required to maintain the token or contracts associated with it, but not DOGE. The founding members have long since moved on, and it has autopiloted its way to glory as our most decentralized coin.[13]

Memecoins are dominated by short-term traders known as degens in this space. Memecoins are highly trendy and volatile. But they can be fun; they provide an easy way for those who don't know anything about crypto to discover it, and some incredible communities have resulted, so we appreciate those who make memecoins their home.

---

13 DOGE is more decentralized than Bitcoin because, although Bitcoin has far more holders, DOGE has no bottlenecks or points of centralization, which Bitcoin still does. It also has no founding team, no centralized group of developers, no core group pushing marketing or a particular direction for the protocol, no foundation, nothing directing it. It literally moves entirely according to the holders.

However, note that these communities often aren't really communities; they are groups of degens focused almost exclusively on price. Conversation about "floors" (lowest market price) or market price will dominate. The problem is that degens tend to dump the coin as soon as a significant price increase is reached. You risk becoming exit liquidity for the degens. A few whales, or large accounts, or founders with large holdings but no restrictions on trading pose the same risk.

There is no real way to determine the innate value of any particular memecoin, because they are expressly designed to have no value. There are, however, some coins that have grown into unique value. ApeCoin is the token that will govern Otherside, the Bored Ape Yacht Club's metaverse, and Shiba Inu will form the basis of a new chain called Shibarium, offering low-cost transactions. Others offer unique educational communities or support for scam victims. They tend to be quite cheap, which is the draw for most people.

These tokens are usually unlimited in supply (which usually means declining value unless a burn program is put into place), extremely volatile, and thinly traded. They are much more likely to be scams, and they may be deemed securities. Average returns are 0, and the risks are that they are either scams or disappear overnight. *Most are scams or will simply go to $0/disappear overnight.*

However, some survive, at least for a period of time. There isn't an agreed-upon way to analyze these for opportunities, so a summary of methods I've seen or read from others generally includes the following.

Things to Consider

I mentioned the fundamentals used by investors. Unfortunately, we don't have things like financial statements and key ratios for cryptocurrency, and certainly not for memecoins. If you are interested in learning more about how to value assets like Bitcoin and cryptocurrency, as well as how to value stocks, I have a course that goes into far more detail (*https://www.alexdamsker.com/offers/noQioukw/checkout*).

Memecoins are a bit odd because of the sheer lack of utility and unique communities that form around them. So we have to substitute other ways to judge the value of any particular token.

The following are a variety of factors to consider, in no particular order. These are only suggestions. Use whichever criteria make sense to you and your investment criteria, and rank and weight them accordingly.

First, check the site of the memecoin for red flags like cut-and-paste language, misspellings, or a general unprofessional appearance. Memecoin sites that aren't run as scams tend to look very good. Marketers are often part (or most) of memecoin teams, and they know how to pull together a decent site quickly.

Second, check the web and social media for information, especially Crypto Twitter (now X) and any Telegram groups. What news can you find out? Focus on news that isn't sponsored or paid for. Note that many Twitter spaces may be paid advertisements that the hosts don't disclose. Also check *CoinGecko* (*http://coingecko.com*) and *CoinMarketCap* (*http://coinmarketcap.com*) for information about the coin.

Find out about the holders. How many holders are there? Do the founders hold an outsized amount? You can find this information on their website or *CoinBrain* (*http://coinbrain.com*). More concentration of holders means greater likelihood of manipulation. Check the security of the smart contracts and the likelihood of a scam, as well as the cost of selling (a sell tax) on CoinBrain while you're at it.

See how much liquidity is in the market. You need a good amount of trading volume in a 24-hour period, which means people are buying and selling. Note that some of this may be bot trading, which can be good (preparing for an exchange listing) or bad (simple price manipulation or the appearance of interest). Also, new memecoins tend to struggle when they are below $10 million in market cap, and start hitting their stride above that. CoinMarketCap and CoinGecko can help with this.

Finally, join the community. Is this a community you want to be part of? Do they seem excited, happy to be there? Do they talk about the coin "mooning" only, or are they really establishing their feet as a community?

These are suggestions only. There are many ways of picking memecoins, at least one of which I suspect consists of a list of coins and a dart, so do what works for you.

Whatever you do, make sure you put in only what you can afford to lose.

Harvesting Profits and Losses

If you've made a profit, that's fantastic! Now pull out your original investment. This is called "harvesting your profits." You need to remember to pull out your original investment and profits regularly, so you don't get caught up in letting things "ride," then watching them ride all the way to zero.

Once you've pulled your original investment, everything you have left is profit. This has significantly reduced your risk, and it allows you to take on riskier bets without taking on more loss than you can afford.

Similarly, if you've experienced a loss, you don't need to wait until it becomes worthless. You can take out the remaining money and turn it into cash or move it into another investment. This is called "harvesting your loss." This also *hedges*, or limits, your risk. Keeping an eye on the value of your investments also prevents emotional excitement from taking over and reducing your ability to logically make decisions with your money. That's a dangerous place to be. Always favor logic over emotion when it comes to money. Especially when that money is yours.

Taxes

Well, we can't leave without this slight bummer of a topic: taxes. It's important to keep track of every transaction in which you convert fiat to crypto, crypto to crypto,[14] or crypto to fiat. These will form either your basis or realization event for US tax purposes. Contact a CPA familiar with crypto who is local to your area to see the exact tax treatment you are subject to if you need to deal with short-term capital gains (usually held less than 12 months), long-term capital gains (usually held longer than 12 months), or personal income tax (usually from salary or "regular earnings").

A more detailed discussion is beyond the purview of this book, but you should note that this is an issue we all have to deal with.

Conclusion

In this chapter, we learned the details of how to earn money in DeFi using various protocols, what their average yields and risks are, the crazy world of memecoins, and how and why to harvest profits and losses. We also discussed taxes from a US perspective, but realize this is an issue in every jurisdiction.

Now that you know what DeFi is right now, next we're going to take a look at what DeFi will become and why it's so incredibly exciting.

---

14 Crypto, here, includes any type of token, such as NFTs or stablecoins.

CHAPTER 6

The Future of DeFi

We learned about the history of blockchain and DeFi, the platforms and ways to interact with DeFi, how to make money with DeFi, and some of the issues with DeFi. But DeFi isn't really dealing with the regulatory issues coming—and some are coming soon. It's also not taking advantage of the biggest assets it will have, and how this will revolutionize finance. So let's talk about the future of DeFi, because where it's going is very different from where it is right now.

The Rise of Asset-Backed Tokens

Right now, we have some asset-backed tokens in the space. These include stablecoins (nonvolatile tokens backed by fiat or another asset, or exchangeable for something in a set ratio) and governance tokens (backed by the right to vote and/or the right to receive additional tokens).

But these tokens are only marginally backed. The stablecoins we have right now are not properly designed, and most do not have any chance at long-term value. Even the fiat derivatives (dollar-backed stablecoins, like Tether and Circle) are fundamentally flawed, as discussed, and will ultimately break their peg to fiat. The governance tokens grant more tokens. But we have no real independent way to value those tokens. We have market value, but those values are highly volatile, especially for tokens on chains or platforms that are barely operational or rarely used.

Purchase and sale of tokens is too often tied to the desire to increase market value rather than the fundamental value of the token itself. And that is the problem—we are stuck in an ouroboros, eating ourselves. People accuse the crypto markets, and the DeFi markets, of false or overinflated value because they have market value (market price), functional value (actual use via the chain), and transactional value (gas fees). These markets have values determined by the token as a security, not as a reflection of revenue or real benefit.

Put another way, our tokens have the problem of generally being valued by buyers and sellers of tokens, not buyers and sellers of the products those tokens represent. Market securities, at their core, are supposed to represent the liquidated value of all the assets of a company, including revenue and equipment, as well as a premium for the potential future sales the company issuing the securities will have.

But there is nothing representing the liquidated value of the chain, platform, or protocol in most tokens. This is primarily because the tokens were issued *before the chain, platform, or protocol was even built.* How do we know what it's worth when it's not even real yet? Then, we often have mature systems that have no real traction. They own no assets. The amount of revenue they draw, if any, is too small to have any significant impact on the market price. Yet their tokens reflect multiples on their initial price. Based on what? This is where we get the accusations of "vaporware" tokens, and it's not unfounded.

However, these truly speculative tokens have a place—it's just not in the bulk of DeFi. Finance is not built on speculation. It's built on funding collateralized speculation, or creating a liability on current assets. This is not what is happening now.

But it could be. And this is where I think DeFi is heading in the future. Let's talk about collateralized speculation, or funding the purchase of real-world assets.

Real-World Assets

Real-world assets (RWAs) are nondigital assets—like real estate, physical artwork, cars, luxury goods, and specialty musical instruments—anything that is an asset you would buy with fiat and use in the physical world, not in the metaverse or online. These assets generally have a well-established market range in terms of price. A hotel property has a value range depending on factors including the quality of the property and building, the location, the management, its age, and the amenities. A car has a value range depending on the age, make, model, condition, and other factors. These RWAs are generally easy to assess and can have third-party valuation that is far less speculative than a relatively new protocol on a relatively new chain with relatively little activity and very little revenue.

Most people have access to an RWA. It may be a housing lease, or furniture, or books, or fine wine, or stock in a company. You could use tokens to purchase more of these, but that really isn't an innovation. You could hold ownership of these on the blockchain in an NFT or other form of token that defines title and rights ownership. But, again, that isn't an innovation.

The real innovation is the ability to use assets you already have to create financing opportunities, using the RWAs as collateral for failure to repay. This approach has many benefits. First, unlike most speculative token collateral, the price isn't nearly as volatile, so the likelihood that you'll be forced to put up more collateral, pay down debt early, or, in the worst case, liquidate your collateral because the value of your collateral dropped too low is minimized.

A second, far bigger benefit is that RWAs with identifiable market value can be used as a method of direct financing. The original holder of the RWA decides to tokenize the RWA and subdivide it into NFTs, with the title and rights held on-chain. The NFTs are then sold to separate holders.[1] Those holders either get the value of their portion of the RWA when it's sold,[2] or they get the value of their NFT plus interest when it is repurchased by the original holder.[3] The original holder, meanwhile, gets to use *all the money invested in the NFTs* for whatever financing needs are required, without having to repay the money and drain operating capital. The only requirement is for the RWA to be legally protected and insured, and whatever is promised at the outset—sale or repurchase—to occur at the promised time. It's a win for everyone but the bank.

This first situation remedies predatory collateral practices, as well as the problems with using volatile assets as collateral. The problem here is the need for financing, but the middle men—here, banks—take advantage by creating terms that require the borrowing party to repay money with the funds just borrowed, and usually significantly less than the value of the collateral. This reduces the risk of the collateral, but also allows predatory lenders to take control of valuable collateral at a very reduced price. This sounds much more complicated than it is, so we'll use examples to clarify.

The site and method described in Situation 1 don't exist yet, but will as DeFi evolves.

Situation 1

If at first you don't succeed, drink bourbon. You'll be amazed at how little you care.
—Anonymous

Shanice is a well-known and highly regarded bourbon manufacturer. She runs a boutique distillery of finely crafted bourbons that are shipped around the world, highly sought after by the moneyed crowd. Her bourbons age for 8 to 18 years and average $12,000 per barrel—more for older vintages and/or particularly charred barrels.

---

1 This transaction would likely be subject to the Securities Act of 1933, as amended, and require registration or exemption in the US.

2 See "Situation 1".

3 See "Situation 2".

She buys her corn mash from local farmers, but inflation and a local mold have hit prices hard this year, and a fire in her distillery used up her cash. She ponders what to do for this year's yield. If she doesn't act quickly, the available resources will be taken up by competitors, and she will have an inferior product coming out of the year—or worse, no product.

Shanice contemplates a loan but realizes the rising interest rates (to combat inflation) will make the payment nearly unmanageable. Also, they allow her only 40% of the value of her collateral at best, which isn't enough for the entire purchase she needs to make. She'll need to use the property and distillery as collateral, and the risk with such high interest rates is extremely high; she could lose everything.

Instead, she decides to use a direct finance DeFi application. She signs up for an account and applies to ask for financing, using one of her 12-year barrels for collateral, currently aged 9 years. A third party confirms that she owns the barrel, that the barrel is what she says it is, and arranges for third-party insurance on the barrel, paid for by Shanice. The barrel is then certified. Shanice offers the certified barrel on the finance marketplace, selling 100 NFTs of the barrel for $80 each, and promising to sell the barrel for no less than $12,000 three years from the date of the NFT sale. This guarantees all NFT holders a minimum 150% return on investment in three years, and access to luxury goods sales that many have never entered at a very low price point.

The sale goes live, and the NFTs sell out quickly. Shanice uses the $7,920 (she kept one NFT for herself) to buy supplies, and has extra to invest in new marketing and complete needed upgrades. The sale, upgrades, and marketing all increase the value of her brand, and in three years, the barrel is sold for $18,000. The funds are directly sent to all NFT holders, the NFTs are burned, and the new barrel owner owns the barrel and bourbon in full.[4]

The next situation takes the place of predatory temporary lending practices like pawnshops, reverse mortgages, payday loans—things that take advantage of the need for immediate cash, disregarding the ability to come up with the necessary funds over time. Here, immediacy is the reason an intermediary (a pawnbroker, a loan shark) takes extreme profit and advantage of someone. The ability to finance and allow reasonable, not usurious, profit will help people with short-term cash flow issues tremendously.

Again, this doesn't exist yet, but it will in the future.

---

4 Note that no banks were paid in this transaction, and the entire value of the collateral was able to be used. Many banks may have been harmed in this transaction. No one cares.

Situation 2

I've always wanted to smash a guitar over someone's head. You just can't do that with a piano.
—Elton John

Your best friend, Todd, comes to you with a problem. He shows you a tax bill of $3,425,000.

You are shocked. "Todd, haven't you ever paid your taxes? What did you do?!" You pour club soda in a glass over ice. Then, glancing over at the paper crumpled in his hand, you grab a bottle of whiskey and dump a bunch over the top, swirling it quickly before handing it to him.

"I don't want to talk about it," he responds dully, taking a long drink. You have no idea whether he knows he's drinking alcohol. You contemplate the pickle juice in the fridge for a bare moment, before deciding the joke wouldn't be worth it right now.

You let out a low whistle. "What are you going to do?"

Todd shakes his head. "No clue. I'm, uh," he coughed, "not exactly liquid right now. I guess I'll have to sell The Guitar." Tears gather in his eyes.

The Guitar is a topic you often discuss with Todd, though not in nearly enough detail to suit you. Somehow, Todd has gained possession of the 1959 Martin D-18E spruce top guitar with the Bartolini soundhole played by Kurt Cobain for his 1993 MTV Unplugged appearance. It was magnificent, and the bastard never let you touch or know how he acquired it.

"Sell it?! I mean, that would do it. It's worth over $6 million. But the market is terrible now—I doubt you'd even get $3 mil for it."

"What else can I do? I need cash. It's due at the end of the month. This is my CPA's best deal." He takes another long drink. "If I had more time, I could refinance and sell a few things. But there's no way I can get it done in time." He looked down. "The, uh, IRS isn't exactly willing to help me out here."

After thinking for a minute, you pull up a DeFi app on your laptop.

"Have you seen this?" You show him the site.

Todd sees that, once he creates an account, he can apply for financing. Once approved, a third party confirms he owns The Guitar in question, the value of The Guitar, and arranges for third-party insurance on The Guitar. Once this is completed, The Guitar is certified.

He then tokenizes the certified Guitar, issuing 1,000 NFTs for $3,000 each. He promises to either repurchase all the NFTs for $4,000,000 within one year of the NFT offering date, or sell The Guitar for at least $4,000,000. Either way, the NFT holders are guaranteed an investment return of 133% within one year.

Todd completes the offering and sells the NFTs. He uses the money to pay off the tax bill, and repurchases all the NFTs six months after the offering date. All the holders take their profits, and Todd reclaims full ownership of The Guitar.

The next time he comes over, he leaves you $1,000 and his eternal gratitude. You pickle juice his drink anyway. Because that's how you roll.

As you can see from these examples, these types of financing—investment/speculation, loan, or a mix of the two—are innovative and allow people to use assets in ways that gain access to money without the predators always waiting to take advantage of people who need money. A pawnbroker would have offered Todd a fraction of the amount The Guitar was worth. A bank would have charged Shanice interest, which would have cut into the funds she had just borrowed, and limited the amount she could borrow to a low fraction of the value of her bourbon.

Instead of getting a predatory, and often inappropriate, reverse mortgage, people with paid-off homes can sell tokenized interests in their homes, keeping a life estate for themselves and their spouse or partner, if they wish. Then, upon their deaths, the life estate is extinguished, and the home is sold. The proceeds go automatically to all the token holders. The house cannot be sold before they die, and the heirs can be part of the token holders, if they want.

Instead of selling land to a developer, environmentally sensitive individuals or communities can sell tokenized assets representing the land, use the funds to develop the land as they wish, and the asset holders can have the right to build on the developed land or sell to someone who will build, as long as the environmental restrictions are maintained.

These tokens, whether NFTs or simple tokens, are themselves securities assets. They can be used as collateral and can be sold and resold before the maturity date—the date of repurchase or sale of the underlying asset. The market price will vary according to the terms of the token and the market conditions underlying the RWA, so holders can profit even before the maturity date. Separate markets will develop for these tokens, as with all securities, and provide liquidity for those who need to exit before maturity.

This isn't imaginary; banks and other collateralization financiers have been doing this for decades. The difference is that now anyone will be able to do it. Well, anyone who can access DeFi financial markets. And right now, that doesn't look like it will be anyone, at least not in the US. So before we rhapsodize further on the glory of financial markets and derivatives, we need to see who can access these tools, who regulates them, and what we need to do to open them up further—assuming that's our goal.

Does DeFi Even Need Regulation?

DeFi right now looks like a giant free-for-all, or the Wild West, as its denizens love to call it—but it's absolutely not. All of blockchain is highly regulated, as are all technologies that are commercialized in the US. It's just not a compliant space.

What about current laws?

In Chapter 2, we laid out an overview of which US entities govern which parts of blockchain transactions; there are quite a few. We also noted that international regulations are changing as a result of FATF and global concerns over money laundering, scams, fraud, and tax evasion. Other than the KYC/AML rules discussed previously, few regulations specifically apply to DeFi markets.

Both the EU's Markets in Crypto-Assets regulation (MiCA)[5] and the US's draft Digital Asset Market Structure seek to provide a more comprehensive framework for regulating cryptocurrency and the markets and providers that surround it.[6] The EU is creating a new structure more in line with the overall FATF view, while the US seems to be seeking to use existing structures, bringing in the function, if not the formal terminology, of the FATF requirements.

Neither addresses DeFi. MiCA specifically exempts crypto assets and transactions that have no intermediaries, have no issuer,[7] and/or are fully decentralized.[8]

Both address stablecoins, a base feature of current and future DeFi and obviously a topic of intense interest for legislatures. They are most interested in crypto assets that are backed by fiat. These assets provide a strong use case for fiat, serving as a derivative of fiat rather than a competitor to it. However, as discussed in "Stablecoins" on page 45, this is one of the worst types of coins. Also, those coins may be regulated, but the use of those coins in DeFi transactions has not yet been defined.

---

5 MiCA was passed May 16, 2023.

6 Digital Asset Market Structure was publicly submitted as a proposed bill June 2, 2023.

7 This presumably includes tokens with fully renounced smart contracts, such as the majority of recent memecoins.

8 See Paragraph (22) of MiCA, May 16, 2023.

RWAs are regulated by MiCA, but the US regulation does not distinguish these assets other than as traditional asset-backed securities, so these would be governed by standard securitization rules. Note that, in the US, this may include perfection of interests and other legal requirements under the Uniform Commercial Code, unless this is superseded by new regulations because blockchain provides similar, or better, protection.[9]

What happens when transactions cross borders?

Interestingly, jurisdictions are working together to enforce financial regulations and prevent safe havens to financial crime, which is a major change in the history of white-collar crime. Traditionally, financial criminals found safe havens in many jurisdictions simply because a generous donation to the local and national government ensured the safety of criminals, while providing a healthy amount of liquidity and solvency to regions that tended to lack such things.

But something changed in 2022. The province of Ontario requested Binance either register its derivative operations or terminate the practice. In response, Binance chose to leave Canada, as it does not wish to be regulated in any jurisdiction. Ordinarily, that would be the end of it. However, something unusual happened: many other jurisdictions joined Ontario in requiring Binance to register or immediately terminate its practice. This included the UK, the US, Japan, Singapore, South Korea, and several others. They even pressured the home jurisdiction of Binance, an island that does nothing but register companies, to find that Binance had "improperly registered." This was an act of coordination between countries for strictly financial corporate activity that was unprecedented.

And it was timely; the impact of the implosion of Celsius (unhedged risk managed by unregistered, unregulated, unidentified money managers), Terra Luna (poorly designed stablecoin paired with Ponzi scheme activities), and FTX (outright fraud backed by top Silicon Valley investors and funds) still impacts both the crypto and traditional investing communities. As it turns out, a Wild West of unresearched, non-compliant financial tools offered to undereducated, poorly funded investors or outright greedy speculators isn't a great idea.

---

9 Blockchain would provide better protection because there wouldn't be any benefit to a *race filing*—people who may have purchased their interest after someone else, but ended up getting a senior interest because they filed their interest with the court first. Getting the interest and registering that interest would be done simultaneously, as the entire purpose of blockchain is the independent recording of an acquired interest.

Is it just because crypto and DeFi attract retail (nonaccredited) investors?

Of course, it's easy to say it's the fault of uneducated retail investors or the evil manipulators who run blockchain companies. But we do have to remember two things: first, most startups fail. And by most, we're talking around 90%.[10] We're very quick to call every failure deliberate, but many are simply the failures that happen in early stages of technology. The difference between a failure and a scam is often the effort the founding team put into the success of the project,[11] and whether the founding team walked away with a profit but the investors or buyers didn't.

Second, traditional investing is full of scams from what may be considered very educated investors, or at least investors with access to all kinds of professional advisors. For example, Silvergate Bank may have been hard hit by the crypto winter of 2022/2023, but the failures of Signature Bank, First Republic, and Silicon Valley Bank (SVB) were simply bad practice, bad management, and hundreds of millions spent to evade regulation—regulation designed to prevent exactly the type of failure that occurred.[12]

Also, the Federal Reserve permitted First Republic to fail completely so that J.P. Morgan could pick through the remains for a fraction of the price, leaving First Republic shareholders with nothing.[13]

SVB had customer bank deposit averages of $1 million, as compared to the national bank deposit average of $41,000. None of the amount over the FDIC limit of $250,000 was insured. Each of those depositors was a de facto accredited investor, and none of them managed to figure out or get advice that everything over $250,001 in their account may disappear without recourse. They took on an enormous level of risk, and they were lucky enough to get bailed out by the taxes of the poor investors who lost money in crypto—and who don't get bailed out themselves.

---

10 According to dozens of sources, including the Bureau of Labor Statistics.

11 Scams are also known colloquially as *rug pulls, rugs, honeypots,* and a variety of other names depending on the type of scam and people targeted.

12 Greg Becker, the former CEO of SVB, was head of a powerful lobby to remove SVB from the regulatory "burdens" imposed by Dodd-Frank and other regulations, saying stress tests and increased oversight added expense and were unnecessary. Until it failed. He sold his stock in SVB weeks before it failed but personally called clients the day before the bank failed "to assure them their money was safe." Hannah Lang, "Who is Greg Becker, the former head of failed Silicon Valley Bank," *Reuters*, May 15, 2023, *https://oreil.ly/cOir0*.

13 Eric Compton, "First Republic/JPMorgan: Deal Brings Benefits for JP Morgan, End for First Republic Shareholders," *Morningstar*, May 18, 2023, *https://oreil.ly/X8i1_*.

Steve Mnuchin, the "Foreclosure King"[14] during his time as chair of the company that owned Financial Freedom, was fined $89 million as a result of his scams against the federal government.[15] He followed this by becoming Secretary of the Treasury.

And, of course, the Great Recession was powered by improperly packaged, extremely risky mortgages, sold by banks and resold by the most respected brokerages on the most respected markets in the world.

The examples are endless. DeFi certainly needs regulation, but so does traditional finance. Neither has clean hands here. The system is broken, so we need to stop blaming tokens and retail investors as though they represent all the risk, scams, and harm in the industry. Let's focus instead on how to make the industry better, and stop assuming some players are immune from criticism and others are repositories for it.

A Better Regulatory Structure for Crypto and DeFi

Let's just acknowledge that the idea of any industry self-regulating successfully with vast sums of money involved is...idealistic. Whether it's traditional finance or crypto assets, politicians and issuers love to talk about the rights and protections of investors, but when it costs them money or votes, they suddenly start to view protection and rights as optional.

Also, most of blockchain, and DeFi in particular, will fall under the new FATF regulations discussed in Chapter 3 and require some type of regulation.

But this regulation doesn't need to be onerous. Every other industry has to deal with the cost and liability; there is no reason to assume that blockchain-based technology should be exempt. Regulations don't kill industries; they kill scams. But we also have to be honest that current regulations are centered on having broker-dealers and regulated parties at the center of all transactions, and that hasn't been true since the late 1990s. They don't really work for anyone, and they aren't fundamentally fair.

---

14 This title was due to his apparent proclivity for forcing homes into foreclosure rather than modifying loans for its "mostly elderly clientele." See Paul Kiel and Jesse Eisinger, "Trump's Treasury Pick Excelled at Kicking Elderly People Out of Their Homes," *ProPublica*, December 27, 2016, *https://oreil.ly/J2Ufu*; Mark Plotkin, "Steve Mnuchin, Foreclosure King, Now Runs Your US Treasury," *The Hill*, February 17, 2017 *https://oreil.ly/cqsJL*; Bess Levin, "Foreclosing on a 90 Year Old Over 20 Cents and Other Heartwarming Tales from Steve Mnuchin's Days at One West," *Vanity Fair*, December 1, 2016 *https://oreil.ly/5JFJn*; Sam T. Levin, "Inside Trump Treasury Nominee's Past Life as 'Foreclosure King' of California," *The Guardian*, December 2, 2016 *https://oreil.ly/39vMu*.

15 Brad Tuttle, "Here's Why Treasury Nominee Steve Mnuchin Has Been Called the 'Foreclosure King,'" *Money.com*, January 19, 2017, *https://oreil.ly/L3Pke*; Ben Lane, "Mnuchin's OneWest Subsidiary Agrees to $89M Settlement for Reverse Mortgage Violations," *Housingwire*, May 16, 2017, *https://oreil.ly/EL55u*.

So, starting with that premise, let's look at an overarching structure for crypto regulations that would work with existing regulations, make sense, and, ideally, is more fair and attainable than what we currently have.

Who Is Issuing Tokens and Coins, Anyway?

One of the biggest issues faced by those involved in DeFi is that regulators and legislators aren't participants in DeFi but are trying to write legislation and regulations as though they have more than a glancing familiarity with its huge variety of issuers and investors. These officials look at traditional offerings and finance and assume that DeFi offerings are similar, if not identical, but just labeled incorrectly. This couldn't be further from the truth.

Issuers in the crypto space are generally an entirely different population than those you see issuing securities for public or private sale in the traditional securities space. They tend to vary significantly in sophistication and intent based on the type of token offered and to whom the token is offered. Many have no intention of offering a security of any sort, but are offering a community token. Some are offering a transactional token. Some are offering a governance token. Some are offering a token that a community member has placed on a marketplace, making it a security. Some are offering tokens that have a mixture of uses. The blurring of these lines is a significant problem, and one of the issues that differs from traditional stock offerings that are clearly meant to do one thing only: raise capital.

So let's begin by clarifying that different types of token offerings exist, and they require different regulatory approaches. Unlike equity, tokens are not just "one size fits all." They can do many things, are used for many purposes, and should be regulated accordingly.

What About Tokens That Do Many Things?

It's true that tokens can be programmed to do many things, and this has been considered a benefit. Vitalik Buterin considered the fact that ETH was used as both a transactional token (the "gas" that powers transactions) and a securities token (exchangeable on markets) as a primary value, as it would ensure the token continued to have demand, even if it wasn't in use. Like excess carbon credits, holders of ETH could sell their tokens to people who wanted to use it, so it would maintain value. However, this assumes some sort of stable market value, not a fluctuating market value. When value fluctuates, the token functions more like an asset. And having a token that is an asset throws a wrench into this otherwise reasonable setup.

When you have a token that functions as a transactional token and a security, you see that you have two forces acting in opposition to one another. When it gains in market price, it loses its utility as a transactional token: gas is too expensive to conduct transactions, so most transactions will stop. Conversely, when the gas price goes down, it comes at the expense of the market price. So you see the price of ETH is banded between a floor and a ceiling: it can't go down too low, because there is market demand, and it can't rise too much, because it destroys fundamental transactional value.

This also applies when you have a token that serves as a governance token and a transactional token, or any other situation where the token has more than one job to do. The interests end up competing, which fundamentally harms the value of both. Accordingly, tokens shouldn't have more than one job. Projects can have many tokens, each with one job, with one tokenomic model, and one set of driving forces. I actually think there is a better approach than tokens for the securities interest that may be sold, which I will discuss later in this chapter. Regardless, this regulatory overview will consider that tokens have one primary purpose, in order to maximize the value of any given token.

Tokens As Securities

The US Securities and Exchange Commission (SEC) regulates securities transactions, the people who enable those transactions, and the markets on which those transactions happen.

That means, generally speaking, if you are buying interest in a company or project or thing because you think that thing may go up in value (though it may go down), whether or not it entitles you to vote or call yourself an "owner," you are buying a securities interest. It doesn't have to be called a security, or an investment contract, or stock, or anything in particular. It just needs to represent one of the things in the federal or state securities laws that are always called securities, however they are offered, or be something that people buy because they think that thing will go up in value— and they don't have to do anything to make that thing increase in value.

Remember that securities can include debt and equities, and, if registered, are freely tradable to others. That free transferability is a *huge* benefit. Most of blockchain pretends we can do it anyway because we currently freely trade tokens—illegally. But the ability to trade tokens that are securities legally brings a lot of investors who need to be sure they can exit their position when they want, and de-risks a lot of these investments. We can get massive amounts of capital into our system just because we don't have the risk of doing something illegal, and they can freely trade. Currently, crypto represents about 2% of investing dollars. That would skyrocket if we could allow people in who don't want to worry about the SEC killing projects just because they didn't register tokens.

And it's not even clear there's a real benefit to not registering, especially for traditionally founded projects with centralized founding teams. We have a disclosure system in the US, which means you don't need permission to do anything; you just have to publicly disclose it after you do it. Also, disclosing your plans and what has happened in your project in a prospectus or disclosure form provides notice to all investors of what you plan to do and the risks associated. If it doesn't work out, they usually can't sue the project or the founders, because you told them what you were doing and the risks. Just something to consider—disclosure protects both the investors and the projects.

Here, we're looking mostly at all the traditional projects that offer tokens before they build, and that token is not the end product. These are the blockchain platform or DApp builds that require many developers and years of work and need funding to get started. They look most like a traditional software build, and they use tokens for multiple purposes. They tend to start out offering tokens as a security offering by a founding team to raise funds for the project. These tokens may have multiple uses eventually, but they generally start off as securities offerings and should be treated that way.

But the regulations need work

We tend to argue extensively about whether something is a security with the SEC. In my opinion, this is a waste of time. The SEC is the ultimate arbiter of determining that something is a security. It gets to decide—that's entirely within its purview.

A better question is, if it is a security, *how do we comply?* Many of the rules don't work for blockchain—or for traditional companies, for that matter. How can anyone comply with a counterparty reporting requirement when the counterparty is a wallet with an alphanumeric string and a couple of cartoon cat NFTs as an identifier?

Also, remember from Chapter 3 that, until 2023, it wasn't even possible to fully comply with the regulations. No regulated exchanges or approved special purpose brokers were available for securities token transactions. So how exactly were companies built before this period supposed to conduct their offerings?

Broker-dealers are the hub of the reporting requirements in the US; it is assumed that they are the core regulated entities that interact with issuers, markets, and investors. And, on that premise, the rules do work. But broker-dealers haven't been a hub requirement since Glass-Steagall ended in 1999. Retail and institutional investors interact directly with markets without broker-dealers. Issuers can now go public directly with primary or secondary offerings, no underwriter required. Crowdfunding, Regulation A/A+, robo-advisors, etraders, and more have undermined the grip broker-dealers have held on markets for generations, and it isn't likely to return.

But our reporting obligations continue with the façade that an intermediary is required. Pretending individual investors, whether accredited or retail, can comply with the broker-dealer reporting requirements when they aren't trained, regulated broker-dealers with access to the accounts, research, oversight, insurance, and resources broker-dealers have seems fairly ridiculous. Investors aren't broker-dealers and shouldn't have to pretend to be.

Why are there so many unregistered securities offerings in crypto, anyway?

It's certainly true that not all token offerings are securities offerings, and not all tokens are securities, but we do have *so many* unregistered securities offerings in crypto. We have those 74 cases the SEC brought from the 2012–2017 ICO (initial coin offering) era, when everyone pretended those coin and token offerings weren't securities, and the cases now forming from the 2017–2020 era, such as the Coinbase and Binance cases.[16] Is everyone just set on acting illegally in crypto?

No. Of course not. We have two big lies in our space that prevent people from understanding the regulations and conducting normal cost-benefit evaluations of offerings when raising capital to fund a project.

Lie number one

The first is what I like to call our Original Lie—and boy, do we love this one. The Original Lie is the one that some idiot(s) told early cipherpunk original developers who were passing tokens back and forth to test early chains. This idiot (or idiots) said, "Hey, those tokens you kick to each other, you could sell those. They aren't securities, so you don't have to register them. You can sell them to anyone. And you can use the money to fund your build!" Lie. 100% lie.

However, the developers, being developers and not lawyers or anyone with any business experience, said, "Fantastic! Let's do it!" And...here we are.

But as many times as I, or any regulator, or any lawyer who has actually studied the law, may shout out; "*Listen! Blockchain is not magical. Tokens can be securities. Selling them to fund your build requires registration or exemption,*" builders and investors continue to claim various stupid responses. These are among my favorites:

But it's on-chain!
So what? On-chain things have investment decisions too. Register.

---

16 The SEC charged Coinbase with operating an unregistered securities exchange, broker, and clearing agency, and making billions of dollars in selling unregistered securities through its staking-as-a-service offering and creating unregistered securities in the process (*https://oreil.ly/e8EzI*). The SEC charged Binance with operating an unregistered securities exchange, broker, and clearing agency, and making billions of dollars in selling unregistered securities through its staking-as-a-service offering, and creating unregistered securities in the process; with intentionally evading US federal securities rules, the Bank Secrecy Act, and international regulations designed to prevent money laundering; with commingling customer funds and diverting them to Changpeng Zhao's personal company; and with Changpeng Zhao illegally managing the US company, Binance.US, which was supposedly independent of his company, Binance.com (*https://oreil.ly/9JZlH*). Note that the CFTC also filed charges against Binance for evading federal commodities laws and international laws designed to prevent money laundering, conducting regulatory arbitrage, and operating as an unregistered futures commission merchant (*https://oreil.ly/t8IK2*).

But it's decentralized!
> Literally nothing in blockchain at the time of this writing is decentralized—see Chapter 1 describing this. If Amazon Web Services crashed, so would blockchain. Also, completely irrelevant to securities designation. Register.

But we have to raise funds!
> Yeah, so does every other company in every other industry ever. Why is blockchain different? Why do we get special rules? Register.

We hate institutions!
> They don't care. Register.

We don't want to!
> Doesn't matter. Register.

It's not fair!
> Cry to your mother. Register.

Lie number two

This isn't really one lie; it's kind of an assortment of lies, misunderstandings, and bad legal advice. The amount of bad legal information and advice ranging from questionable to entirely wrong given to founders in blockchain can't be understated—it's the cause of more loss of crypto than the intent to steal or con, and unfortunately isn't being tallied or reported because so many of the lawyers are aggressively asserting they did nothing wrong, encouraging the natural inclination of many founders and users in crypto to attack regulators, or fleeing the country. Sometimes all three. It's been profoundly harmful to DeFi, and it has set us back at least five years, if not more.

It's also made founders reluctant to consult attorneys, especially those with high fees, because they have no assurance that the advice will provide any protection whatsoever or be useful. This is not because, as they claim, the law is confusing or "regulation is coming" or it's unclear. This is because blockchain involves many very technical areas of law, and the lawyers don't understand what they're doing. Instead of working hard to learn, they are relying on clients to pay them to learn and don't even know enough to understand what constitutes regulatory law. They cite speeches and statements that *have no regulatory weight* as regulatory fact, rather than operating on the law as it stands.

I cannot emphasize enough how incredibly harmful this has been to the industry. There is no accountability for the poor advice offered, and absolutely no guilt from founders who have committed errors for continually using retail investors and their animosity toward government institutions to cover their own failures. Politicians and founders have relentlessly used innocent retail investors to whip up false outrage to maintain token prices and evade consequences for their failure to act legally.

And who is paying the price for this? Retail investors. They are the ones who are being encouraged to protest and buy tokens from failing projects, acting as exit liquidity for troubled founders and promoters, in a fruitless and false narrative that lists public opinion as relevant for regulators, when they and regulators both know public opinion is completely irrelevant.

That said, these specific lies have made compliance so much harder to ensure:

Simple agreements for future tokens, or SAFTS, are legal
These were never legal, and it's unclear why attorneys licensed in securities law thought they would be.

Using tokens to raise funds isn't a security
No idea why anyone thought this was true.

Regulation is "coming"
It's been here for nearly 100 years.

Regulation is unclear
Not particularly.

Having a utility is sufficient to make a token or coin not a security
This does not prevent your token from being a security.

Decentralization exists and provides protection from regulation
It has not been achieved yet, but, more importantly, the idea that decentralization provides protection from any type of regulation, whether securities or otherwise, is untrue.

Not having an entity protects individuals, DAOs, and/or projects from regulation
Regulators just subpoena the individuals involved—it's actually worse.

Without these lies, this space would be much more compliant. However, people *are* trying to be more compliant. But we have to take things as they are, so expect a few more years of cleanup. The tendency to create "copypasta," or copying projects and their open source code from one chain to another, has created multiple identical projects on different chains with identical problems. As a result, litigation is going to look quite savage from the outside but really is just clearing out the mess of output of these past years.

Artificial third parties

We shouldn't have to artificially insert third parties into transactions just because agencies trust people more than immutable technology, even though it's the people who introduce fraud, not the technology. Transfer agents, broker-dealers, clearing-houses—these parties are being artificially forced into a system that does not require them because of an imagined ideal that these parties are free of fraud or mistake. Of course, that's entirely untrue.

And the desire of these parties to remain in securities transactions is extremely high, because they make significant profits on being a formerly necessary intermediary. Many also make significant profits because of their access to asymmetric information, which seems patently unfair. Companies like Virtu and Citadel, which are allowed to serve not only as dealer but also as counterparty to transactions, are fundamentally unfair, and they would be completely eliminated with a blockchain-based system. And isn't that what the regulators are always insisting upon? Fundamental fairness for investors?

The rules need to be streamlined to accommodate the technology, instead of the technology being artificially plugged with antiquated required parties.

What kind of reporting, then?

The disclosure system works in principle. However, the reporting obligations need to be modified to accommodate platforms and DApps as they become more decentralized. For example, to the extent no centralized founding entity controls financial procedures or operations, there should be reporting mechanisms for DAOs and smart contracts. Reports should still be filed, but by the appropriate entity (or lack thereof) rather than have a straw man artificially inserted to sign documents. If an entity or protocol runs autonomously or by committee, that should be the reporting entity.

Whitepapers should be filed as prospectuses, and they should contain information regarding the management of the project, the roadmap, any rights attached to the tokens, risks associated with the investment, any fundraising previously done, a discussion of the technology and projected core use case and users, size and makeup of the initial community, means of primary community communication, plans for decentralization and the timeline attached, the use of hosted or unhosted wallets, the number of wallets currently holding tokens, the number of tokens reserved to the founding team and any partners, any restrictions on sale, the total number of tokens and tokenomics, and the core revenue and financial model of the project. Distribution can be conducted via the project's website, and all insider transactions should be disclosed to prevent manipulation or taking advantage of inside information.[17]

Offerings of $1 million and under with 500 or more holders would be exempt, provided the offering took no more than six months to complete and was not repeated in the 24 months following the end of the offering. The other exemptions, such as offerings to accredited investors and institutional investors, would still remain, and offerings under them would be exempt.

Commodities

The Commodity Futures Trading Commission (CFTC) governs commodities and derivative agreements—two very different things. One is raw materials that go into commerce. The other is securities transactions of varying complexity. How did pork bellies and things like interest rate exchanges get lumped together—and how does crypto even fit in here?

What are commodities?

Generally, *commodities* are agricultural items, raw materials (like oil), services, rights, interests, or other goods that allow you to make contracts for future delivery.[18]

Contracts for the future

This idea of contracting for future delivery is interesting, so let's explore it for a minute. Let's say you own a bakery, and you need flour for your breads and cakes. You can buy flour at the store, but it's expensive, as it's been marked up to make a profit for all the people in the distribution chain of wheat-to-flour process. But if you know you're going to need flour, and approximately how much, in advance, you can go directly to a flour mill and ask for a contract for the amount of flour you need for the next six months or year or whatever period. Since the mill owners know they are going to sell the flour, they can sell it to you much cheaper, because they don't have to pay to have the flour packaged, shipped, stored, and sold in stores. If you have a large

---

17 Insiders would take on the definition in Section 16 of the Securities Exchange Act of 1934, as amended. This primarily targets decision makers and large position holders: accordingly, the founding team, holders of 10% or more of the issued and outstanding tokens, and any independent holder or group of holders performing governance functions beyond voting. This would mean those who have the ability to propose rules (if all holders are not permitted to propose rules) and those who direct the distribution of project resources, enable release of funds or assets, direct hiring or firing of personnel, draw up or submit budgets, and take part in fundraising, financing, or other activities with executory and/or binding power on behalf of the project, except anyone who takes part in any of those functions in a strictly administrative capacity. Node operators, miners, validators, and project developers are not insiders.

18 Not included: onions and box office receipts. I'd love the backstory on what happened with these two items to be specifically excluded from the commodities category forever; you can't trade futures in these.

---

enough amount to buy, you may want to buy the wheat from the farmer directly. That arrangement will be significantly cheaper; you can set up your own contract for milling and save yourself additional cost.

The agreements, which assume the buyer will take physical delivery of the commodity, are called *forward contracts*. They are the basis of commodities, because commodities are, at heart, the raw materials of commerce. Being able to sell raw materials in advance (so they don't go to waste) ensures that products are available for sale, the economy grows, and taxes are paid. These contracts are exempt from many regulations, provided physical delivery happens.

The base assumption here is that the parties are agreeing to sell goods that will be delivered in the future. "I want to buy four bushels of wheat from your fall harvest." "Sure. I will need 10,000 pounds of flour over the course of the next 12 months." The price is set now for future delivery.

The second assumption, and this is an important one, is that the goods themselves are fundamentally fungible. That means you want to purchase something that falls within that category, but the base items themselves are interchangeable. For example, you want to buy coffee beans, but one coffee bean isn't different from another. You don't want *that specific bean*. You may want coffee from Sumatra, or from a particular farm in Sumatra, or from a particular harvest from that farm in Sumatra—but not a specific tree or acre. One of that farmer's beans is identical to another in any given year.

You can always buy commodities at any given time on the spot market, which is basically like the retail market for commodities. It's generally more expensive because you aren't guaranteeing a sale in advance, but you can still make deals if you buy in (very large) volume. And sometimes the spot market is a deal when the price of any particular commodity is rising and you didn't lock in the price in a *futures* contract.

Derivatives

So now let's talk about how these forward contracts turned into complicated financial tools called *futures* and *derivatives*. People realized they had some real value in those agreements. Maybe they had a great price before the price of the commodity shot up.[19] Or the seller locked in a great price before the market dipped into a period called *contango*, or spot market prices that are lower than futures market prices.[20] Or perhaps a buyer realizes they won't use the commodity, or there is more value in selling the rights than holding the right to purchase and exercising it. People realized they

---

19 Southwest gained an enormous advantage over its rival airlines in the mid-1990s by hedging fuel prices at $11/barrel, just before prices skyrocketed to $34/barrel, bankrupting many competitors.

20 In 2010, ETF Securities suffered a massive loss on its oil contracts when the price of oil dropped, and it held high-priced futures.

held rights to something and wanted to sell those rights instead of exercising them. This added a huge amount of liquidity to the commodities market but also a huge amount of risk. And with this risk came significant opportunity.

Now you can trade not just the underlying asset—the wheat, the oil, the stock, etc.—but also the right to purchase or sell that asset.[21] You can exchange your right to receive a benefit for someone else's. For example, say you've loaned out $10 million for 5% interest. However, you wish you'd had the option for adjustable interest, or been able to offer that loan a little later, as interest rates were rising, so you could make more money. Another lender has also loaned out $10 million, but the interest rate is prime rate plus 1.5%, and that lender needs a fixed interest rate loan to hedge their risk in other areas; they need to be certain payments are coming in, and the borrower won't be as likely to have problems making payments if interest rates rise too high. So the two of you decide to swap loans.[22] These swaps typically occur on the over-the-counter (OTC) market and are regulated transactions.

How Does Crypto Come into This?

Well, the SEC decided that Bitcoin and ETH, while not unregistered securities offerings, should be governed as commodities by the CFTC. We have no idea why, and that is deliberate by the SEC—it specifically declined to put forward its reasoning as to why the initial offerings of Bitcoin and ETH were not unregistered securities, why they should be considered commodities, and why they should be governed by the CFTC. All explanations that have been put forward are *speculation only*. No one has any information as to the rationale, and this is not likely to change in the near future.

We can speculate is that BTC and ETH were considered fungible, as that is a fundamental property of the transactions and goods governed by the CFTC. That means that each satoshi can be exchanged with any other satoshi, and each ERC coin can be exchanged with any other ERC coin.[23]

However, that's not currently true. Bitcoin has released Ordinals, or nonfungible inscriptions on satoshis. This is a problem—these inscribed satoshis are no longer interchangeable with any other satoshi. They are priced as unique items and held as unique items. Does this destroy the special exemption that Bitcoin holds as a commodity? Possibly.

---

21 This is known as an *option*.

22 This is known, cleverly, as a *swap*. This is a plain vanilla interest rate swap, but they can take on many forms, as they are an extremely flexible instrument.

23 *ERC* is short for *Ethereum Request for Comment*, and these are the token protocols that are pre-minted and preformatted on Ethereum.

Ethereum has evolved beyond one version of ETH. It created standardized protocols, or ERC tokens, and a wide variety of them. The ERC-20 tokens may be interchangeable, but only if they are of the same platform (Ethereum). The ERC-721 and beyond tokens are, by definition, nonfungible (NFTs). Do these break the exemption held by Ethereum? Possibly. We do know that the DApps within the Ethereum ecosystem are not protected by Ethereum's status, as a number of them have been specifically called out as securities by the SEC in the recent Binance and Coinbase complaints.

So what is the extent of this governance? Does it apply only to the original issuance? Does it apply to future issuances in their respective ecosystems? Is this why exchange-traded funds (ETFs) must only be futures funds, not spot funds—because of the CFTC purview? Or because it is unclear what entity would govern the spot fund?[24]

Smarter Regulation

Future regulation should establish that the CFTC governs futures transactions for all noncommunity tokens (discussed in "Better Regulation" on page 188), including Bitcoin and ETH, as well as all spot market transactions for Bitcoin and ETH.

In addition, the CFTC should govern the rising use of swaps as DeFi moves into actual finance, including credit default swaps and other types of securities swaps. As DeFi moves into more securitization and collateralization of assets, these kinds of swap agreements will help parties hedge their risk, allow for regular instead of fluctuating payment, and adapt easily to changing market conditions. We'll speak more about this in the following section, "Collateral."

Securitization and Collateral

As we've been discussing, most of DeFi will fall in the securitization and collateral area as it relates to financing. This hasn't been discussed in any form, so we'll talk about it now, because it's important to make sure people know what they're getting into and avoid chicanery.

Collateral

We discussed how tokens will be used as collateral for various types of loans, and how they are used as collateral now. But right now, we have a few issues.

---

24 Gary Gensler, current head of the SEC, has indicated that the reason for futures ETFs only is because spot ETFs would impact spot market pricing. But this makes little sense—futures pricing is public and has an impact on spot markets in every market. See, e.g., the *Grayscale* ruling, *https://oreil.ly/gQ6-s*. If people think the price in the future of a commodity or stock will go down and purchase derivatives to reflect that, it often has a downward effect on the daily market price. So this seems like a facetious reason.

Overhypothecation

One problem is *overhypothecation*, or overpromising one asset as collateral to multiple people or protocols. We talked about this earlier—it's the concept that we think we are depositing assets as collateral every time we deposit a token representing an interest in a DeFi transaction pool into another DeFi DApp or protocol, but really we just have one set of collateral, and only the small amount of transactional fees are being deposited as collateral in each subsequent DApp and protocol.

Perfecting your interest

The second is perfection. In the US, we have a requirement for most types of collateral that you make your interest in the collateral "known to the world," and it's governed by the Uniform Commercial Code. You have to complete a process called *perfecting your interest*, and this can be done in various ways, depending on the type of collateral. For most types of personal property, you perfect by taking physical possession. Other methods include recording your interest at the appropriate government office (e.g., recording a mortgage interest in land), taking possession of title (e.g., holding a car title), or automatically perfecting (e.g., buying a consumer good on credit). RWAs will require this.

Why do we need to perfect our interest? To put the world on notice that our interest in the collateral exists, so the borrower can't promise it to another without considering your interest or pretending it doesn't exist. Also, no one can buy any interest in the collateral without considering your interest, because it gives everyone *constructive* knowledge of your interest.[25]

"Considering your interest" can mean a lot of things, but generally it means that if the borrower tries to sell the collateral or recollateralize it, or put any sort of lien on it, all those interests are junior, or subordinate, to yours. If they sell it, you get the value of the outstanding loan the collateral is securing. If they put a lien on it, their lien is subordinate to yours.

What happens if you don't perfect your interest? Generally, unless someone has *actual* knowledge—was specifically told or there was direct disclosure—the next buyer can take without considering your interest. You could be out of luck when it comes to that collateral, especially if the borrower goes bankrupt and the next buyer or lien holder actually perfected.

> *Perfection is not attainable, but if we chase perfection, we can catch excellence.*
> —Vince Lombardi

---

25 *Constructive knowledge* generally means information that may or may not be actually known by the relevant person, but it should have been known by the relevant person. So, even though no one told that person specifically or that person didn't read about it, we treat them as if they did, because they *should have known*.

This perfection issue is tricky, so let's walk through an example.

Botheby's wants to build a new fine art and luxury goods auction house in Oklahoma City. However, interest rates are a bit high, and it wants to keep its balance sheets clean of new debt.

RichFi, a new DApp, offers institutional peer-to-peer financing similar to the bank repurchase market but with more flexibility. Botheby's sets up an account and obtains $20 million financing using two Picasso paintings it owns outright. RichFi digitizes the paintings' provenance and tokenizes them, recording the interest on the relevant blockchain, with the lenders holding the tokens as collateral.

Scandal erupts! It turns out Ashton St. James, the head of Botheby's private art collection, is actually Chas de Graaf IV, a large shareholder of its chief rival, Tristie's! While acting as head of the private art collection, Ashton/Chas sold all the private art, including the two Picassos RichFi lenders held as collateral. The buyers are all known, but they bought the paintings in legitimate transactions, unaware that Ashton/Chas had no authorization to do this. They are all what is known as *bona fide purchasers*. Courts generally try not to interfere with the rights of bona fide purchasers, no matter how malicious or nefarious their sellers were.

The RichFi lenders want to take the paintings back, showing the tokens they hold of their interest. The bona fide purchasers show their receipts. The courts grant the bona fide purchasers the paintings, because the rights in the paintings were not perfected by RichFi—the purchasers weren't informed of the RichFi holders' interest, and there was no reason they should have known of the interest. So, even though RichFi *should* have the superior right to the paintings, they don't, because courts don't want to intrude in transactions with bona fide purchasers.

But instead...

What if, instead of simply recording the provenance on the blockchain, RichFi had taken possession of the paintings, or they were in a museum or other location where possession was difficult, or RichFi had taken hold of the physical provenance of the paintings? This would have had a totally different result!

The paintings would either have been sold without their provenance or in name only (without possession of the physical painting), which would have been a clue that someone had some interest in the painting. This is why notice matters—it's a clue that something isn't right. And buyers have an obligation to do a certain amount of due diligence before buying something. If something doesn't seem right on its face, you must investigate further. If buyers choose not to do that, that's their choice—but they are no longer bona fide purchasers. They are willfully ignorant purchasers.

The court would have said the purchasers had constructive knowledge of the prior interest, even if no one had said a word; they should have known something was wrong and investigated further. The RichFi holders would have prevailed.

Perfection matters. Whether it's rights to tokens, coins, assets, NFTs, or anything else, you have to make your superior interest known. But no one in blockchain is doing it.

Securitization

Sometimes lenders decide they have too many loans on their books. Either they have too much risk (the risk that someone won't repay, or that the interest rates are too low in your loans, and current loan rates are higher, etc.), or they need to diversify their investments, or one of a million other reasons. So they may decide to securitize.

Securitization happens when these lenders take a bunch of loans (car loans, mortgages, credit card loans, etc.) into a group called a *reference portfolio*. These loans in the portfolio all have regular monthly payments but also have risk of nonrepayment. Some have more risk than others, and hopefully the lender has packaged and labeled the risk correctly.[26] That portfolio is then turned into an asset-backed security (sound familiar?), and people can purchase an interest in something that kicks out regular interest payments. It is quite appealing to retail investors who cannot access these kinds of financial tools, and it will be prominent in the future of DeFi.

This turns illiquid assets (sitting collateral, debt) into liquid assets, and it allows people to get access to yet another form of financing. But it also carries a risk of early repayment (the loan is worth less than you thought it would be) or nonrepayment (they don't pay you back), and these aren't always conveyed to the buyers of these instruments.

Better Regulation

First, we should allow securitization of our loans and financial assets in DeFi and turn these assets into securities that provide liquidity to both centralized and peer-to-peer lenders.

Second, perfecting is a good thing: it's a way to establish priority of interests and make sure people who are taking a later interest in something know if there is someone ahead of them in line. This stuff shouldn't be secret.

But two practices need to change. First, anyone taking collateral in any form should be required to take physical possession and hold the collateral in escrow, or register

---

26 One of the problems with the subprime mortgage crisis of 2008 was the number of high-risk, subprime loans packaged with low-risk loans and improperly sold as a package of low-risk loans.

that collateral on a public blockchain identifying the collateral and the owner.[27] Second, this blockchain should be open, optimized for search, easy to interpret (UI/UX for noncrypto users), and available in as many languages as possible. It should also list priority automatically whenever a transaction is entered on the chain related to that collateral.

Once this is completed, registering on this public blockchain should be sufficient to constitute perfection, whether or not there is physical possession (which won't be possible most of the time). This will streamline perfection and make collateralization much simpler to conduct, and open up the world of peer-to-peer financing.

Currency

As discussed in prior chapters, currency requires a mechanism to maintain value within a narrow band. Stablecoins are the likeliest contenders to become a currency, but, as discussed in Chapter 3, most are not particularly well designed to rival fiat at this time.

The regulation for currency is currently being hotly contested in the US, as stablecoins are a primary concern for Congress and the Department of the Treasury. As it currently stands, the only stablecoins legislators are willing to consider are those that are pegged to fiat, which, as previously discussed, is the worst kind of stablecoin.

This serves no one (other than the US dollar), as it merely creates derivatives of the US dollar. In addition, the US is apparently actively working to create a CBDC, which is a direct competitor to these dollar derivatives, as well as an ongoing risk of civil and human rights violations.

We Need Fiat Alternatives

It is vital to have a borderless currency. Anyone who has been subject to state-mandated or state-complicit discrimination or persecution knows that having assets that are trapped in one currency (or, worse, in real estate) destroys the ability to leave the country that is persecuting you or your people. To have truly free movement of capital, resources, and people, to have a global economy that benefits as many people as possible, we need to have borderless money.

A fear seems to exist that an alternative to fiat is intended to be a replacement of fiat. It is not. It is intended to break the control some governments and entities maintain on populations and resources through restrictions on fiat, and allow people more

---

27 I considered a form of masking, to allow people to hide that they are offering collateral, but that defeats the purpose of perfection and allows borrowers to conduct all sorts of nefarious transactions to remove the collateral from a legitimate lender.

opportunity to access capital. More access to capital creates stronger economies, not weaker ones. Stronger economies result in stronger fiat and less drain on government resources to support the population.

In addition, competition is the basis of capitalism. Monopolies make systems sluggish, bloated, and weak. Having an alternative to fiat allows people a place to store value when fiat is suffering, enabling a shorter economic recovery time and easier reduction of supply to quickly reduce inflation. Fiat will provide the same value for a stablecoin requiring a period of recovery. They work together to provide citizens with economic stability even during particularly turbulent periods.

Future Regulation

The FATF regulatory system likely wouldn't change much from the current system of FinCEN regulated money services businesses (MSB) licenses, along with the new custody rules. A new regulatory system could keep these aspects but have the licensing and custodian requirements all managed by FinCEN, not the SEC, and all easy to understand and simple to meet. The timing to obtain a license should be clear and should not be longer than six months. And nonbank, nonbroker entities who have appropriate storage and controls on access should be able to qualify as custodians, provided they have appropriate oversight and an automated system of escrow, deposit, and withdrawal. For example, a platform that wishes to operate a nonvolatile token with an automated, unhosted liquidity pool should be able to obtain the appropriate custodian and MSB licensing without requiring an additional bank or broker.

Promoters

Promoters are those who tell others about projects, help sell those projects, or otherwise use their influential status to convince people to make investment or purchase decisions. Promoters are already regulated in the US by the Federal Communications Commission and the SEC. You must tell people you are a paid promoter, and the terms of your agreement—and you can't mislead people about the nature of your relationship or your benefit.

I don't have a suggestion for future regulation, but I note this as an ongoing issue in blockchain that must be considered in any project. Too many people operate as promoters and pretend to be just "excited to discover" something. It is harming investors and buyers, and it needs to stop.

Community Projects

Community projects are projects like memecoins and PFPs (profile pictures)—NFT-based projects that center communities. The NFTs may provide identification of community, membership benefits, ticketing or access, content access, or similar things.

Fundamentally, however, these tokens are the final product. They do not represent an interest in a future product, they cannot be used to conduct transactions on a chain, they do not offer voting rights or governance positions. They may offer the right to receive free benefits (such as air drops).

The issue here is that, while they are fundamentally a final product, it is also possible to resell them on public marketplaces. Many people purchase them with the hope of reselling them for a profit.

How Should They Be Regulated?

When these tokens are generally not tied to any promise of future value, such as a developing project or building of an underlying company, these should not be considered securities. This is similar to people buying Barbie dolls: some buy them to use as a toy, and others leave them in the box in the hopes that there will be higher resale value in the future as a collector item. There is no clear reason to believe that the doll will be worth more in the future; the buyer just hopes that it is true. So we treat the doll as it is being sold: as a final product, a toy.

Customers Versus Traders

Fundamentally, when you are building for customers, you must treat the product as it is sold: as a final product, access to a service, a token to hold and display, possibly a ticket to gain entry or content. It *may* increase in value in the future, a market *may* develop, but if you are creating and selling a product for customer use, not potential future value, it should be regulated as any other product or service sold.

However, when you are building for a marketplace or current or potential value, whether market-priced or otherwise, you are building for traders. If tokens are tied to the promise of a future build, especially when the sale of those tokens is to raise capital to fund that build, this seems much more like a securities transaction with an investment decision, and it should be treated accordingly.

Centralized Marketplaces

Centralized exchanges (CEXes) are regulated by the SEC, under the Securities Exchange Act of 1934, as amended. These are traditional exchanges, and as we saw from the Coinbase and Binance lawsuits, they are violating rules for combining broker, exchange, and clearance functions.

Typically, brokers and clearinghouses are allowed to handle securities assets, while exchanges are not. It's problematic when these functions are mixed. An exchange can be tempted to start trading illegally on its own behalf (acting as a counterparty) or commingling assets of customers with its own assets, both of which appear to have happened with the companies mentioned. This was a major problem with FTX—I suppose customer funds and assets look like a great way to cover bad bets on the part of the exchange's brokerage activities. And that's what the rules are designed to avoid.

The broker and exchange rules are well defined and understood, and there really isn't a reason centralized marketplaces don't comply. The only issue is with clearance and settlement, as settlement happens immediately upon the transaction closing on-chain; it doesn't require someone checking for the existence of assets, then formally transferring funds from one party to the other, and assets from the second party to the first. The chain does that automatically. This function is irrelevant.

Decentralized Marketplaces

Decentralized exchanges, or DEXes, are considered illegal by the SEC, as they are run by algorithms and smart contracts and cannot be a regulated, compliant exchange that files documents. DEXes allow anyone to start a market in any token, and the theory is that this cannot possibly be a regulated marketplace.

I find this premise to be facetious. The SEC and FINRA (Financial Industry Regulation Authority) permit two market makers to form a market around any security without the consent of the issuer on the OTC market. The market makers just file their own Form 15c-211, and the trading can begin. So markets already exist that don't require the consent or approval (or even the prior knowledge) of the issuer.

In addition, any conceit that DEXes draw more fraudulent or failing tokens than CEXes would assume that the SEC regulatory process somehow weeds out "bad" projects in the review process—a concept that the SEC has repeatedly vehemently denied. Regulated or centralized exchanges are just as likely to have problematic securities as a DEX.

The only argument that has been made that separates a DEX from a properly regulated exchange is the lack of filed documents. But there is no reason algorithms and smart contracts cannot be required to produce appropriate transactional information to submit to the SEC automatically. Alternatively, DEXes can add DAOs with the sole purpose of collecting and filing documents, without attaching liability to the process (provided appropriate safeguards are put into place automating output as much as possible).

Regulation of DEXes may look a bit different CEX regulation, but the risk of abuse is much lower. No one is there to commingle funds, to improperly invest assets, to funnel assets to personal accounts. It's an automated system. If we found a way to make alternative trading systems and AMM systems regulated, we can do the same for DEXes.

These should be appropriately regulated and permitted.

Dark Pools

Dark pools are trading platforms that allow institutional traders and qualified institutional buyers to trade securities or set up positions in derivatives without any market awareness until after the trade is completed. While it's true that large investors will adversely impact price if they publish their intention, that cost is offset by the fact that people who have access to dark pools have significant asymmetric information that is unavailable to most of the investment community.

Dark pools should be prohibited. Large trades should be done by block trade or tranching if holders want to avoid affecting the price, or just accept that they will likely have some adverse pricing in part of the transaction like everyone else in the market. If they hold derivative positions that indicate they believe the price of something—an asset, an interest rate, etc.—will go up or down, then it will be public to see, like all other bets on pricing.

There is no overriding reason to protect the interest of large holders over small holders in hiding these transactions and allowing a privileged few the benefit of knowing this information in advance.

If dark pools must exist, all members of the pool should be prohibited from transacting in any of the assets or derivatives that are the subject of dark pool transactions, other than ones in which they are a party.

Intellectual Property

Intellectual property (IP) is the ownership and transfer of rights relating to creative and artistic work, or "intangible creations of human intellect." IP has four main types: copyright, trademark, patents, and trade secrets. Copyrights and trade secrets don't require any filings, but trademarks and patents require filings with the US Patent and Trademark Office (USPTO).

Without going into the details of what IP rights entail, NFTs are excellent at transferring different types of rights between parties, sometimes with a residual fee, or royalty, going back to the creator of the NFT (who may or may not be the creator of the underlying IP).

Problems and Solutions

However, we have a number of problems with this currently. First, royalty payments typically aren't hardcoded into the tokens; they are offered as a sort of largesse of the platforms on which they are sold. And, as we've seen with Foundation and OpenSea, that offering can be withdrawn without warning or consent of the NFT creators. To use these NFTs as the assets they are, those royalty rights need to be hardcoded into the tokens.

Second, IP rights are being eroded both on-chain and off-chain. The platforms offering NFTs for sale or rent do not offer any assurance that the creator is the owner of the IP that is the subject of the NFT. As we have seen with the rise of narrow AI programs like ChatGPT and Midjourney, there is no regard for ownership rights in the use of these tools. They deliberately disregard metadata, watermarks, and other reproduction limitations in using bits and pieces from the public sphere. As NFTs with AI as a primary or embedded feature become more and more prevalent, we will see more and more violations occurring, and people accidentally or deliberately perpetuating these infringements. Lawsuits have resulted and will continue to result. These programs should be required to abide by IP rights, and clear guidelines should indicate the amount of diligence required by platforms to ensure that the creator has proper rights to the IP that is the subject of the NFT; something greater than the current amount of diligence required, which is none.

Third, cross-chain rights are difficult to establish. We should have requirements that all rights created on one chain should be regarded on all other chains, so people are not tempted to duplicate IP and issue it on another chain, assuming it hasn't been claimed there. Some sort of full and fair credit act for chains providing recognition of rights and an attempt to re-create them in the holder if at all possible, or sequester those rights so they cannot be created at all if not possible. Rights on first use should require a review of active chains to see if those rights have already been established and the rights requested would be an infringement of existing rights.

Fourth, on-chain use should be given the same weight as first use in the off-chain world. And the current professional rights organizations (PROs) should evolve into on- and off-chain monitoring agencies, which distribute takedown notices and cease-and-desist letters, before passing it off to the right holder's counsel of choice.

Fifth, a nonregulatory but useful point: NFTs should offer some point of contact with the creator, in case the current right holder wants to expand their rights. For example, a creator offers a private limited license for the piece of art represented by her NFT. One of the buyers is the head of props for a new television show, and wants to put the art in the background of a main set of the show. With a point of contact, the holder can contact the creator or the creator's estate and ask to expand her specific NFT to a limited commercial license, or even a general commercial license, in exchange for additional compensation. I think creators would prefer that this option be available if the opportunity arises. As the types of rights, goods, and services connected to NFTs expand, this will become more and more common.

All these together will shore up the rights these NFTs offer.

Identity

Quite a few projects are currently working to establish identity protocols, primarily to create some sort of sovereign identity. This is not the type of identity protocol we need for the regulatory space.

A Viable Solution

We need an identity protocol that is a "knowable unknown." By this, I mean a protocol whereby KYC, AML, and other eligibility requirements (such as over 13 years old, over 21 years, accredited investor, or US citizen) can be established privately by any individual.

Let's say we have anonymous tokens held in wallets that identify what qualifications a particular wallet holder has but that provide no other identifying information. Nearly all wallets in most DApps would require some kind of identification and clearance, as discussed—regulations would require it. But that doesn't mean the entire world needs to know everyone's identity and all the transactions you engage in.

So we could issue specific tokens representing particular confirmations of clearance. The tokens could be various ERC protocols, like one for KYC cleared, one for AML cleared, one for over 13, one for over 21, and one for accredited investor. How would that work?

An individual would enter information on a secure, private platform and indicate what they are applying for. Then, the information is randomly submitted to one of several secure third parties for confirmation, then split apart to be stored in different databases in fully anonymous fashion and protected by zk-proof.

Once the confirmation is received, a token-generating protocol is triggered by smart contract. The token generator issues the appropriate token to the public key given, and the information is immediately deleted.

The tokens allow access without providing any information to any of the DApps or protocols, which provides anonymity in transactions but ensures that regulatory obligations are met.

But what if people use that anonymity as a weapon, instead of a shield, as is the case with rugs and hacks? Then the identity of the wallet is broken. You lose your right to anonymity if you commit a crime, and people have the right to know whom to sue.

An injured party would identify the offending wallet, then submit that as the offender to a court with a motion to compel. A court would grant the motion, the protocol would use the zk-proof to reconstruct the identity of the wallet owner, and all the identifying information would be turned over to the court.

The Need for Accountability

This is just an example of a protocol that would work, but anything similar would be a good start. Identities would be kept secret as long as no court order forced reconstruction of the identity for the purpose of accountability. Accountability is something not taken seriously enough in the entire crypto space, and we need to take this very seriously.

If we want people to trust the space, and we want to still maintain the ability to have some form of anonymity, we need to come up with a way to make bad actors accountable for their bad actions. And right now, the common process of saying, "Well, it was a learning experience," after getting rugged is just insufficient. Everyone deserves access and opportunity. But it's the victims that deserve our empathy and protection, not the criminals.

We forget that far too often. Many people dealing with cryptocurrency, founding companies that use blockchain, and both issuers and investors in general are honest people who work hard and are trying to be compliant and fair. But not everyone. And we all know at least a few of the people who are skating through, skimming off of the rest of us.

If we don't stop making excuses for con artists and allowing them to lure others unchallenged and unimpeded, anonymized by cute names and cartoon PFPs, this space and all its opportunity will disappear. And every time someone is turned down for a loan and can't get funding for a business, it will hurt just a little bit more.

Accredited Investor Rules

The accredited investor rules are fundamentally unfair. They essentially say that individual investors must already be wealthy to access the most reliable source of wealth growth available: private company investment prior to going public or purchase. But one can't access the source of wealth growth unless one is already wealthy. How is this fair?

The SEC has traditionally had this wall around investments, with no way in for those who need access the most. Even the current test exception permits taking only Series 7, Series 65, or Series 82 exams—and the Series 7 and 82 exams require a sponsor.

The Series 65 is a step forward, because it is an exam available to anyone. The SEC should expand this exemption, offering more paths to investors to access private investment and higher-risk investments provided they show they understand the basics of the investments involved, the amount of risk, and how to hedge them. As long as people understand and accept risk, why should they be precluded from investing in anything? The SEC specifically does not make any claims or approvals regarding whether any public security is a "good investment." As long as investors know what questions to ask, why can they not assume the same is true of private investments (nothing is necessarily a "good investment")?

I'm not sure if the SEC is assuming that public securities ensure a better investment decision, in which case it thinks accredited investors are poor decision makers, or it assumes retail investors can't take responsibility for their investment decisions, in which case they shouldn't be allowed in public markets either. Either way, this system is flawed. We need to reevaluate this, starting with the accredited investor rules and ending with financial education in schools.

Everyone deserves access to opportunity. No one deserves a particular outcome. If we can agree on that, I think we can make better laws.

Taxes

Taxation is an incredibly complex topic but a very important one. Currently, US federal tax law works generally like this:

Holders are not taxed when they purchase crypto (including NFTs) with fiat. But they are taxed when they convert one crypto to another and when they sell the crypto they hold. They are taxed when they receive tokens from staking when they sell and taxed when they receive tokens from airdrops at the time of the airdrop. They are taxed on receiving payments as a lender or borrower, as the case may be, and on receiving benefits in crypto or fiat. Finally, there is a possibility of an additional collectors' tax for NFTs (that's unclear).

These taxes can be at the personal income rate, the short-term capital gains rate, or the long-term capital gains rate.

Many people trade frequently, for gains or simply for pleasure. The sheer reporting requirements of these events is overwhelming, and the lack of common accounting knowledge in the industry makes it easy to overlook small transactions. This can create liability over very small tax payments.

There should be an exemption in reporting and payment for transactions that result in less than $10,000. Individuals are required to keep records of their liability, and may be required to prove that they had under $10,000 in transactions in any given year via audit. Crypto losses should be able to be carried forward for three years, and back for two years, to offset gains.

Conclusion

In this chapter, we covered the amazing future of DeFi, and my thoughts on the regulatory structural requirements to bring crypto and DeFi into compliance so it can really grow into the powerhouse it's poised to be.

This entire book was designed to be an overview of DeFi and blockchain; it's growing and changing so fast, it's hard to get into details as if it was a stable, mature field. That makes it hard to discuss, but incredibly exciting to be part of and build. I encourage everyone to read more, ask more, join communities. When you're comfortable with the finance portion and the risk involved, jump in slowly. DeFi is one of those fields that require active participation to fully understand.

But if you're looking for a way to give more people more access to capital and more ways to build real wealth, without concern for bias, discrimination, and gatekeepers, DeFi is the path forward. I wish everyone happy stacking!

Index

B

back door, in code, 26
backing tokenomics, 138
bad invitations, 26
bank accounts, 27
bank reserve ratios, 29
Bank Secrecy Act, 91, 94
banking crisis in Asia (1997), 5
banking failure (2007-2008), 88
Bankman-Fried, Sam, 126
banks
    flow of money, 28
    historical practices of, 86
    how they work, 28-31
    money laundering and, 89
    use of your cash, 29-31
Beefy Finance, 158
beta releases, 111
betting protocols, 72
Binance, 124, 172, 178
Binance Smart Chain (BSC), 125
Bitcoin, 8-10
    as asset, 11
    as commodity, 184
        (see also commodity)
    as currency, 11
    deflationary nature of, 11
    as digital cash, 10
    false consensus risk, 26
    as model for blockchain technology, 9
    non-standardized tokens, 39
    Ordinals, 184
    scarcity-based demand in, 83
    Taproot, 88
    as Turing Incomplete, 13
    volatility of, 11
Bitcoin: A Peer-to-Peer Electronic Cash System
    (Nakamoto whitepaper), 8
Bitfinex, 26, 88
BitUSD project, 61
blockchain, 2, 8-27
    (see also Bitcoin; platforms)
    community focus in development of, 16
    complexity of, 2
    core tenets of, 15-27
        anonymity, 27
        consensus, 22
        distribution, 16-22
        open, 15

        permanence, 23-26
        shared, 16
        trustless, 27
    core thesis of technology, 8
    Ethereum, 13-15
    flexibility in platforms, 9
    mass adoption of, 9
    origin of term, 8
    platform selection, 112
    revolutionary aspects of, 10
    smart contracts, 12
    structure of, 9
    transparency in, 15
    trilemma, 36-38
    as trustless system, 2
    weak points in, 25
BlockFi, 64
Bloom protocol, 70
bonding curves, 148, 154-156
borrower-lender platforms, 153-157
    average returns, 156
    pricing, 154
    procedure, 154
    risks, 157
BSC (Binance Smart Chain), 125
bug bounty program, 139
business principles and processes, 109-112
    beta releases, 111
    building community, 110
    design, 111
    examining problems, 110
    finding problems, 109
    public launches, 111
Buterin, Vitalik, 13, 18, 19, 36, 175

C

capital-raising assets, 100
Cardano, 38, 129
cash flow, 3
cash-in/cash-out, 139
CBDCs (central bank digital currencies)
    dollar derivatives versus, 189
    stablecoins versus, 83
CDD (customer due diligence), 93
CDs (certificates of deposits), 31
Celsius, 64, 172
censorship, 117, 120
central bank digital currencies (see CBDCs)
central governing body, 97

O

OCaml language, 127
off-chain credit score integration, 71
off-chain virtual machine, 117, 120
off-season purchasing, 4
Office of the Comptroller of the Currency, 100
onboarding unlimited users, 37
Open ledger, 15
open source code, 16
OpenDAO, 68
openness of DeFi, 32
OpenSea, 193
operators, 116
optimistic rollups, 117, 121
oracles, 43, 77-82
    challenges faced by, 81
    functions of, 80
    problems with, 81-82
Ordinals, 184
Otherside, 161
overcollateralization, in DeFi loans, 66
overhypothecation, 186

P

PancakeSwap, 148
parachains, 129
parallel execution, 132
passwords, forgotten or compromised, 41
Paxos Gold (PAXG), 51
pay as you go blockchain model, 129
peer-to-peer loans, 65
perfecting your interest, 186-188
periodic independent testing, for AML compliance, 94
permanence (immutability), 23-26
permanent ledger, 7
personal network bootstrap, 71
phishing, 26
pin money, 86
plasma, 121-122
    data unavailability problem, 121
    plasma bridges, 121-122
platforms, 35-40, 112
    borrower, 157
    borrower-lender, 153-157
    DApp development, 112-132
        Layer 2 options, 113-123
        non-Ethereum ecosystems, 124-132
        wallets, 123-124

deployment networks, 38-40
    trilemma solutions, 36-38
political decentralization, 20
Polkadot, 129
Poly Network hack, 92
Ponzi schemes, 145
prediction protocols, 72
privacy coins, 87, 89
profitability, 109
programming languages, 38
promoters, 190
proof-of-stake, 24
    combining with proof-of-history, 126
    liquid, 127
    pure, 131
proof-of-work consensus method, 24, 37
protocols, 35, 143-162
    considerations regarding, 161-162
    DApps, 40
    identity, 195-196
    lending, 145-159
        borrower-lender platforms, 153-157
        swap exchanges, 146-153
        yield farming, 158-159
    memecoins, 160-161
    running on Ethereum, 123
    staking tokens, 143-144
public launches, 111, 139
public-private transparency, 15
PulseChain, 64
PulseX, 64
pure proof of stake method, 131

Q

quadratic voting, 62
qualified institutional buyers (QIBs), 107
quantum-like computing, 132

R

Rally "RLY" governance coin, 20
random subsampling, 128
real-time transfers, 10
real-world assets (RWAs), 166-171
rebasing, 59-61
Recommendation 16, FATF, 94
recordkeeping
    financial transactions as, 8
    importance of in history, 4
registration options, 135

Y

Yakovenko, Anatoly, 126
Yearn, 158
Yellen, Janet, 101
yield farming (liquidity mining), 158-159
YouHodler, 68

Z

Zcash, 87
zk (zero-knowledge) rollups, 119-121
zk-SNARKs, 119
zk-STARKs, 119

About the Author

Alexandra Damsker is an experienced securities attorney, having trained at the US Securities and Exchange Commission and international firm Mayer Brown, as well as running a very successful solo practice with clients in eight countries grown entirely by referral and word of mouth. She is a 2x founder (one exit), and has been involved in blockchain since 2016. She is considered a subject matter expert in blockchain best practices, cryptocurrency, NFTs, DeFi, and general token offerings. She currently serves as legal, operations, and strategic advisor to a number of organizations and high net worth individuals, including A-level celebrities and high growth, venture-funded companies.

Colophon

The animal on the cover of *Understanding DeFi* is the Somalian slender mongoose (*Herpestes ochraceus*). This small mammal can be found in Somalia and other adjacent countries, as well as throughout sub-Saharan Africa. They are very adaptable and can live anywhere within this range, but are most common in the savanna and semi-arid plains.

Slender mongooses can live either alone or in pairs. They are diurnal and usually build their dens in crevices between rocks or hollowed logs. Slender mongooses are adept at climbing trees, and will often do so to hunt nesting birds and eggs. They are primarily carnivorous; while insects make up most of their diet, slender mongooses will also eat lizards, rodents, birds, snakes, and occasionally fruit. While no overall population estimate is currently available, slender mongooses are abundant and are not considered an endangered or threatened species.

Many of the animals on O'Reilly covers are endangered; all of them are important to the world.

The cover illustration is by Karen Montgomery, based on an antique line engraving from *Histoire Naturelle*. The series design is by Edie Freedman, Ellie Volckhausen, and Karen Montgomery. The cover fonts are Gilroy Semibold and Guardian Sans. The text font is Adobe Minion Pro; the heading font is Adobe Myriad Condensed; and the code font is Dalton Maag's Ubuntu Mono.

O'REILLY®

Learn from experts.
Become one yourself.

Books | Live online courses
Instant answers | Virtual events
Videos | Interactive learning

Get started at oreilly.com.